# POLLS & SURVEYS

Norman M. Bradburn
Seymour Sudman

# POLLS & SURVEYS

*Understanding
What They Tell Us*

 **Jossey-Bass Publishers**

San Francisco • London • 1989

POLLS AND SURVEYS
*Understanding What They Tell Us*
by Norman M. Bradburn and Seymour Sudman

Copyright © 1988 by:   Jossey-Bass Inc., Publishers
350 Sansome Street
San Francisco, California 94104

&

Jossey-Bass Limited
28 Banner Street
London EC1Y 8QE

**Library of Congress Cataloging-in-Publication Data**

Bradburn, Norman M.
  Polls & surveys.

  (A Joint publication in the Jossey-Bass social
and behavioral science series & the Jossey-Bass
public administration series)
  Bibliography: p.
  Includes index.
  1. Public opinion polls.   I. Sudman, Seymour.
II. Title.   III. Title: Polls and surveys.
IV. Series: Jossey-Bass social and behavioral science
series.   V. Series: Jossey-Bass public administration
series.
HM261.B69     1988        303.3'8        88-42778
ISBN 1-55542-098-2 (alk. paper)

Manufactured in the United States of America

The paper in this book meets the guidelines for
permanence and durability of the Committee on
Production Guidelines for Book Longevity of the
Council on Library Resources.

Credits are on page 249.

JACKET DESIGN BY WILLI BAUM

FIRST EDITION
  *First printing: August 1988*
  *Second printing: October 1989*

Code 8829

A joint publication in
The Jossey-Bass
Social and Behavioral Science Series
&
The Jossey-Bass
Public Administration Series

# Contents

This book is dedicated to the pioneers of public opinion research on whose shoulders we stand, and in particular to two giants: George Gallup and Herbert Hyman. Gallup fought continuously to defend polls and to improve their methodology. His 1940 book (with Saul Rae) *The Pulse of Democracy* is the spiritual ancestor of this book. Hyman reminded us again and again through his life and writings that we could have a great deal of fun conducting opinion research.

# Preface

The telephone rings; a woman with a brisk voice announces that a survey is being conducted and that she would like to ask you a few questions; or, less commonly today, an interviewer appears on the doorstep with a similar request, or a questionnaire arrives in the mail with a request to fill it out and return it to the sponsor. You are about to become a respondent in a survey or poll. (We use the terms synonymously.) But even though you may participate in surveys, and read about the results of polls—and even though your life is increasingly influenced by decisions that are, in turn, influenced by information gathered through surveys—you probably are not very knowledgeable about surveys. Few of us know how to distinguish good polls from bad ones or understand what polls can do and what they cannot do.

*Polls and Surveys: Understanding What They Tell Us* provides answers to questions frequently asked by respondents in surveys, by those who have not yet been selected as participants, and by journalists, businessmen, and many others who have to deal with survey data. It also addresses questions that consumers of poll data should ask but all too frequently do not, because they do not know the right questions to ask.

After repeatedly being asked many of the questions we answer here, we came to realize that no single book for nonspecialists was available to people who wanted to pursue their interest in surveys. When colleagues who wanted their students to know about surveys in a nontechnical way asked us for references, we could recommend parts of several different books, but there was no single work that pulled together the many aspects of surveys and treated the "whys" of polling as well as the "hows." Furthermore, some important issues, such as the appropriate and inappropriate uses of polls, are not usually raised in books, including our own earlier ones, that deal with research methodology. Thus, we decided to write this book.

## Audience

We have always tried to aim our books at a specific audience with specific needs and backgrounds. We see as the primary audience for this book newcomers to public opinion measurement and students in political science, sociology, business, and communications who are studying public opinion or market research. As the title indicates, *Polls and Surveys: Understanding What They Tell Us* is intended as a comprehensive overview for nonspecialists. We have tried to write without jargon, so that the book will also be accessible to the general reader who is interested in polling.

We recognize, as do all pollsters, that the continuing existence and vitality of public opinion research depend on broad public support and willingness to participate in polls. As more and more demands are put on people to participate in surveys, they need to be aware of the importance of good poll data and to recognize bad practices that should not be encouraged. It would be tragic if Gresham's law were to be valid for surveys. Improved public knowledge about polls should help strengthen good survey practice and drive out bad surveys, rather than the other way around.

## The Contents of This Book

After an introductory chapter, which outlines the basics of survey research, we provide a brief history of public opinion polling in Chapter Two. Although polls were used in the nineteenth century and even earlier, the era of modern polling really began in

1935 with the appearance of the Gallup poll. Since then, the use of polls has flourished, and a new profession has come into being to supply polling information. This growth has been slowed at times by major poll fiascos, such as the 1948 presidential election forecasts. Ultimately, however, the need for information to design and manage major social programs and new products has grown rapidly, and the polls have grown simultaneously. Chapter Two concludes with a discussion of the growth of polls outside the United States.

Since the early Gallup polls, there continue to be heated discussions about the legitimate and questionable uses of polls. We discuss these issues in Chapter Three. Presidential uses of polls are especially important, and we attempt to distinguish between presidents who have used polls wisely and those who have not. We then describe a wide range of legitimate poll uses by business, government agencies, and associations. The chapter concludes with some troubling uses of polls as propaganda and in influencing legal cases.

Chapter Four describes the diverse organizations that conduct polls today: newspapers and television networks, private organizations, government bureaus and research centers, policy researchers, university survey organizations, and commercial market researchers. There is also a brief discussion of the major professional associations in the field.

Chapter Five is the first of our methodological chapters. These chapters (Five through Nine) are intended not for producers but for users of survey data. The aim is to make the user aware of adequate and inadequate procedures for data collection and analysis. Although there are many ways to collect data, some are so poor as to make the results meaningless. Chapter Five discusses the organization of interviewing and points out that, despite the cartoon cliché of a male interviewer, most interviewers are women. The chapter describes how interviewers are selected, trained, and supervised and compares the three major data collection procedures: face-to-face, telephone, and mail. Each of these methods is appropriate for some kinds of surveys, but their inappropriate use can result in excessive costs or poor data quality.

Chapter Six describes the right and wrong ways that respondents are selected for surveys. The best way is to use probability methods, such as telephone numbers selected at random and area samples of households. The worst way is to ask readers to send in responses to a questionnaire clipped from a newspaper or magazine or to call in responses to questions posed on television or radio.

Even if a sample is properly selected, it must be well executed if it is to produce reliable results. No survey can get all its selected respondents to cooperate, but conscientious survey organizations use a variety of methods to maximize cooperation. Surveys with low cooperation rates may be subject to as large a bias as those with a poorly selected sample. Such a bias is known as nonresponse bias.

Chapter Seven discusses the different types of questions—factual and opinion—and warns that improper question wording can bias results. For example, double-barreled questions and response categories that introduce different dimensions to a question can produce invalid results. The order of questions and the treatment of "don't know" and "no opinion" answers also will affect responses.

Chapter Eight centers on how to read and use the results from surveys. Some potential problems with survey organizations' presentation of their results include the omission of results, the use of single questions on complex issues, the treatment of "don't know" answers, the reports of sampling variability, and a format that makes the results difficult to interpret. The chapter concludes with a group of examples that illustrate the possible pitfalls in trying to explain survey results.

All measurements are subject to error, and Chapter Nine describes the kinds of measurement errors found in surveys. Some users of survey data are disturbed to learn that measurement error exists, but the sensible user accepts the fact of measurement error and attempts to understand the limitations that such errors may put on the interpretation of data. In addition to sampling error, measurement error may be caused by sample biases and nonsampling errors attributable to the questionnaire (for example, improper question wording), the interviewer (if improperly trained and supervised), and the respondent. Questions that ask about sensitive behavior and require substantial memory effort cause special measurement problems.

Even after fifty years, some critics are concerned that polls harm rather than help a democratic society. Chapter Ten lists the major arguments against polls: (1) They unduly influence elections, especially when exit poll data are released in some time zones before the election booths are closed in other time zones. (2) They constitute an invasion of privacy. (3) They oversimplify issues and place too much pressure on elected officials. (4) Their results are so unreliable as to be meaningless. Obviously, we do not agree with these general criticisms and present data to refute them. We argue against the regulation of legitimate polls, but we do favor some restrictions on phony polls that mislead the public. In most cases, no new legislation is required, simply the enforcement of existing fraud laws.

In the final chapter, we discuss the effects of the polls on the electoral process, government officials, political participation, commerce, and the media. The book closes with our predictions about the future of polling in the United States and around the world.

At the end of the book, we provide a glossary of common terms used in polling, so that consumers can understand the industry's "jargon."

## Acknowledgments

This book has been shaped by innumerable conversations with colleagues, students, friends, and casual acquaintances who have exhibited a lively interest in the way that surveys are conducted and their role in American life today. Although we cannot thank everyone who has contributed to the writing of this book, we are especially indebted to William Kruskal, Warren Mitofsky, Diane O'Rourke, Howard Schuman, Paul Sheatsley, Eleanor Singer, Joe Spaeth, Richard Warneke, and Pearl Zinner, who read and commented on earlier drafts of the manuscript; and to Jean Converse and Hans Zeisel, who commented on Chapter Two. Their critiques have improved the book immensely; any errors remaining are our responsibility.

We are also indebted to Gracia Alkema, a friend and editor, who encouraged us to write the book and who has given us invaluable advice, judicious criticism, and gentle prodding when the project looked as if it might bog down. Dorothy Conway has again proven to be an author's best friend, a peerless editor whose stubborn insistence on clear and exact prose has greatly improved our work and made the reader's life easier. We would also like to thank Carla Buchanan, Linda Connelly, and Bernita Rusk, who typed most of the manuscript.

*June 1988*                                         Norman M. Bradburn
                                                     *Chicago, Illinois*

                                                     Seymour Sudman
                                                     *Urbana, Illinois*

# The Authors

*Norman M. Bradburn* is provost of the University of Chicago. He was awarded B.A. degrees from the University of Chicago (1952) and from Oxford University in philosophy, politics, and economics (1955). He was awarded the M.A. degree in clinical psychology (1958) and the Ph.D. degree in social psychology (1960), both from Harvard University. Since 1960, he has been on the faculty of the University of Chicago. In 1970–71 he was a Von Humboldt fellow at the University of Cologne. And he was formerly the director of the National Opinion Research Center, University of Chicago.

Bradburn is a member of the American Sociological Association and the American Association for Public Opinion Research and is a fellow of the American Statistical Association. Among the books that he has authored or coauthored are *Reports on Happiness* (with D. Caplovitz, 1965), *The Structure of Psychological Well-Being* (1969), *Side by Side* (with S. Sudman and G. Gockel, 1971), *Response Effects in Surveys* (with S. Sudman, 1974), *Improving Interview Method and Questionnaire Design* (with S. Sudman, 1979), and *Asking Questions* (with S. Sudman, 1982). Bradburn continues to be engaged in research on response effects in surveys and in studies of psychological well-being.

*Seymour Sudman* is Walter A. Stellner Professor of Business Administration and Sociology, and research professor, Survey Research Laboratory, at the University of Illinois. He was awarded the B.S. degree in mathematics from Roosevelt University (1949) and the Ph.D. degree in business from the University of Chicago (1962). Before joining the University of Illinois in 1968, he was director of sampling and senior study director at the National Opinion Research Center, University of Chicago (1962-1968).

Sudman is a member of several professional associations, including the American Marketing Association, the American Association for Public Opinion Research (for which he served as president, 1981-82), and the American Sociological Association. He is also a fellow of the American Statistical Association. He has written numerous books, monographs, and articles; with N. M. Bradburn, he coauthored *Response Effects in Surveys* (1974), *Improving Interview Method and Questionnaire Design* (1979), and *Asking Questions* (1982). He has also published *Applied Sampling* (1976) and *Consumer Panels* (with R. Ferber, 1979).

# POLLS & SURVEYS

# 1

# Polling the Public: Purpose & Process

On December 15, 1987, Gary Hart announced that he was returning to the race for the Democratic nomination for president. The next day, the *New York Times* reported that a poll conducted overnight indicated that Hart was the leading choice among Democratic voters. Such a result could hardly have been surprising to Hart, whose decision to reenter the race was influenced by the knowledge that polls containing his name among potential candidates had continued to show him as a leading candidate even after his withdrawal. Hart's campaign, however, never really got off the ground again. The subsequent primary caucuses and elections did not produce the results that those who took the polls at face value might have expected. Does this mean that the polls in December were wrong? Or that they were badly done? Or that they are meaningless? To answer such questions, one needs to know more about polls, about their strengths and their limitations, when they can be trusted and when they should be viewed skeptically.

Polls have become an essential part of our political life and are ingrained in our media and in the business world. Important decisions, such as Hart's decision to withdraw from and then reenter the presidential campaign, are heavily influenced by poll results. Almost daily, we read or hear media reports of a poll or a survey indicating some alarming or fascinating fact about American life or

1

public opinion. In an election year, the normal flow of poll results becomes a flood that threatens to drown us in information overload.

Attention is often given to the way in which spectacular technological innovations, such as transistors or computers, have changed our lives, but relatively little attention is paid to the fact that polls and sample surveys have become a major means by which we learn about our collective selves. We have learned, for example, that orders to factories rose 0.1 percent and that prices paid to farmers for raw products rose 4 percent from October to November 1987; that the proportion of households with vegetable gardens declined from 49 to 37 percent between 1975 and 1985; and that, in 1982, 22 percent of the population eighteen years old and over had visited an art museum. Because of polls, we also know what proportion of the population watches the Superbowl, what proportion opposes abortion under any conditions, and what proportion approves of the way the president does his job—to mention only a few of the many aspects of American life and opinion that are charted by the polls.

Because information based on surveys plays such an important role in shaping major decisions by government officials, businessmen, politicians, and even individuals in their daily lives, we all need to know something about surveys: What, in fact, is a survey? What are its limitations? How can we tell whether a particular survey is good or not? If we are to understand what surveys and polls tell us, we must know how they are conducted, what makes them succeed or fail, and how they are used or misused.

### Definitions and Characteristics of Polls and Surveys

There is no precise distinction between the terms *poll* and *survey*. Both refer to systematic data collection about a sample drawn from a larger population. Probably the most familiar example is the presidential preference poll, a survey of individual opinions. However, surveys also can be made of organizations (such as business firms, universities, or hospitals) or of events (such as purchases, court sentences, or automobile trips). They need not be concerned with humans or their activities. Samples can be drawn of objects, animals, or anything else whose properties can be defined. The method is quite general and has wide applicability. In this book, we confine our attention to surveys of human populations.

The word *poll* comes from the Greek word for *citizen* and has the same root as the word *politics*. In the Middle Ages, the word came to mean "head." In this century, it referred to voting and taxing and then became used to describe opinion surveys on public issues. The word *survey* comes from the Latin (with *sur* coming from *super,* meaning "over," and *vey* from the Latin *videre,* meaning "to see"). "To survey" was "to oversee" something, and the word's meaning spread to a general or comprehensive view of anything. Thus, it might seem that *survey* is a somewhat broader term than *poll,* but very early in their uses the words became intermixed. Polls asked questions about behavior and attitudes unrelated to public issues, and some surveys asked the same political questions that were asked on polls. At this time, there is no clear distinction between the terms.

*Sizes and Number of Polls.* Polls come in many sizes and shapes. They may be small, involving only fifty to one hundred persons, such as an organization's survey of its members; or they may be quite large, involving tens of thousands of respondents, such as the Current Population Survey, a government survey of 52,000 households conducted every month to estimate the unemployment rate.

While no one is certain how many surveys are conducted in the United States each year, the number is probably in the hundreds of thousands. Current estimates are that over 30 million interviews are conducted each year. There are few households that have not been selected as respondents in a survey at least once. Many, if not most, of the readers of this book will have been asked to participate in a survey and, if they are at all like the general public, will have agreed to do so.

Polls have become commonplace in other countries as well, particularly in democracies with competitive elections and market economies, where their uses are similar to those in the United States. Surveys are also conducted in the Soviet Union, China, and other one-party states with centrally planned economies as an adjunct to planning. The existence of private and university-based survey organizations in many countries has made it possible to carry out a number of cross-national comparative studies.

*Polls Versus Interviews.* In some respects, a poll is like other forms of human activity involving questioning. Superficially, a survey interview appears to be a conversation in which the interviewer, by means of a series of questions, tries to find out something about the respondent. Important differences, however, set the polls apart from other types of interviews, such as employment interviews, clinical interviews, or conversations between strangers who meet casually. The most important difference is that the survey attempts to say something about a larger population, of which the individuals being interviewed are members, whereas other types of interviews obtain information about the individuals as individuals.

A respondent in a survey interview may be selected as a member of the adult population of the United States or as a voter in the last election or as someone who has bought a new car in the last year. On the other hand, the person interviewed may be selected as an informant about some organization, such as a business firm or a hospital, or about some geographical unit, such as a neighborhood or a city. Informants are typically asked about the characteristics and activities of an organization or other unit about which they are knowledgeable, rather than about their own personal opinions or activities.

Whether the person selected for an interview in a poll is treated as a respondent or as an informant depends on the purpose of the survey. When the purpose is to say something about a population of individuals, such as probable voters in the next election, the respondents (as representatives of that larger population) are asked questions about their own opinions and probable behavior. When the purpose is to say something about a population of organizations, as in a survey of benefit plans in the insurance industry, the informants are asked questions about the practices and characteristics of their firms.

Surveys rest on a paradox. Although the individual respondents are asked questions about their own behavior or beliefs, survey researchers are not interested in the respondents as individuals. They are interested in them only insofar as their answers, when combined with others, allow the surveyors to make statements about the population as a whole or significant subgroups of the population. In other types of interviews, such as employment or clinical interviews, the purpose is to discover something about the individual as a unique person, so that decisions about the respondents as an individual can be made.

*Standardization of Questions.* Because the answers to survey questions are going to be combined and treated statistically, care must be taken that the questions and the conditions of the interview are as similar as possible. Obviously, if respondents are answering different questions, any attempt to combine their answers would be a meaningless exercise. Similarly, if the conditions under which the questions were asked were very different, or if interviewers behaved in different ways, the answers might not be comparable.

There are many ways, some of them quite subtle, in which the wording of questions or the behavior of interviewers can bias the results of surveys. Reports of polls in the media sometimes carry a small warning that the results are subject to "sources of error that are normal to all surveys," to remind the reader that the results should not be accepted uncritically. Too often, however, even this warning is cut out of the report. Hardly ever is there enough information in the report to assess the nature of such possible errors. In Chapters Seven, Eight, and Nine, we discuss many of the things that can go wrong in surveys and alert the users of surveys to be on the lookout for these possible sources of error.

The most common method used by pollsters to make sure that the questions are the same for all respondents is to standardize the questions. In contrast, in ordinary conversations, employment interviews, or other interviews that attempt to elicit detailed information about individuals, questions on a particular topic may vary from interview to interview, following only a general topic guide; and responses may be followed up with further questions unique to that individual respondent.

The rigid adherence to a standardized interview schedule or a questionnaire, most often with predetermined response categories, is a characteristic of surveys. "Would you say that you are very satisfied, pretty satisfied, or not very satisfied with your Blowhard Hair Dryer?" is not the kind of question you are apt to encounter in a friendly conversation, but it is instantly recognizable to most people as the type of question that is asked on surveys. Because of this exclusive use of questions with predetermined response categories, surveys are sometimes attacked as superficial. How can they get at nuances of opinion when everyone is forced to select from among a small list of set answers? Admittedly, such surveys do not elicit a depth of information about a single individual. However, a well-designed questionnaire *can* measure in depth the distribution of opinion about various topics across a population. It can do so by requiring survey interviewers to ask a number of questions about the topic: How strong are the respondents' opinions? How well informed are they about the topic? How might they feel about the topic under different conditions? Unfortunately, many polls do not take the time to examine topics in any depth; and even many of those that do are not reported in the media with any depth.

*Behavioral Versus Attitude Surveys.* In surveys about behavior, the questions concern actions or events that are, in principle, verifiable: number of years of education, consumer purchases, or vote in the last election. In practice, of course, it is impractical, unethical, or even illegal to obtain such information from sources other than the individuals themselves. Surveys about behavior are conducted because they may be the most economical or the only practical way of obtaining information about the distribution of behavior in the population.

More familiar to the general public are surveys about attitudes, beliefs, opinions, and other psychological states that, in principle, are unverifiable. That is, they are known, if at all, only to the individual respondent. Among the many types of opinion polls are surveys that ask about opinions on current political events, consumer satisfaction or confidence, images of political leaders, or new products.

## Scientific Basis of Surveys

Perhaps the most striking thing about surveys is their claim to make statements about large populations on the basis of data from a small sample of the population. Because these statements are often correct (or nearly so, as in elections), many people view them as if they were produced by the modern equivalent of magic and endow them with a degree of certainty to which they are not entitled. On the other hand, when they fail, as they inevitably do in some cases, we are apt to take pleasure in the discomfiture of the pollsters whose magic has failed and whose predictions have not been borne out. We like the knowledge that surveys give us, but we resent their seemingly uncanny ability to predict the future.

Surveys' claims to validity are based on the statistical theory of sampling. Sampling theory provides a set of rules for making inferences about a total population based on information from only a part (sample) of the population. Sampling theory also provides the basis for the set of procedures by which the samples are selected and inferences drawn. The essential point is that not just any part of the population will do for the sample if one wants to say something true about the larger population; the sample must be selected according to scientifically based rules.

The selection of the sample according to theoretically determined rules sets off scientifically based polls from surveys based on self-selection. Polls that depend on self-selection are frequently conducted by the media or by journalists who want to bolster their conclusions by an appeal to a large number of opinions. A familiar example is the "phone-in" poll, in which viewers of a television program can call in to a special number to register a simple "pro" or "con" vote on some issue.

Self-selection violates the fundamental premise for the validity of sample surveys and makes any inferences from the sample to a larger population illegitimate. Because self-selected samples have a superficial resemblance to scientifically based ones and are cheaper to conduct, some people are misled into thinking that they have the same validity as scientifically based surveys, and the media often make no distinction between self-selected and careful scientific samples.

Chapter Six discusses some of the major issues regarding the selection of samples. Unfortunately, many reports of survey results (and most such reports in the media) do not contain sufficient information about the way the sample for the poll was selected;

therefore, the person who hears or reads the report cannot make an informed judgment about the scientific validity of the poll.

## Do Respondents Tell the Truth?

One of the most frequently asked questions about surveys is: "Do respondents tell the truth?" The answer is: "For the most part, yes," with the qualification: "if they know it." In general—as is shown by the success of surveys in forecasting elections and in other areas where validity checks can be made—deliberate lying by respondents is not the major problem with surveys. In some instances, of course, respondents may not always tell the truth; and surveys about sensitive topics, such as drug use, tax evasion, or criminal behavior, may not elicit the same degree of truthfulness as surveys about consumer behavior or politics. But a potentially more serious problem, for questions about past behavior, is that respondents may fail to recall their past behavior correctly or to make an effort to recall all the past events being asked about. Memory errors are common in everyday life, particularly for events that are not very salient. There is no reason to expect that surveys will be invulnerable to such errors.

With regard to attitude surveys, the biggest problem is that respondents may not have any opinion at all about a topic—especially if they do not know much about it or are not interested in it. Therefore, any "opinions" that they express may be very unstable and may be affected by new information or the wording of the question. Survey methodologists are very much concerned with these problems and are continuing to increase our understanding of the sources of response errors.

## Uses of Surveys and Polls

The results of surveys are used for many purposes. In the most general sense, they serve as aids to planning and decision making in government, politics, business, or the nonprofit sector. More specifically, surveys are often used to help organizations monitor the implementation of decisions and to evaluate the results of government programs or advertising campaigns. Surveys are commissioned by the federal government to measure the costs of medical care and the utilization of medical services, to determine the health status of the population, to evaluate the effectiveness of different types of job-training programs, to assess what is learned in schools, and to measure the unemployment rate. Surveys are used by businesses to help them learn who their customers are, what their customers like or dislike about their products or services, and what other products or services their customers might prefer. Advertising agencies use surveys to test ideas for advertising campaigns and to evaluate their effectiveness.

The media use surveys to measure audience size. The most familiar example is the Nielsen ratings, which are obtained by a device attached to the television sets in a sample of households; this device indicates which station the set is tuned to and, in a recent technological innovation, is able to keep track of who is watching the program. In addition, audience-rating firms conduct a survey involving a large sample of households whose members keep diaries of their television watching. Estimates of audience size based on surveys are used to set advertising rates for both print and electronic media and determine the fate of many television programs and personalities.

The media also use surveys to monitor the development of public opinion related to particular events or government policies and to chart changes in public opinion over time. For the media, results of public opinion polls may be news; and, of course, politicians are interested in surveys to keep abreast of public opinion and, during campaigns, to monitor the reaction of the electorate to their campaign activities.

Surveys are used in legal cases to establish infringement of trademarks and to ascertain whether an advertisement is deceptive. Surveys also have been used to determine the need for a change of venue and to help lawyers in picking juries.

Health planners conduct surveys to measure the use of health services by different groups in the population, in order to plan programs and facilities to meet future health needs. Program evaluators use surveys to measure the outcome of educational programs, job-training programs, and assistance programs.

A broader discussion of the uses and misuses of surveys and

of their effect on contemporary life is presented in Chapters Three, Ten, and Eleven.

## Political Polling: A Special Case

Public opinion polling thrives in a democratic environment. Indeed, some have argued that it is the handmaiden of modern democracy. In modern states, with their large populations, rapid means of communication, and popular dependence on governmental provision of many basic services, effective democratic government depends on a knowledge of public opinion. Although public opinion is expressed in elections, they are not held frequently enough and are not refined enough to give ongoing guidance to popular feeling. Politicians are professional interpreters of public opinion, but they must rely on their own communications with constituents and the information obtained by party workers—all sources that suffer from severe bias. The media vie with one another in their claims to voice public opinion, but their claims are often suspect because of their lack of independence and their need to be economically viable. Public opinion polling provides another means of measuring *vox populi;* furthermore, it lays claim to being based on scientific principles rather than on political or commercial interests.

Polls have become a major factor in modern democratic political life, both in the United States and abroad. Astute political observers in the United States have argued that the president's standing in popularity polls significantly affects his ability to govern. With presidential elections occurring only every four years, the polls become a major means by which the electorate can make its satisfaction or dissatisfaction known on a more or less continuous basis.

Critics of the American political system—as compared with European parliamentary systems, in which governments are replaced when they lose the confidence of the public—point out that presidential popularity polls act to restrain the president from straying too far from his mandate. On the other hand, those who feel that the government should have more latitude to act on policies that are in the best interest of the country, even though not popular, argue that presidential popularity polls do a disservice to the political process by making the president too concerned about the popularity of his actions.

Whatever one feels about this debate, it is clear that polls have provided a means by which public opinion becomes a force in governmental decision making—not necessarily the decisive force but one that must be continually attended to. The president's pollster has become one of his closest political advisers, and no one runs for high political office without working closely with a polling firm. Louis Harris, Patrick Caddell, and Richard Wirthlin have become familiar names in American political life, not because of any office they have held but because of their role as pollsters for successful presidential candidates.

Polls are not the only source of information about public sentiments, nor have they eliminated the other sources. They have proved to be a reliable and valuable source and, in the United States at least, have become the single most important source of information about public opinion. No politician can afford to ignore them; no candidate runs for office without the extensive use of polling.

# 2

# Growth of
# Public Opinion Polling

---

Public opinion polling in the United States began on a regular institutionalized basis in July 1935, when *Fortune* magazine published the first *Fortune* poll, conducted by Elmo Roper with his colleagues Paul Cherington and Richardson Wood. A few months later, in October, George Gallup began a syndicated service to thirty-five newspapers that was soon to be known everywhere as the Gallup poll. Another poll, conducted by Archibald Crossley, was begun in 1936.

### Antecedents

Polls and surveys developed from three widely different streams of activity: journalism (straw polls), market research, and social surveys. In the United States, both George Gallup and Elmo Roper came to polling from market research and journalistic interests. In Britain and Western Europe, the strong tradition of social surveys of economic conditions of the poor and working classes led to the rapid adoption of polls once they were successful in the United States.

*Journalism (Straw Polls).* In democratic countries, there has always been a strong interest in knowing who will win an election.

12

Prior to 1935, newspapers and magazines used a range of informal methods, the most common of which was the straw poll. The first such poll, it is generally agreed, was taken by the *Harrisburg Pennsylvanian* in the summer of 1824. In this poll, Andrew Jackson received 335 votes to 169 for John Quincy Adams, with Henry Clay getting 19 and William H. Crawford 9 (Robinson, 1932). Later that year, the *Raleigh Star* polled 4,256 voters at political meetings and also found Jackson far ahead.

The use of straw polls continued sporadically during the nineteenth century but intensified early in the twentieth century. In 1904, the *New York Herald* polled 30,000 voters in New York City; and major newspapers—including the *Herald*, the *Cincinnati Inquirer*, the *Chicago Record-Herald*, the *St. Louis Republic*, the *Boston Globe*, and the *Los Angeles Times*—collaborated on predicting the 1908 and 1912 presidential elections. The *Farm Journal* began presidential prediction in 1912 and the *Literary Digest* in 1916.

The methods used in these straw ballots varied considerably. Most often, the newspaper or magazine simply printed a ballot and asked readers to cut it out and mail it in. Sometimes, as with the *Literary Digest*, ballots were mailed to millions of names on mailing lists. Today such methods are known to have enormous biases. In other instances, canvassers at meetings or specific locations distributed and collected ballots. Although this was a more careful method, the votes still were generally added together without concerns about sample bias. Results from different locations were obtained at different times and cumulated, so that it was impossible to measure trends. Offshoots of these methods are still used today in shopping-mall intercept studies for some market research studies. Regardless of the method or quality, it was always clear to editors that stories about the results of straw votes sold newspapers and magazines.

*Market Research.* The history of public opinion polling is intimately tied to the development of market research in the United States. Elmo Roper was a partner in a market research firm when he started the *Fortune* poll; in the introduction to that poll, he talked specifically about the adoption of market research methods

to measuring public attitudes. Since his readers were mainly
businessmen with experience and confidence in market research
methods, this link was intended to increase their confidence in this
new idea. Roper's first poll, in addition to asking about public
issues such as taxes and the government's role in providing jobs,
also asked about car ownership and cigarette smoking.

George Gallup was a highly successful advertising researcher
at Young and Rubicam when he started the American Institute of
Public Opinion. In his work for a Ph.D. in applied psychology at
Iowa State University, he had used survey methods to measure the
readership of print media. Among other important findings, he
noted that the comics in newspapers were read by most adults as
well as by children; this finding led to the use of the comics as
advertising media. At the same time, Gallup recognized that market
research methods could be used to obtain newsworthy information
about people's opinions on public issues and on candidates in
elections. Gallup had first applied these methods in 1932, when his
mother-in-law was running for secretary of state in Iowa. Gallup
did informal polling in key districts, tried to discover the major
issues and perceptions of the two candidates, and helped her plan
a successful campaign.

Market research as an organized activity started in the United
States in 1879, when the N. W. Ayer and Son advertising agency
wired state officials and publishers requesting information on
expected grain production (Lockley, 1950). Sporadic activity
continued for the next thirty years. The first market research firm,
the Business Bourse, was founded in 1911 by J. George Frederick,
who was also the first to hire and maintain a group of interviewers
in strategic locations. At the same time, the Harvard Business
School established a Bureau of Business Research. One member was
Paul Cherington, who was later a partner of Elmo Roper. In 1911
also, the Kellogg Company undertook the first readership survey, a
mail postcard survey to determine which magazines were read by
different types of people. Simultaneously, the Curtis Publishing
Company started a commercial research department under the
direction of Charles Coolidge Parlin. This department grew to be
one of the largest in the country; at one time, Curtis had a staff of
about 1,200 part-time interviewers.

Although the growth of market research was interrupted by World War I, by the middle 1920s many large manufacturers and advertising media had market research groups. Pressure from these researchers led to the first Census of Distribution, conducted by the Census Bureau in 1929, which reported on the number and characteristics of retail and wholesale establishments. With the introduction of radio as a commercial medium, there also grew a need to measure listenership.

The market researchers and advertising agencies were always interested in academic developments that might improve the quality of their product or provide a new service. Many of their methods, however, had been developed empirically as they produced information for clients. They recognized that relatively small samples could be used to predict results with sufficient accuracy for action purposes. They knew from Robinson's (1932) *Straw Votes* that some attention must be paid to the demographic composition of their sample, although the quota methods they used to control for characteristics were later shown to be problematic. They were also aware that question wording mattered. Indeed, the second *Fortune* poll included a brief technical discussion of question wording as a far greater source of bias than sampling. One notable researcher on question wording was Henry C. Link, who established the Market Surveys Division of the Psychological Corporation in 1930. This group provided consulting and interviewing assistance to market researchers and thus helped transmit some of the results of work with attitude questionnaires on college students into a broader arena. In 1932, Link started the Psychological Barometer, a service to advertisers that periodically measured attitudes on public as well as business issues.

*Early Social Surveys.* Since ancient times, governments and rulers have used censuses to help govern and tax populations, especially in newly conquered territories. Reference to such censuses are found in the Bible; in the eleventh century, William the Conqueror's general census of England was recorded in the Domesday Book; censuses also were taken in Venice and Florence in the Renaissance; and in the United States, the first census was taken in 1790. Aside from the census, however, there was no well-established tradition of national social surveys in the United States prior to the 1930s, although hundreds of local studies had been conducted to gather basic statistical data and to arouse public interest in reform measures (Parten, 1950). The rapid growth of national social surveys occurred in the late 1930s, after the polls were introduced and successful.

In Britain, the dislocations of the industrial revolution led to investigations of the poor and working classes starting in the middle of the nineteenth century. It can be argued whether this was social research or journalism, but the techniques of interviewing are very similar. The two best-known examples of this work are Henry Mayhew's *London Labour and the London Poor* (1861) and Charles Booth's more methodologically sophisticated study, *The Life and Labour of the People of London* (1889–1903).

This work continued during the twentieth century. Benjamin Rowntree (1902) interviewed every wage-earning family in York and obtained information on housing, occupation, and earnings. A decade later, Arthur Bowley made a study of working-class conditions in Reading, the first of a series of poverty studies. His major contribution was the use of careful sampling, and his work influenced all future British social surveys (Bowley and Burnett-Hurst, 1915). In the worldwide depression of the early 1930s, surveys of working-class poverty were common. Similar studies were also common throughout Western Europe. A famous example was the study of attitudes of the unemployed in Marienthal by Marie Jahoda, Paul Lazarsfeld, and Hans Zeisel ([1933] 1978). The local studies in the United States may also have been influenced by this work in Europe.

An obvious question is whether the American market research and journalistic traditions had any impact on Western Europe. Apparently, they did not. Market research did not begin in Europe until the 1930s, probably spurred by the success of the polls. The British and Western European parliamentary systems also made it more difficult and less interesting journalistically to attempt to predict national election outcomes.

## Developments in the 1930s and 1940s

It is often noted that, when the time is ripe, scientific discoveries are made simultaneously by several researchers. This was the case with public opinion polls, which, if not a basic discovery, were a major extrapolation from existing methods. By the mid 1930s, the questionnaire, interviewing, and sampling methods (imperfect as they were) could support public opinion polling. Indeed, the *Literary Digest* had conducted three large mail ballots on attitudes toward prohibition in 1922, 1930, and 1932. One might ask why the polls had not begun a decade or more earlier. One possible answer is that George Gallup and Elmo Roper had not yet had sufficient training or experience. A structural explanation independent of individuals is that interest in public opinion, which had diminished during the return to normalcy, rose sharply after the great depression and President Roosevelt's New Deal.

The most influential writer on public opinion in the 1920s was Walter Lippmann (1922, 1925). Lippmann was essentially an elitist who doubted that public opinion could be useful in helping a society to govern itself. During this era, the defenders of public opinion were mainly silent. In the 1930s, however, an upswelling of populist sentiment infused the work of all the early pollsters, but especially George Gallup, who became the spokesman for polls through his book *The Pulse of Democracy* (Gallup and Rae, 1940) as well as in many articles and speeches. Gallup was eloquent, even poetic, in his defense of the use of polls:

> What the mass of the people thinks puts governments in and out of office, starts and stops wars, sets the tone of morality, makes and breaks heroes. We know that democrats think public opinion is important because continuous efforts have been made throughout the history of popular government to improve and clarify its expression. We know, too, that autocrats think public opinion is important because they devote vast sums and careful attention to curbing and controlling it.
>
> Throughout the history of politics this central problem has remained: shall the common people be free to express their basic needs and purposes, or shall they be dominated by a small ruling clique? Shall the goal be the free expression of public opinion, or shall

efforts be made to ensure its repression? In the
democratic community, the attitudes of the mass of
the people determine policy. "With public opinion on
its side," said Abraham Lincoln in the course of his
famous contest with Douglas, "everything succeeds.
With public opinion against it, nothing succeeds"
[Gallup and Rae, 1940, p. 6].

It may not be a coincidence that George Gallup was born in
Iowa and Elmo Roper in Nebraska within a few months of each
other at the turn of the century. Although they both became
sophisticated Easterners, their roots were clearly in Midwestern
populism. Roper, although connected with the leading business
magazine of its time, was an ardent New Deal Democrat. Gallup,
although he claimed never to have voted in a presidential election
after he started his poll, was a moderate Republican. They both
shared, however, a strong belief in the value of knowing what the
public felt.

*The First Gallup Poll.* The initial report of the Gallup poll
on October 20, 1935, received substantial attention in the nation's
press. The first question asked was "Do you think expenditures by
the government for relief and recovery are too little, too great, about
right?" The data were reported not only nationally but also by
persons on and not on relief, by region, and by party preference.
Results were also compared with those obtained by unpublished
polls on the same question in February and July 1934.

The *Washington Post* gave these results a full page at the
front of its features section (see Figure 1). There were also articles
explaining how the polls were conducted and a quote from James
Bryce, the famous British authority on American government: "The
obvious weakness of government by opinion is the difficulty in
ascertaining it." The *Post* had also featured several full-page
advertisements prior to the first poll with pictures of Woodrow
Wilson, Theodore Roosevelt, James Bryce, and Walter Lippmann.
The ad headline read: "A contribution to the science of government.
America speaks." At the end of the ad was an invitation to subscribe
to the newspaper so that the reader would not miss any of the poll

results. In addition to being a contribution to the science of government, the polls were seen as a circulation builder.

*The* Literary Digest *Fiasco.* The new public opinion polls had their first test and triumph in 1936, when all three polls—the Gallup, the Roper, and the Crossley—predicted a substantial victory for President Roosevelt. Since Roosevelt carried all states except Maine and Vermont, it should not have been too difficult to predict his victory. Actually, the new polls substantially underestimated the size of that victory. What made these predictions impressive was that the *Literary Digest* poll, which was based on a huge mail-in sample and which had been correct in every presidential election since 1920, had predicted a Republican victory. Using methods that it had used earlier, the *Literary Digest* mailed ten million ballots to households listed in telephone directories or state auto registrations. Of course, there were very large biases in favor of upper-income households, since in 1936 lower-income households did not have telephones or cars. Of the mailed ballots, some 2.4 million were returned, an impressively large number but only a quarter of all mailed. Again, nonresponse biases strongly favored those who were the most committed Republicans. The *Literary Digest* predicted that Alfred Landon, the Republican candidate, would get 57 percent of the major party vote. In fact, he received only 38.5 percent.

What made the correct prediction by the polls still more impressive was that Gallup had warned his subscribers that the *Digest*'s methods would point to the wrong man. As reported in the *Saturday Evening Post:*

> Landon was nominated on June 11, 1936. On July 12, Gallup warned his subscribers that the Digest's old fashioned methods would point to the wrong man.
>
> Almost as an after-thought he mentioned that its totals would show about 56% for Landon, 44% for Roosevelt.
>
> Inasmuch as the poll was not to begin for six weeks, Wilfred J. Funk, editor of the Literary Digest,

Figure 1. The First Gallup Poll.

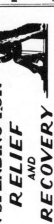

The results of these polls are being published for the first time today in leading newspapers—representing every shade of political preference—from the Atlantic to the Pacific. The results show that public opinion on the spending issue has shifted as follows:

**Persons Saying:**

| | Too Great | Too Little | About Right |
|---|---|---|---|
| February, 1934 | 37% | 17% | 46% |
| July, 1934 | 48% | 16% | 36% |
| October, 1935 | 60% | 9% | 31% |

That is, almost twice as many persons now believe the Government is spending too much as did a year and a half ago. In the same time, the number of persons who think the Government is spending too little has dwindled by half. Of every three persons who thought the Government's spending "about right" in February, 1934, only two think so today.

The degree of opposition to Government spending varies considerably by sections of the country as shown on the map above. New England, where the Democrats recently lost an important Congressional election, leads the protest. The East Central and Middle Atlantic sections are next in vehemence, and the South, the West Central region, and the Pacific Coast States are bunched well above the protest line. By contrast, the Rocky Mountain region, where several States have swollen relief rolls as the result of drought and dust, defines Government spending as "about right":

**Persons Saying:**

| Section | Too Great | Too Little | About Right |
|---|---|---|---|
| New England | 75% | 6% | 19% |
| East Central | 62% | 9% | 29% |
| Middle Atlantic | 61% | 13% | 26% |
| South | 60% | 5% | 35% |
| West Central | 58% | 7% | 35% |
| Pacific Coast | 58% | 9% | 33% |
| Mountain | 44% | 11% | 45% |

Finally, the institute polls demonstrate that, in the amount of Government spending for relief and recovery, the Republicans have an issue they can unite on. The following table shows how party members view the President's spending policy:

| | Too Great | Too Little | About Right |
|---|---|---|---|
| Republicans | 89% | 4% | 7% |
| Democrats | 36% | 11% | 53% |

How this issue of Government spending for relief and recovery, and other issues, have affected President Roosevelt's majority will be reported by America Speaks next Sunday.

The American Institute of Public Opinion has exerted unusual efforts in order to answer that question. Not content with a special tally of ballots from this lowest income group, trained interviewers have sought out the voters in relief areas.

This, then, is the way persons on relief answer the questiion of Government spending:

**"Too little," say 40 per cent.**
**"Too great," say 21 per cent.**
**"About right," agree 39 per cent.**

For every two persons on relief who are satisfied—who think the Government is spending the right amount—there are two other persons on relief who believe the Government is not spending enough. From their number comes virtually everyone in the United States who thinks Government expenditures for relief and recovery "too little."

More surprising—for every two persons on relief who are satisfied, another person, also on relief, thinks the Government actually spends too much. This person joins the Nation-wide majority which calls Government expenditures "too great."

Why does this one man in five on relief rolls think the Government is spending too much in his behalf?

From interviews and from penciled postscripts on scores of ballots come these typical answers:

**"Too much is spent on red tape."**

**"It would have been cheaper to give us work right from the start."**

**"The Government will go broke, and then where will we all be?"**

The persons on relief who think the Government should spend more express themselves this way:

**"There's not enough to get by on. I'm only existing—not living."**

**"The Government might be spending a lot, but folks on relief ain't getting it."**

**"The wrong ones are getting it."**

**"The Government has lots of money and should help the people more."**

Two out of every five on relief think the Government is sending about the right amount. These are the reasons they give the American Institute of Public Opinion:

**"The country is better off now than it was before."**
**"I feel pretty much O. K. myself now."**
**"Those over us must know their business."**

# Bryce Named Poll as Best Opinion Test

More than 44 years ago in 1891 James Bryce, one of the great authorities on American government, wrote prophetically:

"The obvious weakness of government by opinion is the difficulty of ascertaining it."

Bryce did not foresee the exact machinery of America Speaks, the national weekly poll of public opinion, but he did predict that some method of registering public sentiment on the issues of the day would be devised.

Students of government will now examine his analysis of 44 years ago with renewed interest. Quoting a few paragraphs from his famous book "The American Commonwealth":

"No other people now stand so near the goal of government by public opinion as the Americans."

"The referendum is the logical resource, but it is troublesome and costly . . . the choice of persons for office is only an indirect and often unsatisfactory way of declaring views of policy . . . elections come at fixed intervals, and time is lost in waiting for the popular judgment."

"It may even be said that one of their chief problems is to devise means whereby the national will shall be most fully expressed, most quickly known, most unresistingly and cheerfully obeyed."

"Toward this goal Americans have marched with steady steps. No other people stand so near it."

# Gallup Directs Institute Polls For the Public

Dr. George Gallup, managing director of the American Institute of Public Opinion, is known in American journalism as the man who first devised a scientific way of measuring "reader interest" for newspapers and magazines.

He adapted the same method to measuring the effectiveness of advertising and later he undertook the measurement of the size of radio audiences and their reactions to different programs.

Dr. Gallup has now devised and put into operation a method for determining popular sentiment on political and economic questions of the day. Dr. Gallup has been taking Nation-wide polls of opinion on major issues since December 1933. It was not until he had conducted 54 such polls over a period of nearly two years that the American Institute of Public Opinion was willing to offer its present weekly project to the public.

## 11,000,000 Jobless.

Eleven million were jobless in the United States at the beginning of the transfer from direct relief to work relief last May, according to estimates by Harry L. Hopkins, Federal Emergency Relief administrator. The number is exactly half the estimated figure for world unemployment, as reported at the bor Office at Geneva. same time by the International La-

columns of The Washington Post considers that, irrespective of its editorial convictions, it owes a duty to its readers to publish the facts about Nation-wide opinion.

Joined with The Washington Post in making possible this new venture in the field of journalism are many of the leading newspapers of the country. These newspapers, which print the results of the weekly polls at the same time they appear in The Washington Post, represent all shades of political belief. Some are rock-ribbed Republican, some are ardent supporters of the New Deal, some are independent.

But all these papers have one thing in common with The Washington Post. They believe their readers are entitled to know the opinions of the great mass of citizens of this country on controversial issues of the day. None of these papers, however, has anything to do with the machinery of conducting the polls or of tabulating the results. All that is handled by the American Institute of Public Opinion, a fact-finding organization that has no affiliation with any political party or with any economic group.

## Roosevelt Strength Is Tested in Survey

If the Presidential election were held today, for whom would you vote?

The American Institute of Public Opinion has asked United States voters that question every month since February, 1934. In next Sunday's Post, AMERICA SPEAKS will tell you whether President Roosevelt is gaining or losing today and how the Presidential "batting average" has shifted during the last 20 months.

itures too great. (See chart.)

Six months later Congress had thrown in another $1,400,000,000. This time approximately one-half of the people felt the Government was spending too much.

Now, in October, 1935, when President Roosevelt has virtually finished allotting his $4,800,000,000 emergency fund, two-thirds of the people—60 per cent to be exact—think Uncle Sam is spending too much.

Political observers believe that several recent pronouncements from the White House indicate that President Roosevelt is himself in agreement with this view. In his San Diego speech early this month the President declared that the Federal Government must plan to reduce expenditures for emergency relief as swiftly as is humanly possible.

Although it was Norman Thomas, Socialist candidate for President, who in the 1932 campaign first advocated a $5,000,000,000 appropriation to help the destitute, the relief program became a war-cry of loyal Democrats less than a year later. Republicans quickly took up the opposition, and at the time of the first poll in February, 1934, virtually 90 per cent of the voters who designated themselves as Republicans thought the Government was spending too much. Democrats at that time believed the amount was about right, or, if anything, not enough. The solid Republican front remained unbroken in the second and third polls.

Soon, however, a dramatic shift of sentiment began to take place among Democrats. In the first poll only 1 Democrat out of every 12 thought Government spending excessive. In the second poll, one out of every six thought so. In the third poll, in October, 1935, the proportion jumped to one out of every three.

## Wilson Wanted Guidance.

In 1911 Woodrow Wilson said: "I would rather hear what men are talking about on trains and in the shops and by the firesides than hear anything else, because I want guidance and I know I could get it there."

## 'Fewer Mistakes.'

In 1906 Theodore Roosevelt said: "I believe the majority of the plain people of the United States will day in and day out make fewer mistakes in governing themselves than any smaller class or body of men will make in trying to govern them."

## An Investment in Youth

*CCC camps maintained half a million young Americans last year at a cost of three hundred million relief dollars. Is American youth receiving full benefit from these expenditures? Should they be continued?*

# Poll Is a National Election on a Small Scale

*Since February, 1934, the American Institute of Public Opinion has conducted 54 consecutive Nation-wide polls on political and social issues of public interest.*

*The poll reported today and every poll conducted by the American Institute of Public Opinion is a national election on a small scale. Ballots come from every State in the Union, the large cities, the towns and rural districts and from high and low income groups. Each group is allotted the same proportion of votes as it casts in a national election. The number of votes from any State is in direct proportion to its population and electoral vote.*

*The population of the United States is usually classified in five economic levels, ranging from the highest income group down to and including those citizens on relief. As one out of six individuals is on relief, a proportionate number of ballots must be secured from this group in order to insure a perfect cross-section of the Nation.*

*Secret ballots are sent to voters by air mail, letter and postcard, in addition to personal interviews by a Nation-wide staff of trained interviewers.*

*The result of this method is that the reports of the National Weekly Poll of Public Opinion are within a per cent or two of what would be obtained if the whole country voted on the same question.*

## Power and Protection

*Grand Coulee dam on the Columbia River is [illegible] such public works projects which the Government hopes will be [illegible] for providing employment, and incidentally, power and irrigation.*

was outraged. "Never before has anyone foretold what our poll was going to show even before it started!" he snapped. "Our fine statistical friend" should be advised that the Digest would carry on "with those old fashioned methods that have produced correct forecasts exactly one hundred per cent of the time" [Rich, 1939, p. 9].

The 1936 election led to the demise of the *Literary Digest* (which was already in financial difficulty) and to the almost overnight acceptance of public opinion polls by politicians and the general public. From this point, the growth of polls in the United States and Western Europe was rapid, indeed explosive.

*State Polls.* With the success of the national opinion polls came a demand from regional newspapers for use of the same methods within state and local areas. In 1940, the Texas poll was established by Joe Belden and funded by a group of Texas newspapers; in 1943–44, the Iowa poll (sponsored by the *Des Moines Register*) and the Minnesota poll (sponsored by the *Minneapolis Tribune*) were established. The California poll followed in 1946 under the direction of Mervin Field.

*Department of Agriculture Surveys.* Late in 1936, the Department of Agriculture, under the direction of Henry Wallace, an Iowa populist and later vice-president of the United States, set up an experiment in which a sociologist traveled through various rural areas talking to farmers about the effects of USDA's farm programs (Skott, 1943). The information was so useful that the interviewing staff was expanded to five the following year. The work was conducted in the Program Planning Division of the Agricultural Adjustment Administration. Sampling was not systematic, interviews remained mainly unstructured, and very little quantitative analysis was done; but the results received ever wider attention, and a decision was made to put this function in the central planning group. Therefore, a Division of Program Surveys was established in the Bureau of Agricultural Economics in 1939. Rensis Likert, already well known for his work on attitude scales, was named as the new head of this division, and it expanded rapidly until its growth was slowed by competing demands during World War II. Although the division concentrated on surveys of farmers and the rural population, it also studied the general population to measure public knowledge about farm issues.

A major development in this new agency was the use of area probability samples, which were ultimately to replace the quota methods then in use. The questionnaires, however, continued to be very unstructured and depended heavily on the work of Carl Rogers, who later developed the clinical procedures of nondirective therapy. In contrast to the earlier studies, answers to questions were coded and quantified. There was still little recognition of problems of interviewer and coder variability introduced by these methods.

The interviewers used in these studies were full-time social scientists, almost all with advanced degrees. The core staff included some who would be ranked among the most distinguished sociologists, social psychologists, and statisticians in academic social research and commercial market research in the decades after World War II. When plans were made to reduce the activities of this group near the end of World War II, Rensis Likert began looking for a university setting to establish a new facility. He finally established his group at the University of Michigan in the summer of 1946 as the Survey Research Center.

*Bureau of Applied Social Research.* In 1933, Paul Lazarsfeld, who had been trained in psychology and mathematics in Vienna and had conducted the first broadcast-listening study in the 1920s, came to the United States to escape the rise of the Nazis. He established the Office of Radio Research at Princeton University with Hadley Cantril and Frank Stanton as associates. (Stanton was then research director of CBS and later became its president.)

When Lazarsfeld moved to Columbia University in 1940, the Office of Radio Research became the Social Research Laboratory of the Department of Sociology. Its program was expanded to include the study of other media of mass communication, and an investigation of the effects of these media on voting inaugurated a continuing program of research on political behavior. During World War II, many studies were undertaken on behalf of the government, particularly under the direction of Robert K. Merton. In 1944, the organization was renamed the Bureau of Applied Social Research. The new name symbolized the bureau's efforts to support large-scale social research by linking it to the practical problems of public and private organizations. The bureau became the training ground for a very large number of the most distinguished quantitative sociologists over the next several decades.

*Public Opinion Quarterly.* The first issue of the *Public Opinion Quarterly* was published in 1937, with Harwood Childs as its editor. Childs was one of several distinguished scholars in this field at Princeton University. Since Gallup and Claude Robinson also lived nearby, Princeton, New Jersey, became the first major center of public opinion activity in the United States and has remained so to this date. Another significant Princeton scholar was Hadley Cantril, whom we discuss in greater detail in the next chapter.

*National Opinion Research Center.* NORC was founded in 1941 by Harry H. Field with money from the unrelated Field Foundation and housing and a small subsidy from the University of Denver (Sheatsley, 1982). Field was born in Britain and came to the United States after World War I. He was introduced to research when he went to work for Young and Rubicam in 1935. It was Field who was asked by Gallup to establish the British Institute of Public Opinion.

Although Field had little formal education, he conceived of the idea of a nonprofit research center affiliated with a university. This center would do no commercial research or election forecasting but would offer its services at cost to nonprofit organizations and university researchers. Three leading commercial researchers, Gallup, Roper, and Crossley, encouraged his efforts. Field also had strong support from Hadley Cantril of the Office of Public Opinion Research at Princeton and from Gordon Allport at Harvard and Samuel Stouffer at the University of Chicago as well as from Paul Lazarsfeld at Columbia. Stouffer, Allport, and Hadley Cantril were on the founding Board of Trustees.

The first activity of the newly formed NORC was to hire and train a staff of interviewers. Although interviewers worked only part time as needed, from its onset NORC used only interviewers who had been hired and trained personally. This was also the procedure used by Roper, who loaned NORC some interviewers until it could hire and train its own. This interviewing staff was extensively utilized during World War II as NORC became the field organization for the Surveys Division of the Office of War Information (OWI). Among the topics studied during the war years were labor problems, absenteeism, morale, inflation, price controls, shortages and rationing, war news and the media, and the role of women in the war effort. Since OWI was located in New York, NORC opened an office there. After 1942, this office was headed by Paul Sheatsley.

*Research Branch, U.S. Army.* While civilian attitudes were being measured by Gallup, Roper, Crossley, and the newly organized NORC, the United States Army measured the opinions of enlisted men and officers through the Research Branch of the Information and Education Division, which was established in October 1941, just two months before the United States became involved in the war. This group was headed by Samuel Stouffer, who had been a sociology professor at the University of Chicago. Joining him in the initial planning were Rensis Likert and Quinn McNemar, a professor of psychology at Stanford.

Under Stouffer's leadership, a distinguished staff was assembled, including Edward Suchman, Shirley Star, Robin Williams, Jack Elinson, and Arnold Rose, all of whom became leaders in the field of opinion research after the war. Consulting for the Research Branch were a large number of sociologists, psychologists, and statisticians who were already distinguished: Hadley Cantril, John Dollard, Edwin Guthrie, Philip Hauser, Paul Lazarsfeld, Louis Guttman, Robert Merton, Frederick Mosteller, and Frank Stanton.

The work that was done by this group has been very ably summarized in the classic work in four volumes, *Studies in Social Psychology in World War II,* often called *The American Soldier,* the title of Volume 1 (Stouffer and others, 1949). The main purpose of the Research Branch was to provide the army command with facts about the attitudes of soldiers as well as inferences that might be helpful in policy formulation.

The Research Branch was involved in some far-reaching research:

1.  Development of the point system for determining order of demobilization (based on the wishes of soldiers, as determined in surveys)
2.  Survey of the postwar plans of soldiers, used for establishing the new GI Bill that made it possible for millions of soldiers to attend college
3.  Development of a psychoneurotic inventory—the first such effort at mass screening for mental health
4.  Measurement of attitudes and stress of combat, both before and after, to determine the relation between these and combat losses
5.  Studies of morale problems in the infantry
6.  Development of a job classification and assignment system

The findings of these studies are described in detail in *Studies in Social Psychology in World War II,* and these books are still essential reading for social scientists as well as for military men and historians. In a lengthy review in *Public Opinion Quarterly,* Lazarsfeld (1949, pp. 383, 386) pointed out the major contributions of this work:

> The Stouffer volumes contributed to our under-standing of at least three aspects of the role of primary groups:
>
> a)   the way in which primary groups shape the thinking of the individual,
> b)   the way in which they provide emotional support,
> c)   how the loss of contact with such groups creates emotional disturbances in the individual.
>
> The manner in which such inner controls function and develop is summarized by the concept of a "frame of reference." Stouffer and his associates have

devoted a great deal of attention to clarifying and documenting the importance of these inner controls.

For the purposes of preliminary orientation we can make the following distinctions, which rank the effects of frame of reference in an order of increasing complexity:

a)   selective perception,
b)   level of expectation,
c)   relative deprivation,
d)   role of uncertainty.

In addition to the substantive contributions of the Research Branch, there were major methodological contributions. Most noteworthy were the development of scalogram analysis, which soon became known as Guttman scaling (after its developer, Louis Guttman), and the development of latent structure analysis by Paul Lazarsfeld. There were also important experiments in mass communication by Carl Hovland and his colleagues that are beyond the scope of this book.

Stouffer fully recognized that the methods used by his group were derived from "the techniques of public opinion research and marketing research, involving systematic questioning of representative samples of respondents about concrete problems" (Stouffer and others, 1949, p. 37). However, the Research Branch's procedures were not the personal interviews used by the pollsters. The questionnaires were self-administered in 10,000 sessions with about 500,000 soldiers, so that on average fifty soldiers were in a room at the same time. Those who could not read or understand the questionnaire were interviewed by an enlisted member of the branch, who was at the session along with an officer. Sampling was done very carefully, by means of random sampling procedures from army rosters. As is always the case in such studies, which are still conducted in much the same way, some men were not available because of special assignments or field exercises, but there were virtually no refusals.

*Current Population Survey.* Surveys had been conducted prior to 1940 on a sporadic basis by the United States government, in addition to the Department of Agriculture work already mentioned. For example, a national consumer expenditure survey and the first national health survey were conducted with crude samples in 1935–36. In 1936, the Bureau of Labor Statistics began a continuing series of surveys to determine the extent and characteristics of unemployed workers. These surveys, transferred to the Census Bureau in 1942, have been conducted steadily, with modifications, and are now known as the Current Population Survey. Much of the work on area probability sampling was developed as part of this activity. While this study, and most of the wide range of surveys conducted since then by the Census Bureau, dealt with behavioral and demographic information, it soon became evident that many problems, such as interviewer and question-wording effects, were as troublesome in demographic as in attitude surveys.

*Founding of American Association for Public Opinion Research.* By 1946, the rapidly growing field of public opinion was ready for a professional organization to facilitate communication between the academic and commercial researchers. Harry Field, the director of NORC, convened a conference at Central City, Colorado, which was attended by many leading academic, government, and commercial pollsters, media researchers, and other academics; and in 1947, the American Association for Public Opinion Research (AAPOR) was formally founded in a conference at Williams College in Williamstown, Massachusetts. Many of the policy and methodological issues addressed there would continue to be addressed at future AAPOR conferences. In particular, sessions on bread-and-butter issues related to questionnaire wording and interviewer performance have been standard at all AAPOR conferences. The organization has now grown to about 1,200 members and continues its mix of academic, nonprofit, and commercial researchers, with representation from all the major media and governmental users and providers of survey data.

### The 1948 Disaster: A Setback for Polls

The polls had continued to predict presidential elections with great accuracy in 1940 and 1944, but the 1948 election was a disaster and led to substantial, but temporary, loss of confidence in poll results, as well as a reevaluation of methodology by the pollsters themselves.

All three major national polls, Gallup, Roper, and Crossley, predicted a substantial victory for Thomas E. Dewey over Harry S. Truman, who was running for his second term after taking office as vice-president in April 1945, when Franklin Delano Roosevelt died. Table 1 shows the predictions of the three major polls and the actual election results. As can be seen, Truman won comfortably. The most complete study of the failure of the polls in this election was conducted by the Social Science Research Council (1949). This study pinpointed the following major reasons:

1. The pollsters stopped interviewing too soon and combined early and late poll results. Thus, they missed a strong late trend to Truman.
2. The sample procedures being used led to oversamples of higher- and middle-income voters, who were more likely to be Republican.
3. The methods in use were not adequate to determine whether the poll respondent would actually vote in the election.
4. The pollsters did not allocate the undecided voters to the different candidates in an objective or consistent way.
5. Simple random variability caused sample results to differ from population results by chance.

**Table 1. 1948 Presidential Election Poll Predictions
(Percentage of Total Presidential Vote).**

|               | Dewey | Truman | Thurmond | Wallace | Total[a] |
|---------------|-------|--------|----------|---------|----------|
| National vote | 45.1  | 49.5   | 2.4      | 2.4     | 99.4     |
| Crossley      | 49.9  | 44.8   | 1.6      | 3.3     | 99.6     |
| Gallup        | 49.5  | 44.5   | 2.0      | 4.0     | 100.0    |
| Roper         | 52.2  | 37.1   | 5.2      | 4.3     | 98.8     |

[a]Exclusive of percentages for minor candidates. Gallup percentages calculated on total vote for four principal candidates.

The 1948 election led to major changes in methods used by polling organizations. Since 1948, the polls have been conducted until election day, and trends are watched carefully. The sampling procedures changed from loose quota samples, which made interviewers responsible for respondent selection, to modified area samples (discussed in Chapter Six), where interviewers were told to visit specified households. (The new samples adopted were not strict area probability samples, since, if no one was home at a specified address, the interviewer was permitted to go next door.) Finally, all the pollsters adopted more detailed methods for determining likelihood of voting. These technical revisions were made to satisfy the sophisticated critics of poll methodology, who were basically sympathetic to the idea of public opinion polling.

The 1948 poll failure also led to a short-term disenchantment with the entire polling process. Several newspapers canceled the Gallup poll, and some questions were raised about market research surveys as well. In a short time, however, the users of poll and survey data agreed that they really needed this kind of information, although they tended to treat it with greater caution.

Since 1948, the election polls have been right most of the time, but there have been sufficient errors to remind us that the process cannot be perfect. At the least, random variability will always be a factor. Also, there is still no objective method for treating undecideds or for determining whether a respondent will actually vote. The polls in recent years have recognized these problems and have toned down their claims to infallibility.

### Recent Trends: 1960s–1980s

*Use of Polls by Candidates.* The use of pollsters hired by persons seeking political office first received extensive publicity in the 1960 presidential election, when John F. Kennedy hired Louis Harris and Richard Nixon used Claude Robinson, the head of the Opinion Research Corporation and former partner of George Gallup. Since that time, every presidential candidate has hired a polling organization, and the use of hired pollsters has spread to state, local, and congressional district races. A pollster for a successful candidate, especially a presidential candidate, can obtain substantial new business and exert substantial influence, as may be seen in the careers of Louis Harris and Patrick Caddell, Jimmy Carter's pollster.

The use of political polls for fund raising, particularly in primary elections, has led to a concern that poll results reported by candidates may be deliberately distorted. This concern is discussed in the next chapter, where we also give our views on how politicians should and should not use poll results.

*Use of Polls for Program Planning and Evaluation.* The Kennedy-Johnson era also introduced the extensive use of surveys for the purpose of program planning and evaluation. As an example, the Model Cities Program required administrators to obtain the views of residents in the selected areas, and these views were obtained through surveys, mainly conducted by indigenous interviewers. Evaluation studies were mandated by Congress for most "Great Society" programs, such as the Job Corps, Manpower Development Training Programs, and Neighborhood Health Centers.

The existing survey organizations in the 1960s were not large enough to handle all of the new work generated by federal and local social initiatives, although they grew rapidly in this period. In addition, several new survey organizations flowered. The Rand Corporation, which had been an Air Force think tank, moved into civilian issues as defense contracts were reduced. The Research Triangle Institute of North Carolina began work on the National Assessment of Educational Progress, which soon led to extensive surveys on health and other social problems. It was also at this time that several state universities—including Illinois, Wisconsin, and California—formed survey organizations to conduct state and local surveys.

*Wide Use of Telephone Surveys.* The example of the *Literary Digest* fiasco in 1936, when it mailed questionnaires to the minority of households who had telephones, was sufficient to discourage the use of the telephone during the 1950s and earlier. It became clear, however, to those who watched trends in telephone ownership after World War II that the time would come when almost everyone would have a phone. By the late 1960s and early 1970s, phone ownership had increased to about 90 percent. (Currently, it is about 95 percent.) Thus, while small biases caused by persons without telephones were still a problem, telephone methods began to get active consideration.

Phone methods became attractive because—for a number of reasons—the costs and difficulty of face-to-face interviewing had greatly increased. Many more women were working and could not be found at home as they had been earlier. Moreover, because of the growth of crime and violence in cities, many interviewers were reluctant to visit some areas, and many potential respondents were reluctant to open their doors to strangers. In contrast, phone surveys could be conducted rapidly and cheaply—especially since the introduction of WATS (wide-area telephone service) lines had substantially reduced long-distance charges. Although sampling from telephone directories could be a problem because substantial numbers of persons had unlisted numbers, this problem was overcome by the use of random digit dialing, which bypassed directories entirely and simply selected telephone numbers as in a lottery.

As experience with telephone surveys grew, most researchers concluded that telephone and face-to-face methods usually pro-duced the same results, so that researchers with limited resources almost always preferred the telephone. Political pollsters, in addition, learned that they could get results faster and poll until the last minute more easily with telephones. The last to adopt the telephone technology were government data collection agencies, but even there phone methods are now widely used. In the past decade, the major development in telephone technology has been the use of computer-assisted telephone interviewing (CATI, discussed in detail in Chapter Five). Of course, some kinds of studies, such as those that require reading of material by respond-ents, cannot be done by telephone.

*Renewed Interest in Question-Wording Effects.* As one gets nearer to the present, it is more difficult to determine the important trends, and different observers are less likely to agree. From our perspective, an important recent development in the area of survey methodology has been the renewed interest in question and questionnaire effects. This topic was of concern in the early Roper and Gallup polls and has been discussed at virtually every conference of the American Association for Public Opinion Research. What is new are the current efforts to obtain a deeper theoretical understanding of what is happening.

We believe that this work has been stimulated by our book *Response Effects in Surveys: A Review and Synthesis* (Sudman and Bradburn, 1974). Schuman and his colleagues at the Survey Research Center, University of Michigan, have been conducting continuing experiments of effects of question-wording order and method of administration (Schuman and Presser, 1981). Most recently, and perhaps most significant for future developments, there have been meetings of survey researchers and cognitive psychologists to set research agendas for common problems.

## Developments Overseas

Our history of survey and opinion research has been focused on the United States, but that history was repeated in most developed countries with a few years' lag. The British Gallup poll was established in 1937 and the French poll in 1938. By the outbreak of World War II, opinion polling was well established as a part of the fabric of democratic societies. Under George Gallup's leadership, polls continued to develop during and shortly after World War II. Polls were established in Australia in 1940; in Canada in 1941; in Denmark in 1943; in Switzerland in 1944; and in the Netherlands, West Germany, Finland, Norway, and Italy in 1945–46. All these polls used roughly similar methods and asked some of the same questions, so that opinion comparisons across countries could be made for the first time.

In Britain, the Government Social Survey was founded in 1941 to provide information on home-front morale and attitudes during World War II. After 1970, the Social Survey, which was then an independent department, was merged with the General Register Office to become the Office of Population Censuses and Surveys. The range of activities of this group is comparable to that of government data collection groups in the United States.

Market and audience studies have been conducted at the same level of sophistication as in the United States. Indeed, new methodologies flow in both directions, so that several of the audience measurement methods used in the United States were initiated in Britain.

The opinion polls in Britain had a history similar to the history of polls in the United States. Thus, after several successful election predictions, the polls in Britain went wrong in 1970, predicting a large Labour victory when, in fact, the Conservatives won. An examination of this election suggests that the same issues plagued the British as the United States pollsters: possible last-minute changes, the difficulty in determining who would vote, and decisions on how to treat the undecided respondents. Again as in the United States, there was a temporary drop in confidence in the polls, but confidence has since been restored.

It is probably fair to say that British and European social scientists have usually been somewhat more theoretical and less quantitative than their United States counterparts. Nevertheless, academic survey organizations exist in some European countries—notably, Social and Community Planning Research in London and the Zentrum für Umfragen, Methoden und Analysen (ZUMA) at the University of Mannheim in West Germany. The Institut für Demoskopie/Allensbach, founded in 1948, has been a leader in quantitative social research in West Germany, although it is an independent organization not directly affiliated with a university.

There are three major international organizations of professionals in public opinion and survey research. The World Association for Public Opinion Research (WAPOR) corresponds in its interests and activities to the American Association for Public Opinion Research, and the two organizations have a joint meeting every other year. The International Association of Survey Statisticians is composed primarily of statisticians in government offices that conduct censuses and surveys. The European Society for Opinion and Marketing Research (ESOMAR) is composed of marketing, public opinion, and communications researchers in Europe. It meets with WAPOR every other year.

Survey methods and opinion polling are now found everywhere in the world, even in Communist countries such as the Soviet Union and China and other totalitarian regimes.

## Surveys and Social Science

The history of polls and surveys has been intertwined with that of the other social sciences, especially sociology, political science, and survey statistics. One needs only compare the contents of major scholarly journals today to those of a half century ago to see the quantitative revolution that has occurred. A large fraction of all the articles use survey research data and manipulate the data with the aid of powerful computer programs. While some social scientists, especially in Europe, bemoan this trend and continue to prefer theorizing without data, they have become a distinct minority.

Survey statistics has developed a new set of problems dealing with sampling methods, estimation procedures, and the computation of sampling errors from complex designs. Solutions to these problems have been widely adopted by survey data collectors and analysts. Initially, much greater emphasis was placed on multivariate methods than on the analysis-of-variance procedures used in experiments. Ultimately, however, researchers have realized that both analysis-of-variance and multivariate procedures are examples of the broader set of linear models, so that the distinction between surveys and experiments is not as great as once thought.

It is unproductive to try to assign a one-directional cause-effect relationship to what is a mutually interactive process. The social sciences have both affected and been affected by survey methods, and both have been affected by outside technical developments such as computers and telecommunication equipment.

## Additional Reading

Anyone interested in more details on the origins and history of academic survey research in the United States should consult the excellent new book *Survey Research in the United States: Roots and Emergence, 1890–1960* (Converse, 1987). Claude Robinson's (1932) history of the straw polls is the standard reference on the early history of polling. We have also borrowed heavily from *The Pulse of Democracy* (Gallup and Rae, 1940) and *The Sophisticated Poll Watcher's Guide* (Gallup, 1972b). Readers fortunate enough to have available a library with early volumes of the *Public Opinion Quarterly* will find not only the articles of historical interest but also the full descriptions of the early conference of the American Association for Public Opinion Research. For a history of survey research in Britain, see *Survey Methods in Social Investigation* (Moser and Kalton, 1972); and for a useful short history of the early days of polling, see *Surveys, Polls and Samples* (Parten, 1950).

# 3

# Proper & Improper
# Uses of Surveys

Surveys, like other scientific and technical tools, can be well made or poorly made and can be used in appropriate or inappropriate ways. In this chapter, we discuss the wide range of uses of surveys and give examples of some uses that to us are clearly appropriate, some that are clearly inappropriate, and some that are questionable.

The most widely known uses of survey opinion data are in the political arenas, and we shall pay special attention to the uses of opinion data by presidents of the United States and legislators. If one measures use by amount of money spent, however, much more money is spent by businesses and nonprofit organizations in trying to satisfy customer needs through market and advertising research. The federal government is the single largest user of survey data, and we discuss this use. Surveys are also widely used for gathering data in the social sciences.

In recent years, advocacy groups have increasingly made use of opinion measurement in developing programs for obtaining their goals. Some of these uses are completely appropriate, but others are not. A little-known, but growing, use of surveys is as information for legal cases and administrative hearings before commissions, such as the Federal Trade Commission. Again, there are some questionable uses here, particularly related to jury selection.

Finally, there is the extensive use of polls as a source of news in the media. Preelection and exit polls in particular are being challenged as inappropriate or questionable uses of opinion measurement.

All the procedures we discuss here are legal. Whether they are ethical and appropriate must ultimately be a subjective judgment. We present reasons why we think some uses are or are not appropriate, but it is ultimately public opinion that will decide.

### Use of Opinion Data by United States Presidents

The early rapid growth of opinion polls occurred during the administration of Franklin Delano Roosevelt, and that was hardly coincidence. The pragmatic character of FDR and the brilliant staff that he collected around him provided an atmosphere in which the seedling profession of opinion research could grow and flourish. Just as FDR reached out to the American people with his fireside chats, he listened to them through opinion polls. Although he had no earlier experience to guide him, FDR intuitively used opinion research as we believe it should be used, not to promote programs and policies because they would be popular but to help the president decide how to lead the American people. Roosevelt's use of opinion data is illustrated in Hadley Cantril's (1967) fascinating and informative memoir, *The Human Dimension: Experiences in Policy Research.*

Roosevelt first used polls in 1940, when he carefully studied trends in public attitudes on aid to England. Specifically, he wanted to gauge public opinion on whether the neutrality law should be changed to permit American ships to carry war supplies to England, whether the United States should lend war materials to the British through a lend-lease bill, and whether—in general—his efforts to help Britain were approved of. He was always ahead, but not too far ahead, of public sentiments.

After Germany invaded Russia in June 1941, Gallup used a split ballot to see what the public thought about aid to Britain. The first slanted question was: "Some people say that since Germany is now fighting Russia, as well as Britain, it is not as necessary for this country to help Britain. Do you agree or disagree with this?" Seventy-three percent of the American people disagreed with the proposition. The other question, slanted a different way, was: "Some people say that, since Germany will probably defeat Russia within a few weeks and then turn her full strength against Britain, it is more important than ever that we help Britain. Do you agree or disagree with this?" Seventy-one percent agreed. It was quite clear that opinion was solid. Both questions revealed practically identical majorities in the same direction. Furthermore, analysis of the replies of respondents with different religious and economic backgrounds showed no appreciable differences of opinion. Roosevelt was particularly relieved to learn of the uniformity of opinion within the population.

Roosevelt also used polls for domestic purposes. In 1943, for example, he requested a survey of farmers on the issue of farm subsidies. Those arguing against farm subsidies maintained that the farmers themselves did not want subsidies. After Cantril conducted the survey (with an especially designed national sample of over 2,000 American farmers), he found that most farmers were unaware of the administration's farm program, although farm groups in Washington apparently assumed otherwise. In the letter transmitting the findings, Cantril recommended that the primary aim in a speech should be clarification—sacrificing, if necessary, emotional oratory for simple phrasing. A few days after turning in the report, Cantril got a letter from the president commending the report as both surprising and instructive.

Cantril (pp. 41-42) summarizes Roosevelt's use of polls as follows:

> Roosevelt regarded the reports sent him the way a general would regard information turned in by his intelligence services as he planned the strategy of a campaign. As far as I am aware, Roosevelt never altered his goals because public opinion appeared against him or was uninformed. Rather he utilized such information to try to bring the public around more quickly or more effectively to the course of action he felt was best for the country. I am certain he would have agreed with Churchill's comment that "Nothing is more dangerous than to live in the

temperamental atmosphere of a Gallup poll, always
taking one's pulse and taking one's temperature. . . .
There is only one duty, only one safe course, and that
is to try to be right and not to fear to do or say what
you believe to be right." . . . I want to emphasize that
no claim is made that the data provided the President
were crucial in his decisions. But actions taken were
certainly very often completely consistent with our
recommendations.

The two presidents who followed Roosevelt did not make
much use of polls, but for quite different reasons. Harry Truman
had serious doubts about the polls' accuracy in 1948 and was
delighted to be proved right. Nonetheless, it was the early poll
results that, in part, persuaded Truman to get out and make the
vigorous whistle-stop campaign that ultimately brought him
victory. While there is little public evidence of how Truman used
the polls before or after 1948, he was certainly kept aware of public
opinion during the Korean War.

Dwight D. Eisenhower was clearly the most popular United
States president in recent times. Given a steady high level of
approval and the absence of any major new programs that he
wanted adopted, he seems to have made limited use of opinion
polls. Nevertheless, there is evidence that he was briefed on public
attitudes toward Korea and on Senator Joseph McCarthy.

John Kennedy's use of polls is reported by Theodore
Sorensen, who was his special counsel. In his book, Sorensen (1965,
pp. 332–333) writes about Kennedy's political behavior and sources
of political intelligence:

He was a President willing, if necessary, to risk
defeat for his principles, but he preferred preserving
both his principles and his power to effect them.

Consequently, politics was an ever-present
influence in the Kennedy White House. Kennedy
retained in the White House his unusually acute
political antennae, with which he sensed the public
mood both quickly and accurately. He understood

what moved people, what touched their hearts and what touched only their pocketbooks. He was good at distinguishing their momentary whims from their enduring convictions.

There was no single source of this sensitivity. He read every fiftieth letter of the thirty thousand coming weekly to the White House as well as a statistical summary of the entire batch, but he knew that these were often as organized and unrepresentative as the pickets on Pennsylvania Avenue. "Mail, unfortunately," he told a 1962 press conference, "is not true as an indicator of the feelings of the people . . . I got last week 28 letters on Laos . . . [and] 440 letters on the cancellation of a tax exemption for a 'mercy' foundation."

He also remained an avid consumer of public opinion polls. He did not commission any polls directly, as rumored, but Louis Harris and others reported findings of many polls taken for their political clients, and the published polls of Gallup and his colleagues were studied with care. Nevertheless, the President remained a skeptic. He told Orville Freeman that a survey of farmers showing Kennedy's job performance rating higher than his Secretary of Agriculture's merely proved that the latter was doing a good job—but that the whole poll was dubious, since it also claimed that Bostonian Kennedy ranked higher than Kansan Eisenhower. He told a press conference that a Gallup Poll showing 72 percent against a tax cut which produced deeper debts might have had a different result had it asked opinions on a tax cut necessary to prevent a recession, unemployment and consequently greater debts.

He relied on more than mail, public petitions and polls. He talked with hundreds of people every week in the White House. He read newspapers and magazines from all over the country. He judged the reactions of his crowds when he traveled (although

not necessarily their size, which was partisan and
planned). He observed the pressures reflected in
Congress and heard reports from his Cabinet on their
trips. But somehow his political intuition was an
amalgamation of all these that was greater than the
sum of its parts.

It is obvious that no president will rely entirely on public
opinion polls but will depend on all the sources of information
about what different publics want. Among all the sources, however,
only the polls and the president's closest friends provide disinterested information, and there is always at least a little doubt about
friends.

Kennedy made one of the major errors in his reign of a
thousand days when he approved the invasion at the Bay of Pigs in
1961. This invasion was based on the hope that the Cuban
population would rise up in revolt and join in the invasion. In
reality, however, the Cuban public was strongly behind the Castro
regime at that time. A careful survey of Cuban public opinion in
urban areas conducted in 1960 indicated that 86 percent of the
population was pro-Castro and only about 10 percent was opposed
to him. This report was published in July 1960, and copies went to
the White House and the State Department. Since all this took place
at the end of the Eisenhower administration, it is possible that the
report got lost in the change of administrations and was not seen
in time by the Kennedy advisers. One need not believe strongly in
conspiracy theories, however, to speculate that this report was
buried within the CIA and the State Department because it disputed
some of the claims of those who supported the invasion.

Lyndon Johnson, whose hero was Franklin Roosevelt,
initially used the polls as his Democratic predecessors had. In the
period just after his election in 1964, he was at his height of
popularity in the polls and was therefore encouraged to press
through Congress the major civil rights and war-on-poverty bills
for which he is remembered. But, as he writes in his memoirs, *The
Vantage Point: Perspectives of the Presidency* (1971, p. 440), he
ignored the polls when he attempted to stem inflation with a tax
increase in 1966: "On the subject of taxes, the people were extremely

vocal. Mail on the hill was running heavily against a tax increase. [As a footnote, he adds:] Even as late as January 1968, a Gallup Poll showed that 79 percent of the American people were opposed to raising taxes." Nevertheless, on the basis of advice from the Council of Economic Advisors, he continued to press for a tax increase during the period 1966–1968. As he put it: "I was aware that history's judgment would be based not on the Gallup Poll of 1966 or 1967 or 1968 but on what I did to steer the economy between the shoals of recession and the rocks of runaway inflation" (p. 440).

The great tragedy of the Johnson administration was, of course, Vietnam. During 1964 and 1965, as the United States greatly expanded its forces, public opinion was still uncrystallized, but people generally approved of the United States' involvement. Public opinion seems to have played little role in Johnson's decisions about Vietnam and is barely mentioned in his memoirs. As the war escalated and America was drawn ever deeper into the quicksand, public opinion became more and more negative toward our Vietnam activities, but by then Johnson could see no way out. His approval rating dropped from 70 percent in 1965 to 39 percent in August of 1967. Johnson was a very proud and sensitive man, and this loss of popularity rankled. He commissioned private polls to prove that he was still popular, but the polls, as well as early primaries, proved otherwise; so he decided not to seek reelection. He learned, as did subsequent presidents, that it is ultimately the success of a policy that determines a president's popularity and that you can't get repeat purchases of a product that people don't like.

It is important to distinguish between the use of polls to get elected and the use of polls to govern wisely. Since the Kennedy era, virtually every successful politician has used polls to develop election strategies. Let us again use Lyndon Johnson as an example, quoting from *The Making of the President, 1964* (White, 1965, p. 257):

> Johnson during campaigning had most of all wanted to know "How'm I doing?" and polls in his earlier career had been useful only as measures of personal impact. This attitude began to change slowly in the spring with the record of George Wallace in the

Northern primaries, for the President of the United
States, so intent on passage of his Civil Rights Bill,
could not but be concerned with the meaning of the
surprising Wallace vote in the Democratic primary.
He had read, like every political figure, the Gallup
and the Harris polls, generally published. But he had
read them as personality readings.

Now, in the spring, Walter Jenkins commissioned for the President a confidential poll on the
Maryland primary—where Wallace had won 43 percent of the Democratic vote—conducted by Oliver
Quayle and Company. Out of it, Quayle had produced
a fifty-five page technical report heavy with the
terminology of the pollster: themes, voter profiles,
issue measurements. Johnson read the poll overnight
and was delighted; calling for more, he was supplied
with Quayle polls on the Indiana and Wisconsin
results which confirmed the original Maryland poll:
that backlash was a potential threat, not yet a real
threat. The studies fascinated Johnson with their
contrasts of Republican and Democratic attitudes,
with their measures of voter concern (number one: the
frustration of Americans at the endless cold-war vexa-
tions) and approval (Johnson was doing a marvelous
job on bread-and-butter issues). Backlash and the
Negro revolt were indeed chipping away some Democratic strength in the big urban centers—but this was
more than overmatched by a contrary drift of Republicans to Lyndon Johnson himself. By June, Johnson
had become converted to polls, with the conversion of
a man discovering a new science. From Maine, Quayle
brought back a survey indicating that Johnson might
pull as high as 77 percent of a vote held at the
moment; and that Nixon voters of 1960, by a measure
of roughly 50 percent, were willing to consider
Johnson as their likely choice! From a survey of
Wisconsin dairy farmers, traditionally Republican,
came remarkable indication of Johnson strength.

But most of all Lyndon Johnson learned from the polls, which became his favorite reading material by June, that he was completely free to choose as Vice-President any running mate he fancied. No name suggested in any Quayle poll as Johnson's partner added to or diminished the President's winning margin more than 2 percent. Theoretically free, as any President always is, to impose his own man as Vice-President, he was politically free, too.

We do not believe that this use of polls in elections is in any sense an immoral or unethical practice, but neither do we believe that it substantially advances the skill and wisdom with which our leaders govern. A really serious concern arises when a president or any elected official is so concerned about what the polls are saying that he advocates or opposes programs on the basis of the polls, rather than attempting, as Roosevelt did, to lead the public in the direction he thinks is right. This type of behavior usually comes from presidents who cannot exert effective leadership.

Questions about the value of polls may have arisen because the elected presidents since Johnson have generally not used polls well. There are strong and unhappy similarities in the uses of polls by Presidents Nixon and Carter. Both were faced at some point with dropping popularity because of unpopular programs. Rather than using the polls as information about their programs, they concentrated on efforts to improve their images.

Here is how Evans and Novak (1971, p. 388) describe President Nixon's reaction when his popularity dropped during the Laos operation in 1971: "Shortly after that Gallup finding, it was decided by Nixon's public relations experts to give the American people the largest concentrated dose of this President on television and in interviews with journalists. The purpose was to stimulate an immediate upward movement in the polls and thus prevent further deterioration of the President's position on Capitol Hill and in the nation."

In a period of six weeks, the president made seven major television appearances, but none of these had any impact on public opinion. As Evans and Novak report: "All to no avail. The mid-

March Gallup Poll . . . showed Nixon down to . . . still another new low" (p. 389). No matter how much propaganda poured out of the White House, Nixon could not prevent a nightmarish mass psychological reaction in the country.

The similarity between Nixon's use of opinion polling data in this crisis and Lyndon Johnson's use of polls to evaluate his Vietnam policy is striking. The emphasis was on retaining or recovering presidential popularity rather than making wise policy judgments.

One of the heaviest users of polls in recent times was Jimmy Carter. Unfortunately, he was not an effective president, nor did he use polls wisely. A graphic description of his use of polls is given by Elizabeth Drew in the *New Yorker* (1979).

In June 1979, the gasoline shortage, which resulted in long waiting lines, dropped Carter's approval rating to only 30 percent; by July, it had dropped to 25 percent. The president's pollster, Patrick Caddell, first persuaded Mrs. Carter and then President Carter that the president was in terrible political trouble and that he needed to take bold, "breakthrough" actions. The president was scheduled to make an energy speech at the beginning of July. Unfortunately, there was no new energy policy. Caddell felt that it would be disastrous for the president simply to make another energy speech, and he urged Carter to address broader cultural issues. After reading a memorandum from Caddell and the draft of the energy speech, the president canceled his speech. Caddell also recommended that the president get tough with OPEC, so that he could once more get the nation's attention. He recommended actions that would have both theater and mystery, since, he argued, these are important elements of leadership.

Carter and his advisers met at Camp David. To correct the perceived public malaise, the president asked for the resignation of his entire cabinet. The storm of protest that followed still further reduced Carter's ability to deal with Congress or lead the American public on energy issues. In retrospect, it is clear that Carter's use of polls was similar to Nixon's and almost the direct opposite of Roosevelt's. It is also obvious that a slavish use of polls can never substitute for leadership.

The Reagan administration got off to a spectacular start, at

least in part because of a highly effective use of polls, as reported
in an article by Sidney Blumenthal (1981, pp. 41-43):

> Ronald Reagan . . . is applying in the White
> House the techniques he employed in getting there.
> Making more effective use of media and market
> research than any previous President, he has brought
> into the White House the most sophisticated team of
> pollsters, media masters and tacticians ever to work
> there. They have helped him to transcend entrenched
> institutions like the Congress and the Washington
> Press corps to appeal directly to the people.
> This does not mean that the President goes by
> the polls rather than by his own conservative ideology.
> The polls don't change his beliefs or shape his
> policies; they tell him how to plan his strategies.

As a specific example, when the polls showed strong
opposition to United States policy in El Salvador, Reagan quickly
pulled back from highlighting the topic because it would drain
support from his economic programs. Reagan's tactics were highly
successful in obtaining approval for the first year's budget and tax
cuts.

So far, this description of President Reagan's use sounds
much like our earlier description of Roosevelt's wise and effective
use of polls. Unfortunately, as a president's popularity falls because
a program is not working well, there is a tendency to search for an
easy solution. In the spring of 1982, a prolonged economic slump
caused a sharp drop in presidential popularity, and Reagan's
behavior was distressingly similar to Carter's. As reported in
*Newsweek* (Williams, Howard, and Maier, 1982, p. 86):

> When Ronald Reagan's advisors gathered at
> Camp David earlier this year to review his latest polls,
> they discovered that he was slumping badly with
> Roman Catholics. Last week they came up with what
> they hoped might be a quick fix. The President flew
> to Chicago, home of the country's largest Catholic

school system, and announced his intention to give
tuition tax credits to families that send their children
to non-public schools. Congress, however, is almost
certain to turn a deaf ear, at least for this year. At a
time when Federal aid to public education is falling
and when the projected Federal deficit is about $100
billion, not many legislators are in the mood for more
tax relief of any kind.

Since then, Reagan has continued to use polls extensively.
Mostly he has used them appropriately, not to shape policies but
to help plan implementation strategies. Although, on a few
occasions, the polls seem to dominate the policy, Reagan has been—
on the whole—an effective user of poll data.

The use of polls does not depend on political party affiliation. Since Roosevelt, most presidents—regardless of party and of
location on a liberal-conservative spectrum—have used polls to
govern and, since Kennedy, to be elected. The use of polls, however,
does not guarantee that a president will govern well.

To summarize:

1.  No elected official can govern wisely without knowing what
    the public thinks on major issues. Public opinion research is
    one source, but not the only source, of such information.
2.  The use of opinion information does not ensure that wise
    decisions will be made; that depends on the wisdom and
    political leadership of our elected officials and our wisdom in
    selecting them.
3.  A president who uses opinion polls as measures of presidential
    popularity and then shapes his behavior and policies to
    increase that popularity is treating the symptoms and not the
    cause. Popularity results from the public perception that the
    policies being proposed are sensible and will be well imple-
    mented. To repeat, one cannot use polls or surveys to get repeat
    buying for a bad product—be it a cereal or a presidential policy.
4.  Finally, skill in using the polls to get elected does not ensure
    wisdom in office once one is elected. A mindless use of public
    opinion polls to retain political power while in office usually

leads to weak, ineffective governing. Fortunately, most politicians who follow this strategy do not get reelected.

## Congressional Polls

Except during elections, presidents do not often conduct polls for their own use; instead, they depend on the many polls that are conducted on a regular basis. Members of Congress who need information on the attitudes of residents in their district are not so fortunate. Aside from some state polls that can be used by senators, there are seldom polls for districts unless the congressman (or congresswoman) conducts them.

In a study conducted in 1970, about three-fourths of all congressmen reported that they used polls, and the percentage has probably increased in the 1980s (Stolarek, Rood, and Taylor, 1981; Jewell and Patterson, 1977). More and more, polls of constituents are being conducted by congressmen. Unfortunately, since they conduct these polls largely for public relations purposes, the data are not well collected or well used. If the primary purpose of the poll is to act as a personal advertisement rather than as a method for gathering data, the voter is being deceived. An example of such a poll was received by one of us a few weeks before an election (see Exhibit 1).

Let us describe the typical method used in a congressional poll. Using the franking privilege of Congress, the congressman sends a copy of the questionnaire to every registered voter in the district. Since questionnaires are not pretested, question wordings are often biased or confusing. Respondents who wish to mail the questionnaire back are required to use their own postage; as a result, only a small fraction of voters (10–15 percent) will return the questionnaire. The results will typically confirm the congressman's stands on various issues, since the people most likely to respond are those with favorable attitudes toward the congressman. Indeed, if the congressman is only interested in the attitudes of strong supporters, the mail method is probably satisfactory, although inefficient (Stolarek, Rood, and Taylor, 1981). If the data are taken at face value, however, they simply reinforce the congressman's existing views.

## Exhibit 1. A Congressional Poll.
## Congress of the United States

Please answer the following questions, circling the responses that best express your opinion.

All of your answers will be kept strictly confidential. Please note that there is room for two persons ("Respondent #1" and "Respondent #2") to answer.

Your opinions will be studied by Congressman Dan Crane to guide him in better representing you in the U.S House.

Please return your completed survey immediately. Thank you for your cooperation.

| | Respondent #1 | Respondent #2 |
|---|---|---|
| 1. To eliminate the nearly $200 billion deficit, cuts in spending have to be made. We spend about $237 billion on defense and $616 billion on domestic programs. Which should be cut most? | ☐ Domestic ☐ Defense | ☐ Domestic ☐ Defense |
| 2. Has the quality of education in your school district (choose 1): improved; worsened; or stayed the same in the past 10 years? | ☐ Improved ☐ Worsened ☐ The Same | ☐ Improved ☐ Worsened ☐ The Same |
| 3. Congressman Crane is the leader of the "workfare" program, under which able-bodied welfare recipients age 16–65 must work at public service jobs for their benefits. Do you think this program should be in your community? | ☐ Yes ☐ No ☐ Undecided | ☐ Yes ☐ No ☐ Undecided |
| 4. Should we tax everyone 10% on their net income, no matter what the size of the income (called the flat rate, or fair share tax)? | ☐ Yes ☐ No ☐ Undecided | ☐ Yes ☐ No ☐ Undecided |
| 5. Should we have another payment-in-kind (PIK) program? | ☐ Yes ☐ No ☐ Undecided | ☐ Yes ☐ No ☐ Undecided |
| 6. Should teachers be allowed to strike? | ☐ Yes ☐ No ☐ Undecided | ☐ Yes ☐ No ☐ Undecided |
| 7. Should forced retirement at age 65 be abolished? | ☐ Yes ☐ No ☐ Undecided | ☐ Yes ☐ No ☐ Undecided |
| 8. Does the U.S. have a vital interest in Latin America? | ☐ Yes ☐ No ☐ Undecided | ☐ Yes ☐ No ☐ Undecided |

Name _____ Address _____ Zip _____

This information is for acknowledgement purposes only. Your answers will be kept strictly confidential.

This entire form is to be returned. Please see reverse. Thank you for your cooperation.

Many congressmen admit that they pay little or no attention to the surveys of their constituents, but simply use them to increase their own name familiarity. Even those who use them take only a small sample of the returns, and most place limited trust in the results. This attitude is justified given the major sample biases that exist. The few congressmen who are most enthusiastic about such polls and use them extensively are probably the most likely to be misled.

In addition to congressional polls, nearly all congressmen commission professional polls when they seek reelection and use these results in planning their campaigns. Also, on many issues they may use the national polls as indicators, adjusting national results mentally to reflect what they know of their own constituencies.

It is possible for congressmen to obtain useful poll data that can help them serve their constituents more effectively. Small sample surveys of 300–500 voters in the district contacted by telephone or in a carefully conducted mail survey with follow-ups are not very costly. Sometimes data on issues can be obtained as part of the polls that the congressman conducts for election purposes. It takes some understanding of polls to recognize that a careful sample of a few hundred constituents is superior to a badly biased sample of thousands. (See Chapter Six, which discusses sampling.) Ultimately, however, even accurate polls must be used by congressmen as an aid to judgment rather than as a substitute for judgment.

### Federal Government Surveys

The federal government is the single largest user of surveys. In Table 2, we list and briefly describe some of the major federal surveys, excluding censuses. Federal surveys are intended to be used not only by the legislative and executive branches of government but also by users of all kinds throughout the United States.

Table 2 is derived from Appendix III of the *Statistical Abstract of the United States* (United States Bureau of the Census, 1987). This is probably the single most useful initial source of information about types of federal surveys, providing not only summary information but also detailed references to the basic sources.

**Table 2. Major Federal Surveys.**

| Subject | Description |
| --- | --- |
| 1. U.S. Bureau of the Census | |
| a. Current Population Survey (CPS) | Nationwide monthly sample survey of civilian noninstitutional population, fifteen years old or over, to obtain data on employment, unemployment, and a number of other characteristics. |
| b. Surveys of State and Local Government | Sample survey conducted annually to obtain data on revenue, expenditure, debt, and employment of state and local governments. Universe is all governmental units in the U.S. (about 80,000). |
| c. Survey of New Construction | Survey conducted monthly of newly constructed housing units (excluding mobile homes and nonhousekeeping residential buildings, such as motels, hotels, courts, and cabins). Data collected on the start, completion, and sale of housing. (Annual figures are aggregates of monthly estimates.) |
| d. Housing Survey | Conducted nationally in the fall of each year to obtain data on the approximately 92 million occupied or vacant housing units in the U.S. (group quarters are excluded). Data include characteristics of occupied housing units, housing inventory changes, vacant units, new housing and mobile home units, financial characteristics, recent mover households, housing and neighborhood quality indicators, and energy characteristics. |
| e. Survey of Manufacturers | Conducted annually to provide basic measures of manufacturing activity for intercensal years for all manufacturing establishments having one or more paid employees. |
| f. Surveys of Wholesale Trade, Retail Trade, and Service Industries | Annual surveys to obtain estimates of retail and wholesale sales and end-of-year inventories in the U.S. All employers and nonemployer retail establishments operating during the calendar year are represented. Service industry survey for receipts begun in 1982. |
| g. Current Business Surveys | Monthly estimates of retail sales by kind of business and geographical area; end-of-month inventories of retail stores; wholesale |

## Table 2. Major Federal Surveys, Cont'd.

| *Subject* | *Description* |
|---|---|
| g. Current Business Surveys (cont'd) | sales and end-of-month inventories; and receipts of selected service industries. (Service industries monthly survey discontinued after Dec. 1981.) |
| 2. National Center for Health Statistics (NCHS) | |
| a. National Health Interview Survey (NHIS) | Continuous data collection covering the civilian noninstitutional population to obtain information on personal and demographic characteristics, illnesses, injuries, impairments, chronic conditions, and other health topics. |
| b. National Master Facility Inventory (NMFI) | Periodic surveys of nursing and related care homes with three or more beds and other inpatient health facilities to update file. Information obtained on names, locations, and types of facilities, and number of beds and residents or patients. |
| 3. Center for Education Statistics (CES) | |
| a. Revenues and Expenditures for Public Elementary and Secondary Education | Annual survey of state education agencies to obtain data on revenues and expenditures for public elementary and secondary education. Includes the fifty states, District of Columbia, and the outlying areas. |
| b. Statistics of Public Elementary and Secondary School Systems | Annual survey of state education agencies to obtain data on pupils enrolled, staff employed, and number of schools. Includes the fifty states, District of Columbia, and the outlying areas. |
| c. Higher Education General Information Survey (HEGIS) | Annual survey of all institutions and branches listed in the *Education Directory, Colleges and Universities* to obtain data on characteristics of institutions, including control (public or private), type (university, other four year and two year), and student charges. |
| d. Fall Enrollment in Institutions of Higher Education | Annual survey of all institutions and branches listed in the *Education Directory, Colleges and Universities* to obtain data on total enrollment by sex, level of enrollment, type of program, racial/ethnic characteristics (in alternate years) and attendance status of students, and on first-time students. |

Table 2. Major Federal Surveys, Cont'd.

| Subject | Description |
| --- | --- |
| e. Financial Statistics of Institutions of Higher Education | Annual survey of all institutions and branches listed in the *Education Directory, Colleges and Universities* to obtain data on financial status and operations, including current funds revenues, current funds expenditures, and physical plant assets. |
| f. Degrees and Other Formal Awards Conferred | Annual survey of all institutions and branches listed in the *Education Directory, Colleges and Universities* to obtain data on earned degrees and other formal awards, reported separately by field of study, level of degree, sex of recipient, and (in alternate years) by racial/ethnic characteristics. |
| 4. U.S. Bureau of Justice Statistics (BJS) National Crime Survey | Monthly survey of individuals and households in the U.S. to obtain data on criminal victimization of those units for compilation of annual estimates. |
| 5. U.S. Bureau of Labor Statistics (BLS) a. Current Employment Statistics Program (CES) | Monthly survey covering about four million nonagricultural establishments to obtain data on employment, hours, and earnings, by industry. |
| b. Consumer Price Index (CPI) | Monthly survey of price changes of all types of consumer goods and services purchased by urban wage earners and clerical workers prior to 1978, and urban consumers thereafter. |
| c. Producer Price Index (PPI) | Monthly survey of producing companies to determine price changes of all commodities produced or imported for sale in commercial transactions in primary markets in the U.S. Data on agriculture, forestry, fishing, manufacturing, mining, gas, electricity, and public utilities. |
| 6. U.S. Energy Information Administration Residential Energy Consumption Survey | Annual survey of households and fuel suppliers. Data obtained on energy-related household characteristics, housing unit characteristics, use of fuels, and energy consumption and expenditures by fuel type. |

Table 2. Major Federal Surveys, Cont'd.

| Subject | Description |
|---|---|
| 7. U.S. Department of Agriculture Statistical Reporting Service (SRS) | |
| a. Basic Area Frame Sample | Two annual sample surveys of U.S. farm operators: June survey collects data on planted acreage and livestock inventories; December survey collects data on livestock inventories and fall-seeded crop acreage. |
| b. Multiple-Frame Surveys | Surveys of U.S. farm operators to obtain data on major livestock inventories, selected crop acreages and production, and farm labor characteristics; and to obtain farm economic data for price indexing. |
| c. Objective-Yield Surveys | Surveys for data on corn, cotton, potatoes, soybeans, and wheat to forecast and estimate yields. |

*Source:* Adapted from United States Bureau of the Census, 1987, Appendix III.

Since federal programs change over time, the list of surveys given here may have been slightly modified since the 1987 *Statistical Abstract* was published.

Readers who have not previously been aware of the scope of the federal government's statistical programs may be surprised by the variety of surveys that are conducted by or for the various departments of the federal government. They may wonder whether all these surveys are necessary or whether they exemplify wasteful federal spending. The same concerns were evidenced by President Reagan and his budget staff, who sharply reduced federal spending on surveys in the first year of the Reagan administration. The president soon discovered, however, that the surveys were essential for measuring the impact of the changes he made in policies, besides having strong support from the business, agricultural, and medical communities. By the end of his first term, President Reagan had not only restored the budget cuts but in some cases had increased the amount of money spent on surveys.

## Market Research

The use of surveys in market research preceded their use in measuring public opinion, and currently the dollars spent on market research far exceed those spent on measuring public opinion. According to a careful estimate made by Honomichl in 1982, total survey research expenditures in the United States were then about $1.2 billion. Other estimates go as high as $2 billion. Of this amount, less than 10 percent was for public opinion research; the rest was for market research.

The term *market research* refers to the information-gathering activities that enable organizations to match the needs and preferences of the market with the products and services they provide. As this broad definition suggests, such organizations include not only businesses but also nonprofit organizations, such as hospitals and universities, and local and state governments that provide services such as transportation, recreational facilities, and libraries.

In this section, we briefly describe some of the major market research applications: new-product testing, customer satisfaction with products or services, use of media, and the polls as economic indicators. All these uses are completely legitimate when conducted for honest purposes and indeed help our economy function more efficiently. It is sometimes claimed that research is used to manipulate the consumer; and, of course, unscrupulous organizations can use surveys for dishonest purposes. But an organization that tries to determine what the consumer needs is not manipulating the consumer; rather, it is attempting to shape the economy to maximize consumer satisfaction.

*New-Product Testing.* A major part of the marketing effort of any organization is determining whether a new product or service will be a success. A firm may use several different surveys before deciding to launch a new product or service. Initially, there may be some fairly general surveys to determine what consumers are doing currently and what needs they have that are not being satisfied. If unmet needs are discovered and a new product or service is being considered, there will then be concept tests to see what consumers think of the idea. Finally, small quantities of the product or service will be offered to consumers on a trial basis, and information about attitudes and likelihood of purchase will be obtained. As an organization moves nearer and nearer to a costly decision to market a new product and service, the quality and size of the survey sample will increase.

A special aspect of new-product testing should be mentioned. If questions are asked only about the new product, there will be a strong possibility of a favorability bias. That is, respondents who are not required to actually buy the new product but simply to report on their likelihood of purchase probably will overstate that likelihood—so that actual sales after the product is introduced will be less sizable than the survey responses had suggested they would be. Favorability biases disappear, however, when respondents are asked which of two products they would be likely to buy: the new one or one already in the marketplace. (Other response effects in surveys are discussed in greater detail in Chapter Nine.)

*Customer Satisfaction with Products or Services.* For many products and services, organizations conduct periodic surveys of customers as part of a program to keep quality at a satisfactory level. Especially important in this respect are the customers who purchase durable goods such as automobiles or appliances; although such purchases are made infrequently, dissatisfaction with the current product can lead to a lost customer in the future. Customer satisfaction surveys also are being conducted by various services— for example, telephone companies, banks and other financial organizations, hospitals, and government offices such as Social Security offices and even offices of the Internal Revenue Service.

*Use of Media.* Advertisers need to know the characteristics of the audience for specific magazines or radio and television programs, as well as their frequency of reading, listening, or viewing and their attitudes toward the specific media. Most often this information is obtained by the media and given free to advertisers in an effort to sell advertising space. In the past, the quality of media information has been variable. Studies conducted for multiple clients have usually been fair and of reasonable quality. Some studies conducted for individual media, however, have been

deliberately distorted in design or analysis, to increase the advertising revenue of a magazine or a station. An even more difficult
deception to detect is the withholding of unfavorable information.
Obviously, deliberate attempts to mislead by slanting surveys
constitute an illegitimate use of survey methods.

*Polls as Economic Indicators.* Almost all businesses are
affected by the business cycle, the growth and decline in the
economy. An important use of surveys is as lead indicators that help
predict when the economy will change. Currently, this information
is provided by the Survey Research Center at the University of
Michigan, which has conducted surveys of consumer sentiment
since 1946, and by the Conference Board, which has conducted
similar surveys since 1967. Aggregate estimates of consumer
sentiment are good predictors of the future of the economy,
although the accuracy of specific estimates—notably, estimates of
the purchases of specific durables or the buying intentions of
individual consumers—is quite low. (An excellent review of surveys
of consumer sentiment is found in the Fall 1982 *Public Opinion
Quarterly:* see articles by Graber, Curtin, Linden, and Roper.)

### Associations and Interest Groups

Every profession and trade has its own association, and
almost all of these associations conduct regular surveys of their own
members and other relevant publics. Well-known examples are the
annual surveys of physicians by the American Medical Association,
the annual survey of hospitals by the American Hospital Association, and the various surveys of dentists, lawyers, accountants, and
teachers. These surveys are conducted to determine current practices
and the economic condition of members, as well as their views on
controversial issues affecting the association or interest group.

Periodic surveys also are conducted to determine the general
public's attitude toward a profession or trade (advertising, nursing,
teaching, and the like) and public opinion on controversial issues
involving the profession or interest group. When such surveys are
used to help determine what the public knows and thinks, so that
an educational or persuasion program can be mounted, their use is

fully justified. Questions arise when associations use survey results for propaganda purposes. Depending on how the survey is designed and how the questions are asked, the results may or may not give an accurate view of public opinion. Later in this chapter, we give more concrete examples of misuses of surveys for propaganda.

## Use of Surveys in Legal Settings

The use of surveys in legal cases has increased sharply in the past two decades, largely because the courts now are willing to accept survey data as legal evidence. In the 1940s and 1950s, polls frequently were excluded as legal evidence because of the "hearsay" rule; that is, a witness reporting poll results was considered to be telling secondhand what other witnesses would report. In recent years, however, courts have accepted the idea that there is an entity called "public opinion" that can be measured. Consequently, witnesses are now allowed to report about how they measured opinion in specific cases and what the summary results were.

In this section, we describe three legitimate uses of surveys in the legal setting and discuss a growing use of surveys that we find troublesome.

*Determining Need for a Change of Venue.* In major criminal cases, local media coverage may be so intense that most members of the community are aware of the case and may have formed judgments that would prevent them from reaching a fair verdict if they were selected for the jury. The judicial solution in this case is a change of venue to another location, where prospective jurors are unlikely to be aware of the case. Changes of venue are inconvenient for witnesses and increase trial costs; consequently, judges are reluctant to grant a change of venue simply on the unsupported claims of the defendant.

A widely accepted solution is to conduct a survey of the members of the community, to determine what fraction have heard of the case and have developed attitudes toward the defendant that would prejudice them as jurors. If this fraction is so high that it would be difficult to impanel a jury, almost all judges will approve a change of venue.

*Preventing Deceptive Advertising.* The Federal Trade Commission has as one of its missions the prevention of deceptive advertising. The question of whether an advertisement is or is not deceptive ultimately depends on what the readers or viewers of the advertisement think that it means. Current FTC policies encourage the use of surveys to determine public beliefs, rather than depending simply on expert opinions. In these surveys, the advertisement is shown to respondents, and they are asked questions about it.

*Protecting Trademarks.* Firms that spend millions of dollars to promote their trademark wish to protect this investment and are obviously upset if another company infringes on this trademark. In a few cases, the infringement is direct; that is, a different firm will use the same name for exactly the same product. In most cases of alleged trademark infringement, however, the name may be slightly different and for a somewhat different product. Thus, in a case some years ago, American Motors contested the use of the trademark "Holiday Rambler" for a camper, alleging that the name infringed on the trademark name "Rambler" for automobiles.

In such cases, the question is whether there is substantial confusion in the minds of potential consumers between the two trademarks. This question is usually answered by a survey that asks questions about both products and attempts to determine what fraction of consumers think both products are made by the same company. What is meant by "substantial" confusion is a decision for the individual judge. Most courts have ruled that confusion on the part of 15 percent or more of the consumers constitutes "substantial" confusion. Confusion rates of less than 5 percent have been ruled as not "substantial." The range of 5–15 percent is a gray area.

*Selecting Juries.* In large civil and criminal trials, lawyers have a wide latitude in dismissing potential jurors without cause. In the past, they have selected jurors on the basis of social characteristics such as age, race, sex, occupation, and family status, to maximize the favorability of the jurors toward their own clients. Currently, some lawyers—instead of basing their jury selection on previous experience—conduct large sample surveys before an important case begins. In these surveys, respondents are told briefly about the issues and asked for their opinions on who they think is right. They are also asked for demographic information. Then, if it turns out that middle-aged male blue-collar workers are most sympathetic to the lawyer's client, the lawyer will make every effort to get as many jurors of this type impaneled while excusing jurors with characteristics that the survey showed would be less friendly to the client.

As nonlawyers, we find such procedures troubling, since we believe that a jury is supposed to represent all segments of the public. Instead of banning of the use of surveys by lawyers (which would be a difficult rule to enforce and would not reach to the root of the problem), we suggest that judges be allowed to play a greater role in jury selection, perhaps by selecting half or a majority of the jurors. If surveys are to have any role in jury selection, they should be available to both sides and to the judge.

## Social Science Use of Surveys

Surveys are the most widely used method of collecting data in the social sciences, especially in sociology and political science. A count of articles in the *American Sociological Review* for a year indicated that almost half of them were based on surveys (Sudman, 1976b). In psychology, experimental methods dominate, but in many experiments there is a survey component; that is, subjects are asked to express their opinions before and after the experimental manipulations. When these manipulations occur in a real-world setting, as is often the case with market research studies and some social science studies, one has a field experiment that combines survey and experimental methods. Surveys are used in many situations where it is impossible to conduct true experiments because individuals or groups may be harmed.

The use of surveys for research may be direct (that is, to answer questions that the survey was designed to answer) or secondary (that is, to answer questions other than the ones for which the survey was originally designed). Secondary analysis of existing surveys is increasing in popularity as archives of survey data have expanded and become better known. Generally, archival data are inexpensive, and relatively little time is required to obtain them. On the other hand, data gathered for other purposes are often less than ideal for questions being studied by secondary analysis. Following is a list of major survey archives:

> Behavioral Sciences Laboratory, University of Cincinnati, Cincinnati, Ohio 45221
>
> Data and Program Library Service, University of Wisconsin, 4451 Social Science Building, Madison, Wis. 53706
>
> Institute for Research in Social Science, Manning Hall, University of North Carolina, Chapel Hill, N.C. 27514
>
> Inter-University Consortium for Political and Social Research, University of Michigan, Ann Arbor, Mich. 48106 (Institute for Social Research archives are at same address)
>
> National Opinion Research Center, University of Chicago, 1155 East 60th Street, Chicago, Ill. 60637
>
> Roper Center, University of Connecticut, Storrs, Conn. 06268
>
> Survey Research Center, University of California, Berkeley, Calif. 94720

To be done well, primary data collection using surveys requires a substantial staff of experienced people and outside funding, although some small surveys have been conducted by professors using student interviewers. The funds for basic social science research rose sharply in the two decades after World War II but have declined in the 1980s. Concomitantly, there has been a decline in the funds available for surveys for basic research. As pointed out earlier in the chapter, there has been no decline, and in fact some increase, in the funds spent for policy purposes. One solution that is always available to enterprising researchers is to include basic social science research questions within the framework of a survey conducted for policy purposes. This combining of goals has an illustrious history, a classic example being the work by Stouffer and his associates in *The American Soldier* (1949).

### Using Polls to Persuade

It is not illegal or even necessarily unethical for lobbyists or interest groups to attempt to persuade legislators or others that the public favors their position on abortion, nuclear disarmament, taxation, or any other issue. Certainly, public opinion is one of the factors that must be considered, although not the only one. The problem is that, in an effort to persuade, interest groups may deliberately design or analyze surveys so that the results turn out as they wish them. As in the famous cliché, surveys are used as a drunk uses a lamp post, for support rather than illumination.

Interest groups can manipulate surveys to give desired results by selecting a biased sample or straining the analyses of results or— the most usual form of manipulation—"loading" the question. Particularly on new issues, where views have not crystallized, major changes in results are obtained by wording changes. We give below some fairly obvious examples of "loaded" questions. These are real examples taken from political surveys where fund raising is also being conducted.

- Do you support appropriations for modernizing our defenses, which became dangerously obsolete as a result of cutbacks by the Carter/Mondale administration?
- Should Congress appropriate funds for a space-based missile defense system to give the United States protection we do not now have against a Soviet nuclear attack?
- The Soviets have amassed the largest naval force in the world and have increased the number of submarines patrolling the U.S. coast. Should the U.S. Navy receive more funding to replace our aging sea force and build more Trident nuclear submarines?
- Do you feel there is too much power concentrated in the hands of labor union officials?
- Are you in favor of forcing state, county, and municipal employees to pay union dues to hold their government jobs?
- Are you in favor of allowing construction union czars the power to shut down an entire construction site because of a dispute with a single contractor, thus forcing even more workers to knuckle under to union agencies?
- Do you want union officials, in effect, to decide how many municipal employees you, the taxpayer, must support?
- Should all construction workers be forced into unions through

legalized situs picketing, thus raising the cost of building your
schools, hospitals, and homes?

- Would you vote for someone who had forced public employees
  to join a labor union or be fired?

These questions are obviously "loaded" with nonneutral
terms, such as "dangerously obsolete," "knuckle under," "forcing,"
and "union czars." In addition, the questions present arguments on
only one side of an issue.

We do not believe that any regulation of polls could prevent
deception without also impinging on free speech. Nor is it likely
that interest groups will desist from efforts to shape survey results
unless these efforts are counterproductive. At least for now, the only
solution to misleading polls is to make poll users aware of the
possibilities for bias. These possibilities are minimized when the
data come from independent sources, such as the syndicated polls
or federal or university sources. When the source of the poll has an
axe to grind, the burden of proof is on that source to demonstrate
that the results have not been deliberately manipulated.

What has been said about issues applies equally to candidates. Candidates have an obvious stake in obtaining favorable poll
results, because such results have a strong impact on their ability
to raise funds. Favorable poll results also raise the morale of a
candidate's workers and lower the morale of workers for the
opponent. Given these incentives, candidates frequently distort poll
results. In the simplest case, a candidate may simply misreport the
results of a survey, to indicate greater support than he or she
actually has. As with issues, samples and questions can also be
distorted. Samples may be deliberately selected from areas where the
candidate is strongest. Questions may be worded in such a way that
the candidate is asssociated with the side of an issue that most voters
favor, and then voters are asked about favorability toward the
candidate.

Not all candidate surveys are distorted. Candidates may
conduct a careful study of constituents to plan their campaigns. If
the results are favorable, they may then be made public, whereas
unfavorable results are buried. Again, the only reasonable solution
is for the users of these poll results to be cautious. The burden of

proof is on the candidate to demonstrate that the poll was taken carefully. As a general impression, we believe that a large number of all candidate polls that are made public for persuasion purposes are seriously flawed.

### The Polls as News

The use of polls by the news media has sharply increased in the past decade. Earlier, newspapers subscribed to one of the syndicated polls, such as the Gallup or Harris poll; in recent years, many major newspapers and the major television networks have in addition started their own polling operations. These polls are of two major types: issues and candidate preference. We have no concern with and indeed are heavy users of the polls dealing with issues. Such polls provide information that increases public awareness of important public issues, as well as providing unbiased information for policy makers and useful data for secondary analysis by social scientists.

Our concern, and that of many serious students of polls, is with the "horse race" aspects of polling; that is, the almost exclusive attention that is given at all times—but especially just before an election and in exit polls—to who is winning or has won the election. We do not believe that such polls influence the election (an issue discussed in Chapter Ten) or that the media should stop all such polls. On the other hand, we do not believe that such polls contribute greatly to the democratic process. In our view, these polls serve primarily "a nondisruptive, entertainment function" (Ladd, 1980).

Unfortunately, most news editors believe (and they are probably right) that the public is more interested in people than in issues. Reports about who is winning an election are easier to do and are likely to attract a larger audience than reports of attitudes on issues. Thus, "horse race" reporting tends to drive out the more useful issue reporting—especially in television news programs, where the available time for any story is limited. Some of the best national newspapers—notably, the *New York Times*—have continued to place a strong emphasis on issues, but most local newspapers pay attention only to the "horse race" aspects of polling. To the extent that this emphasis trivializes public perceptions of the purposes of polls and surveys, it may also reduce public willingness to cooperate.

Our discussion applies also to the exit polls that are conducted with voters as they leave the polling place. Again, there is little evidence of any major impact of these results on persons who have not yet voted, but one might ask whether it is worth all the effort to have the results available a few hours earlier than they would be otherwise, which is about all that the networks do. The analysis of why people voted as they did provides valuable information and is featured in major newspapers in the days following the election.

In a symposium in the winter 1980 *Public Opinion Quarterly,* "Polls and the News Media," several authors point out the difference between journalists and the survey research community. Journalists are always concerned with speed and tend to concentrate on personalities rather than issues. Survey researchers tend to be more concerned with issues and less concerned with speed. In our view, the media should attempt to balance their need to provide "hot" news with society's need for a fuller understanding of public issues. That a balanced presentation is possible is illustrated in the use of polls by some of the best newspapers and magazines in the United States and other countries where polls are used in both ways.

### Summary

In this chapter, we have discussed a broad range of applications of survey and poll procedures. Most of the applications are useful to society; but, as with every tool, there is always the possibility of misuse or use for trivial purposes. We believe that the use of surveys is justified for decision and policy purposes, even if some groups may be embarrassed by or unhappy with the results. Concerning the use of surveys for jury selection, we raise questions about whether the judicial system needs reevaluation in the light of modern survey methods. The most questionable uses of polls, in our opinion, are their use for propaganda purposes and their overuse to indicate who is winning in primaries or elections.

## Additional Reading

There are two journals especially related to surveys and polls: *Public Opinion Quarterly* and *Public Opinion*. Both contain many examples of the uses of polls as well as poll results.

Descriptions and results of federal surveys are found in the various bibliographies published by the U.S. Government Printing Office. A useful start is with the *Statistical Abstract,* published annually by the Census Bureau.

The most difficult survey applications to obtain are those in market research, since most of this information is considered confidential by clients. Syndicated data on media usage and other media information may be obtained in research libraries or directly from the media. Sometimes, survey results are reported in the trade press.

Results from the syndicated news polls may be found in the data archives discussed earlier. In particular, Gallup poll results are summarized in *The Gallup Poll: Public Opinion, 1935-1971* (Gallup, 1972a) and *The Gallup Poll: Public Opinion 1972-1977* (Gallup, 1978), with annual updates from 1979 to the present. Monthly summaries also appear in issues of the *Gallup Report.*

Social science research illustrations are, of course, found in the journals of the field. Data from the widely used General Social Survey, conducted by the National Opinion Research Center for the social science community, are available from NORC.

# 4

# The Organizations
# That Do the Polling

In this chapter, we describe some of the diverse organizations that are conducting polls today: newspapers and radio/ television networks, private polling organizations, surveys conducted by bureaus or departments of the federal government, organizations employed by the federal government to conduct surveys on policy issues, university survey organizations, and market research organizations. As this listing amply demonstrates, opinion polling and surveys are conducted by many different types of organizations; the media polls are simply one important subtype.

## Media Polls

*Gallup Polls.* The Gallup poll is the only poll that has been conducted continuously for more than fifty years. Although George Gallup died in 1984, the poll is still conducted by the Gallup Organization and is syndicated in hundreds of newspapers. (The Gallup Organization is now headed by Andy Kohut, and the poll is conducted under the direction of James Shriver and two of Gallup's sons, George Gallup, Jr., and Alec Gallup.) Although these polls are heavily concerned with political issues, and particularly with the performance of the president, one is impressed by the broad range of topics that have been covered over the years. For example, Gallup has periodically asked about religious beliefs and behavior and is the single best continuing source of information on this topic. It has also reported on attitudes toward smoking, drinking, and exercise; readership of books and magazines; attendance at sports events and movies; public knowledge of geography and famous people; automobile ownership and driving behavior; birth control practices; child-rearing practices; race relations; sleeping behavior; favorite vacations; Christmas gifts or carols; and even attitudes toward skirt lengths.

The Gallup poll results have been used extensively by students of opinion research, because Gallup's practice of asking questions with the same wording makes trend analysis possible. Also, the Gallup results have been widely published and archived, so that they are easy to use. Books summarizing Gallup poll results from their beginning to the present time are published every few years (see Gallup, 1972a, 1978). In addition, poll results are summarized in annual volumes (see Gallup, 1979–present) and monthly in the *Gallup Report*. All Gallup polls are archived at the Roper Center, University of Connecticut, Storrs, Connecticut.

The Gallup polls usually consist of face-to-face interviews with approximately 1,500 adults. From a designated starting point, usually a street corner, interviewers follow a specified travel pattern, omitting households where no one is at home, until assigned numbers of interviews with men and women have been completed. In some cases, especially when time is short, Gallup polls are now conducted by telephone. Along with others who use such methods, Gallup polls have some biases caused by failure to reach people who are not at home when called. Gallup questions are generally asked in a straightforward, unbiased way, although problems sometimes arise, especially on issues that are new and not well understood by the public. Because of the proliferation of media polls, Gallup does not stand out as it once did, but it still remains highly respected by the public and by opinion research professionals.

*Gallup Polls Abroad.* The Gallup organizations in countries around the world are operated by local researchers, who provide syndicated information to newspapers in their own countries on issues of national interest. In addition, all Gallup organizations collaborate to ask identical questions on agreed-upon topics, so that cross-national comparisons are possible. Some of these cross-national results are presented in the books mentioned above. More current information is available bimonthly in the *Gallup Report International*.

*Harris Polls.* The other major syndicated polling service in newspapers is the column by Louis Harris, which appears twice weekly in about two hundred newspapers. The column is based on polls conducted by the firm Louis Harris and Associates. Harris, who got his start as the private pollster for President Kennedy, has continued to emphasize political and policy issues, and his polls are highly regarded by policy makers.

Harris was a graduate of the University of North Carolina, and his poll results are archived there at the Institute for Research in Social Science at Chapel Hill. A sourcebook listing the archived studies is available (Martin, McDuffee, and Presser, 1981). As with Gallup, Harris polls from 1963 through the 1970s were conducted face to face, using modified area samples without callbacks. Since then, random digit dialing telephone methods have been used with samples of about 1,500 respondents.

Some critics of Harris have suggested that his polls are colored by his liberal Democratic leanings, but this charge is not well supported. Most of the time, when similar questions are asked by Harris and Gallup or others, the results are similar. In a few cases, subtle differences in question wording can lead to sharp differences in results, particularly on newly developing topics. In such cases, Harris results are sometimes more liberal than those of the other pollsters. Such differences do not indicate that one set of results is correct while the other set is biased but, rather, that the public does not yet have firm views on the topic. To some extent, Harris's political perspectives are revealed in the topics selected for polls—such topics as product safety and consumer protection, labor and business regulation, environmental concerns, the behavior of young people, women's status, right to privacy, euthanasia, and abortion.

*Network Polls.* Since 1967 for CBS and 1973 for NBC, the networks have had major polling operations and have reported poll results on their evening news and in special news programs. Early in 1981, ABC established its own polling operation. These network polls were established primarily to provide election coverage and postelection evaluations. The methods used on election day, however, are substantially different from those used in the usual national polls, since on election day voters are interviewed after they leave selected polling places.

Each of the three networks has a print partner that helps design the surveys and shares the cost. CBS collaborates with the *New York Times,* ABC with the *Washington Post,* and NBC with the Associated Press from 1978 to 1983, and now with the *Wall Street Journal.* The Associated Press now conducts continuing surveys in cooperation with the Media General company.

All network polls include continuous measurement of presidential popularity; they also measure consumer attitudes on the economy and a wide variety of issues. Trends are measured on selected topics only. The topics are selected primarily by the news departments and are, of course, influenced by evaluations of what is news. Overall, a broad range of important topics has been covered. Table 3 lists the topics included in the published versions of these polls since their inception. This is not a complete listing, but it should give a good flavor of the topics covered and of the overlap between polls.

All the polls use some form of random digit dialing telephone surveys and have capable staffs developing the questionnaires and interviewers who are well trained and supervised. Readers who wish to examine the results can find them in either the cooperating newspapers or in printed form that the networks send to selected libraries. All these polls are archived at the Roper Center at the University of Connecticut.

The two major objections to the network polls have to do with the exigencies of television news. Polls are frequently taken in short time periods when an issue is developing. As a result, superficial questions sometimes are asked on complex topics, and there may be a sample bias against people who are not home when the interviews are occurring, although limited callbacks are conducted. An even more serious objection is that only a very short time period is available on a news program for poll results, so that

**Table 3. Topics Covered by Network Polls.**

| | |
|---|---|
| All three polls | Abortion, civil defense, crime, Cuba, death penalty, economy, education, elections, El Salvador, Falkland Islands, gun control, A. Haig, immigration, international relations, labor, Middle East, party identification, Poland, presidential popularity, sex/pornography, Social Security, Soviet Union, taxes |
| CBS and ABC | Air traffic controllers, busing children, confidence in American institutions, important problems facing the U.S., racial attitudes |
| CBS and NBC | Balanced budget, baseball strike, Congress, draft, Iran, oil, space program, wilderness policy, women/ERA |
| ABC and NBC | Moral Majority |
| CBS | Afghanistan, air conditioning, atomic energy, China, energy, environment, health insurance, Medicare, Mexico, Olympic Games, Panama Canal, travel |
| ABC | AWACS, boxing, insanity defense, invasion of privacy, Nancy Reagan, television news coverage |
| NBC | Housing, Supreme Court nomination, Watergate revisited, wilderness policy |

only superficial analyses are possible. The later published or archived material is more substantial and useful.

*State and Local Polls.* The Iowa and Minnesota polls, which were established in the 1940s, continue today, with slightly reduced frequency. The Iowa poll, sponsored by the *Des Moines Register and Tribune,* conducts about four surveys a year in nonelection years with samples of 1,200 respondents. The Minnesota poll, sponsored by the *Minneapolis Star-Tribune,* conducts surveys about ten times a year with samples ranging from 600 to 1,200. Both of these polls now use random digit dialing telephone interviews. The frequency of polls and the sample size are increased in election years. Many other state and local polls are conducted by the media during elections and when special local issues arise. These are not regular polls and are not archived as are the Iowa and Minnesota polls, which provide data to the Roper Center. In addition, the

Minnesota poll materials are archived by the Minnesota Historical Society.

The California poll continues to be conducted by Mervin Field, and the results are syndicated in several California newspapers. In addition, the *Los Angeles Times* conducts a regular monthly poll of persons in Los Angeles County, with typical sample sizes of around 2,000. Both the Los Angeles and the California polls use random digit dialing telephone methods and are archived at the Roper Center. In addition, information from the Los Angeles poll is released in printed form to libraries.

### Private Polls

Private polling organizations ask the same kinds of questions about public opinion as the media polls do. Their clients are associations, private companies, political parties or candidates, and federal or state governments. The organizations described in this section are only representative. For a complete listing, a directory would be required. (Such directories are available and are described in the section on "Additional Reading" at the end of this chapter.)

Harris, Gallup, and Field also work for private clients as well as the media. Harris has worked for many political candidates, mostly Democrats, as would be expected. Gallup and Field do not do polling for political parties or candidates but work for many other organizations. There is general agreement that, although news polls such as those conducted by Gallup and Harris have many important functions, survey organizations do not make money from them.

*The Roper Organization.* Although Elmo Roper died in 1971, his research organization continues under the direction of his son, Burns Roper, a former president of the American Association for Public Opinion Research and a respected spokesman for the field. In addition to the custom work done mostly on the telephone, the Roper Organization has a syndicated service, *Roper Reports,* which conducts 2,000 face-to-face interviews ten times a year on trends in American life, mostly for business clients. As one might expect, nonconfidential Roper Reports are archived at the Roper Center.

*Yankelovich and Associates.* Daniel Yankelovich, a social psychologist, has had an extremely successful market research business but became publicly known through his surveys during the 1970s for *Time* magazine and the *New York Times.* His best-known continuing activity is the syndicated *Yankelovich Monitor,* an annual report on the changing social climate in the United States. This information is purchased by many large corporations, as an aid in long-range planning, and is widely reported in the media.

*Opinion Research Corporation.* One of the largest of the private polling organizations is the Opinion Research Corporation, founded by Claude Robinson and located in Princeton, New Jersey. The firm continues to specialize in opinion surveys for large business firms.

*Response Analysis Corporation.* As an example of the continuous splitting process, the Response Analysis Corporation, also located in Princeton, was formed by researchers who left the Opinion Research Corporation. Response Analysis has both commercial and government clients. It is especially well known for its work on drinking, alcoholism, and drug use, and more recently on household energy consumption. (Several other firms in Princeton were formed by researchers connected with Gallup. As a result— and because of its proximity to New York and Washington, D.C., the largest centers of survey research activity in the United States— Princeton remains an important center of this activity. Other large centers are Chicago and Los Angeles.)

*Small Regional Organizations.* The field of opinion and survey research has always been easy to enter. Individuals who wish to offer their talents to clients need not make large initial investments in capital goods. Virtually all parts of the process except for the design and client contact can be subcontracted, including sampling, data collection, and data processing. Thus, along with some very large organizations, opinion research has also always had hundreds of small firms. Some of these firms have grown or been absorbed into larger organizations, but most have stayed small. An example of this type of firm is Hollander, Cohen Associates, established in Baltimore in 1949. Sidney Hollander, its founder, was president of the American Association for Public Opinion Research in the 1970s and was highly instrumental in developing and implementing AAPOR's Code of Ethics. As with Joe Belden in Texas and Mervin Field in California, his clients have tended to be regional.

To the extent that these small firms have now adopted random digit dialing methods from central locations, the quality of sampling and interviewing has probably improved over earlier studies, when most of the work was subcontracted to field organizations of varying quality. Since entry is easy, it is inevitable that some small firms will be started by persons with little experience and training, and there is much greater variability in the quality of the work done by the very small firms than among the giants. Nevertheless, the best of the work done by the regional researchers is every bit as good as the best work done by the well-known national organizations.

Ultimately, the quality of work done by a survey organization is determined by the client. Unsophisticated buyers of research who use only price as a criterion are similar to individuals who choose a physician or lawyer simply on the basis of price. The major requirement is that the organization be able to produce a study whose quality is sufficiently high for the uses that will be made of the results. If there are several organizations that meet this criterion, then price becomes a factor. We have often observed studies unable to meet their major objectives because they were so underfunded that the research design that emerged was inadequate. Such research results in wasted money and decreased confidence in the use of opinion and market research and is best left undone if it cannot be done right.

## Government Surveys

The federal government in the United States and the central statistics offices in most countries in the world are the largest

producers of survey data in their respective countries. The major
feature that characterizes almost all government surveys is that they
deal with demographic and behavioral topics and avoid attitude
questions as well as controversial topics. Thus, in the United States,
no Census Bureau survey is permitted to obtain the religion of the
respondent as a characterizing variable, although private polls
obtain this information routinely.

Another major feature of most government surveys is that
they are usually conducted with large samples and with very high
completion rates, so that sample biases are very small. Data from
these surveys are usually available in inexpensive published form
and on computer tapes, so that they can be used for additional
analyses. In Chapter Three, we described several of the major
statistical surveys that are available. Here we discuss the major
collectors of this information in the United States.

*U.S. Bureau of the Census.* Everyone is aware of the function
of the Census Bureau in conducting the decennial censuses, but few
people realize that most of the bureau's activity is related to ongoing
surveys of households and businesses. The best known of the
continuing Census Bureau surveys is the Current Population
Survey, conducted in 52,000 households each month, that is used to
determine the level of unemployment. Selected households remain
in the sample for eight months. This survey is conducted initially
face to face and subsequently by telephone, if possible. The
cooperation rate on this survey is about 97 percent, which is far
higher than on private surveys. This very high cooperation rate is
obtained partly because respondents respect the Census Bureau and
some may believe erroneously that cooperation is required by law.
(Cooperation is required legally on decennial censuses but not for
continuing surveys of households.) Also important are the training
and experience of the Census Bureau's interviewers, who work
almost full time and are carefully supervised.

Recently the Census Bureau has started a continuing Survey
on Income and Program Participation, to measure the effect of
federal programs on poverty and income distribution. Not surprisingly, the cooperation and quality of data on this survey are
somewhat lower, because income and savings information is

considered sensitive by many respondents and is difficult to report accurately without extensive reference to records.

The bureau conducts both censuses and continuing surveys of businesses, including manufacturing, wholesale trade, retail trade, and service industries. The results of these surveys form a major part of the data used to compute changes in the gross national product. Business establishments are required by law to cooperate in these surveys. The same law requiring cooperation by businesses requires the bureau to keep data confidential, so that reports from one firm cannot be identified by its competitors.

The Census Bureau is also the data-gathering agency for other government departments. The Current Population Survey is conducted in cooperation with the Bureau of Labor Statistics. The Census Bureau also conducts an important continuing survey of consumer expenditures for the Bureau of Labor Statistics, which is used for determining the weights for the Consumer Price Index. Data on consumer expenditures have wide applications by commercial and academic researchers studying consumer behavior.

In the health area, the Census Bureau conducts the National Health Interview Survey for the National Center for Health Statistics. This annual survey of 32,000 respondents collects information on acute and chronic illness. Attached to the survey is a subpart, the National Health and Nutrition Examination Survey, in which individuals are invited to visit a central location where they receive a complete medical examination.

In a different field entirely, the Census Bureau conducts the annual National Crime Survey of 60,000 households for the Bureau of Justice Statistics. These data are collected to supplement official police statistics, which substantially underestimate crime because many victims do not report crimes and many reported crimes are not entered into police records.

For a brief description of other surveys conducted by the Census Bureau, such as the Housing Survey and the Survey of New Construction, see Table 2 in Chapter Three.

*National Center for Health Statistics.* In addition to obtaining data from the Census Bureau and other contractors, the National Center for Health Statistics has developed its own data collection system. Interviewers at a telephone center, using the same methods as the most careful private polls, conduct national and regional surveys, mainly with households. While all telephone methods miss the few percent of households without telephones, the center has demonstrated that for most policy applications the telephone methods are adequate, as well as being far less expensive.

*Center for Education Statistics.* Unlike the Census Bureau and the National Center for Health Statistics, the Center for Education Statistics collects almost all its information by self-administered mail questionnaires sent annually to state education agencies, which collect data from local elementary and secondary schools, from individual schools participating in federal programs, and from colleges and other institutions of higher education. Here data quality depends mainly on the respondent, although editing checks are used to identify any unusual changes reported from one time period to the next. While it is likely that data on enrollment and staff size are reliable, data on financial operations and staff practices are subject to substantial response errors.

*Statistical Reporting Service, Department of Agriculture.* We saw in Chapter Two that the Department of Agriculture pioneered the use of surveys in the federal government. These surveys continue today. Most of them are conducted by mail, with some telephone follow-ups and face-to-face interviews. The most newsworthy of these surveys are those conducted periodically to predict yields of corn, soybeans, wheat, potatoes, and cotton; the results of these surveys have immediate effects on the futures markets for these commodities. Other surveys obtain farm economic data, and these face much the same problems as surveys of household economic conditions.

### Policy Researchers

In this section, we somewhat arbitrarily group a number of large organizations, both profit and nonprofit, whose major activity is conducting surveys for the United States government. Not surprisingly, these organizations have concentrated on issues of income redistribution and health. They have not been the initiators of this research but have grown by being responsive to federal research directions. All these organizations have faced rapid expansion and shrinking as federal funds for policy research have risen or shrunk. Most recently, there was a sharp decline in funding and in the size of all the policy research organizations at the start of the Reagan presidency, but since then most of them have expanded again as the demand for data continues, especially in the health area.

*Westat.* Westat is an employee-owned private company headquartered in the Washington, D.C., area. This company had an interesting start. It was formed by a group of former employees from the U.S. Bureau of the Census, including the eminent statisticians Morris Hansen and Joseph Waksberg. In accordance with its Census Bureau tradition, Westat has always been noted for its careful samples and high-quality interviewing. At one time, Westat became part of a large conglomerate, Container Corporation of America, but that firm soon realized that it did not have the management skills to run a large survey organization and sold Westat to its employees.

*Mathematica Policy Research.* Another major private company is Mathematica Policy Research, which has been noted for its economic work—particularly, the large experiments conducted in New Jersey on the effects of income supplements to those below specified poverty levels. Mathematica is located in Princeton, New Jersey, and was initially formed by economists and statisticians associated with Princeton University.

*Research Triangle Institute.* The Research Triangle Institute (RTI) is a nonprofit research organization located in an area in the middle of three major universities, the University of North Carolina, North Carolina State University, and Duke University. Although the institute is completely independent from these universities and is now supported by project funds, it was originally started on land and facilities provided by the state of North Carolina. The formation of the Research Triangle Institute led, as the state hoped it would, to an explosion of research and high-technology organizations in what had previously been a depressed area. The survey research activities of RTI are about half of the total research conducted. RTI has been noted for its activities in educational and health surveys. It conducted the first surveys for the National Assessment of Educational Progress, where children and adults were given tests of subject matter knowledge.

*Rand Corporation.* The Rand Corporation, located in Santa Monica, California, was started initially as a civilian think tank for the United States Air Force. As work from the Air Force declined, the leaders of Rand decided to shift their emphasis toward policy issues in the civilian sector. The economists, statisticians, and social scientists on Rand's staff turned their attention to such issues as housing supplements for the poor and medical insurance. Recently, Rand has also been examining the judicial process.

### University Survey Organizations

The university survey organizations may be distinguished from the nonprofit policy research organizations in that they combine teaching and research functions with data collection and analysis. Surprisingly, the two best known of these organizations, the National Opinion Research Center (NORC) of the University of Chicago and the Survey Research Center (SRC) of the University of Michigan, are both financially independent of their universities; that is, all their funds for staff and equipment must be generated totally from project funds. On the other hand, the large number of state and local survey organizations affiliated with universities receive some support from their universities in recognition of their role in promoting teaching and research.

At one time, only NORC and SRC among the university survey organizations were capable of conducting large national surveys with their own trained field staffs. This is still the case for face-to-face surveys, since these organizations continue to maintain national field forces of interviewers. Currently, however, the state survey organizations can and do conduct national telephone surveys as well as regional, state, and local face-to-face interviews.

All these organizations have as one of their important missions providing advice and help, within available resources, to inexperienced researchers. Table 4 (at the end of this section) gives a listing of these organizations as of 1987. More than thirty state organizations have joined together into the National Network of State Polls. This network enables researchers to obtain data from multiple state organizations using similar methods and coordinating their activities.

*National Opinion Research Center.* NORC was the first of the university survey organizations and continues today as a leader in the field. One of its best-known projects is the General Social Survey, which is conducted annually with funds from the National Science Foundation and which provides access to the data to all interested social scientists. The General Social Survey is directed by James Davis, now at Harvard but formerly director of NORC.

NORC is divided into centers. The Cultural Pluralism Research Center (no longer operating) studied ethnic and religious groups; some of its best-known work was conducted by Andrew Greeley about American Catholics. New centers on economic research and social policy have broadened NORC's mission beyond simply survey research, but the survey group continues at the core of the organization.

NORC has always been noted for obtaining interviews on difficult topics from difficult populations. In its early days, NORC conducted studies on drinking and alcoholism in Chicago's skid row. More recently, several studies have been conducted on drug abuse among persons already identified as users.

NORC has also been a leader in the field of methodological research. Its studies in this area include the classic work conducted in the 1950s by Hyman and his colleagues on interviewer effects and, in the 1970s, our work on response effects and the general issue of questionnaire design. More recently, NORC has been heavily involved in efforts to merge survey and cognitive psychology insights to find methods for improving answers to complex questions. NORC has now established a Center for Methodological Research to continue its focus on methodology.

A bibliography of all NORC studies is available from Patrick

Bova, the NORC librarian. NORC also archives its studies and makes either computer or print forms available to researchers at cost.

*Survey Research Center, University of Michigan.* The Survey Research Center, which was formed in 1947 at the University of Michigan, is now the nucleus of the expanded Institute for Social Research, which also includes the Center for Political Studies and the Research Center for Group Dynamics. The Survey Research Center is in many ways similar to NORC. In the past few years, the two organizations have had a common national area probability sample and share some interviewers for face-to-face national studies.

SRC has conducted both substantive and methodological research. A major continuing survey of consumer behavior and expectations, led for many years by George Katona, was responsible for the expansion of economics into the area of consumer behavior. The presidential election studies, in which panels of respondents are interviewed before and after each election, have become the most widely used source of information on election behavior. The wide availability of these data through the Inter-University Consortium for Political and Social Research has encouraged their use by researchers and students.

Methodologically, Michigan was an early leader in efficient area probability sample designs under the leadership of Leslie Kish. Experiments on interviewer effects and question wording have been conducted on a regular basis by Charles Cannell and Howard Schuman and their colleagues.

SRC has become known around the world because of its summer institute, where new researchers are trained in all aspects of survey methodology. Many of the participants in this program are from universities and government statistics offices in developing countries, although some of the advanced courses are attended by faculty and graduate students from other universities in the United States, who find these short courses an efficient way of learning about the latest developments in data collection and analysis.

*Survey Research Laboratory, University of Illinois.* The Survey Research Laboratory at the University of Illinois (SRL) was founded in 1964 by Robert Ferber, an internationally known statistician, economist, and market researcher. It has conducted hundreds of studies for the state of Illinois and the city of Chicago, and in conjunction with university faculty at both Chicago and Champaign-Urbana campuses. A major part of SRL's work is devoted to methodological research on improving questioning and sampling methods. Among its best-known research projects are those on the uses of diaries for collecting consumer expenditures and health behavior and more recently on the uses of network sampling methods for improving reporting of rare events. Earlier than most national survey organizations, SRL recognized the value of telephone procedures and has continued to use and develop them.

*Survey Research Laboratory, University of Wisconsin.* The Survey Research Laboratory at the University of Wisconsin, Madison, was founded by Harry Sharp shortly after the founding of the Illinois laboratory. Most recently, the Wisconsin SRL has become a center of innovation in the use of computer-assisted telephone interviewing.

*Survey Research Centers, University of California at Berkeley and Los Angeles.* These two California centers are independent, although they often work in close cooperation on state surveys, such as the large study of disability conducted for the state of California. The Survey Research Center at UCLA is now part of the Institute for Social Science Research, while the Berkeley center remains free standing. Both centers have worked closely in the development of computer-assisted telephone interviewing methods, although most of this activity is currently centered in Berkeley.

*Center for Survey Research, University of Massachusetts, and Center for Urban Studies of MIT and Harvard.* As its name suggests, this center has concentrated on urban studies in the Boston area. Major methodological research has been conducted on interviewer effects and improved methods for training and supervising interviewers.

*Institute for Survey Research, Temple University.* This center was one of the first to be founded on the East Coast, but its

**Table 4. Academic Survey Research Organizations in the
United States and Canada.**

*Alabama*
Capstone Poll
University of Alabama
P.O. Box 587
Tuscaloosa, Ala. 35486

Division of Behavioral Science
  Research
Carver Research Foundation
Carnegie Hall
Tuskegee University
Tuskegee, Ala. 36088

Institute of Higher Education
  Research and Service
University of Alabama
P.O. Box Q
University, Ala. 35486

*Arizona*
Public Opinion Research
  Program
Stauffer Hall
Arizona State University
Tempe, Ariz. 85281

Survey Research Laboratory
Department of Sociology
Arizona State University
Tempe, Ariz. 85287

*California*
Center for Survey Research
Public Policy Research
  Organization
310 Social Ecology Building
University of California, Irvine
Irvine, Calif. 92717

Institute for Social Science
  Research
University of California, Los
  Angeles
9240 Bunche Hall
405 Hilgard Avenue
Los Angeles, Calif. 90024

*California (continued)*
Survey Research Center
University of California
2538 Channing Way
Berkeley, Calif. 94720

Survey Research Service
School of Health
Loma Linda University
Loma Linda, Calif. 92350

*District of Columbia*
Center for Assessment and
  Demographic Studies
Gallaudet University
800 Florida Avenue, N.E.
Washington, D.C. 20002

*Florida*
Center for Organizational
  Communication Research and
  Service
Department of Communication
University of South Florida
Tampa, Fla. 33620

Policy Sciences Program Survey
  Research Center
Room 68 Bellamy Building
Florida State University
Tallahassee, Fla. 32306

*Georgia*
Center for Public and Urban
  Research
Georgia State University
University Plaza
Atlanta, Ga.

Survey Research Center
544 Graduate Studies Building
University of Georgia
Athens, Ga. 30602

**Table 4. Academic Survey Research Organizations in the United States and Canada, Cont'd.**

*Illinois*
NORC: A Social Science Research Center
University of Chicago
1155 E. 60th Street
Chicago, Ill. 60637

Northwestern University Survey Laboratory
Northwestern University
625 Haven
Evanston, Ill. 60608

Public Opinion Laboratory
Northern Illinois University
DeKalb, Ill. 60115

Survey Research Laboratory
University of Illinois at Chicago
910 W. Van Buren Street, Suite 500 (M/C 336)
Chicago, Ill. 60607
or
University of Illinois at Urbana-Champaign
1005 W. Nevada Street
Urbana, Ill. 61801

*Indiana*
Center for Survey Research
Indiana University
1022 E. Third Street
Bloomington, Ind. 47405

*Iowa*
Center for Health Services Research
University of Iowa
S517 Westlawn
Iowa City, Iowa 52242

Center for Social and Behavioral Research
University of Northern Iowa
Cedar Falls, Iowa 50614

*Iowa (continued)*
Statistical Laboratory
Iowa State University
Ames, Iowa 50011

*Kansas*
Institute for Public Policy and Business Research
607 Blake Hall
University of Kansas
Lawrence, Kans. 66045

*Kentucky*
Survey Research Center
12 Porter Building
University of Kentucky
Lexington, Ky. 40506

Urban Studies Center
College of Urban and Public Affairs
University of Louisville
Louisville, Ky. 40292

*Maryland*
Institute for Governmental Service
Suite 2101 Woods Hall
University of Maryland
College Park, Md. 20742

Survey Research Center
1103 Art/Sociology Building
University of Maryland
College Park, Md. 20742

*Massachusetts*
Center for Survey Research
University of Massachusetts-Boston
100 Arlington Street
Boston, Mass. 02116

*Michigan*
Survey Research Center
University of Michigan
P.O. Box 1248
Ann Arbor, Mich. 48106

**Table 4. Academic Survey Research Organizations in the
United States and Canada, Cont'd.**

*Minnesota*
Minnesota Center for Survey
  Research
University of Minnesota
2122 Riverside Avenue
Minneapolis, Minn. 55454

*Mississippi*
Survey Research Unit
Social Science Research Center
P.O. Box C
Mississippi State University
Mississippi State, Miss. 39762

*Missouri*
Public Policy Extension
Public Policy Administration
406 Tower
University of Missouri-St. Louis
8002 Natural Bridge Road
St. Louis, Mo. 63121

*Montana*
Survey Research Center
1-108 Wilson Hall
Montana State University
Bozeman, Mont. 59717

*Nevada*
Center for Survey Research
FDH Building 615
University of Nevada, Las Vegas
Las Vegas, Nev. 89154

*New York*
Center for Management
  Development
School of Management
323 Jacobs Management Center
State University of New York,
  Buffalo
Buffalo, N.Y. 14260

Center for Social and
  Demographic Analysis
Social Sciences
State University of New York,
  Albany
Albany, N.Y. 12222

*New York (continued)*
Center for Social Research
City University of New York
33 West 42nd Street, Rm 625
New York, N.Y. 10036

Center for the Social Sciences
Columbia University
420 West 118th Street
New York, N.Y. 10027

Division of Sociomedical Sciences
Columbia University School of
  Public Health
600 West 168th Street
New York, N.Y. 10032

Survey Research Facility
Cornell Institute for Social and
  Economic Research
323 Uris Hall
Cornell University
Ithaca, N.Y. 14853

*North Carolina*
Center for Urban Affairs and
  Community Services
P.O. Box 7401
North Carolina State University
Raleigh, N.C. 27695

Institute for Research in Social
  Science
Manning Hall 026A
University of North Carolina
Chapel Hill, N.C. 27514

Center for Survey Research
Research Triangle Institute
P.O. Box 12194
Research Triangle Park, N.C.
  27709

*Ohio*
Communication Research Center
Cleveland State University
1983 E. 24th Street
Cleveland, Ohio 44115

**Table 4. Academic Survey Research Organizations in the
United States and Canada, Cont'd.**

*Ohio (continued)*
Institute for Policy Research
Mail Location 132
University of Cincinnati
Cincinnati, Ohio 45221

Polimetrics, Laboratory for
   Political and Social Research
Department of Political Science
Ohio State University
156 Derby Hall
154 North Oval Mall
Columbus, Ohio 43210

*Oregon*
Survey Research Center
Oregon State University
Corvallis, Oreg. 97331

*Pennsylvania*
Institute for Survey Research
Temple University
1601 N. Broad Street
Philadelphia, Pa. 19122

University Center for Social and
   Urban Research
1617 Cathedral of Learning
University of Pittsburgh
Pittsburgh, Pa. 15260

*Puerto Rico*
Social Science Research Center
Faculty of Social Science
Rio Pledras Campus
University of Puerto Rico
Rio Pledras, P.R. 00931

*Tennessee*
Urban Observatory of
   Metropolitan Nashville-
   University Centers
P.O. Box 25109
Nashville, Tenn. 37202

*Texas*
Office of Survey Research
College of Communication
CMA 6.144
University of Texas
Austin, Tex. 78712

*Utah*
Social Research Institute
130 Social Research Institute
Graduate School of Social Work
University of Utah
Salt Lake City, Utah 84112

Survey Research Center
2120 Annex
University of Utah
Salt Lake City, Utah 84112

*Virginia*
Survey Research Laboratory
Virginia Commonwealth
   University
901 W. Franklin Street
Box 3016
Richmond, Va. 23284

*Washington*
Social and Economic Sciences
   Research Center
Wilson Hall #133
Washington State University
Pullman, Wash. 99164

*West Virginia*
Applied Research, Evaluation and
   Planning
411 Knapp Hall
West Virginia University
Morgantown, W.Va. 26506

*Wisconsin*
Wisconsin Survey Research
   Laboratory
University of Wisconsin-
   Extension
610 Langdon Street (Lowell Hall)
Madison, Wis. 53703

**Table 4. Academic Survey Research Organizations in the
United States and Canada, Cont'd.**

| | |
|---|---|
| *Canada* | *Canada (continued)* |
| Centre de Sondage | Institute for Social Research |
| University of Montreal | York University |
| P.O. Box 6128, Station "A" | 4700 Keele Street |
| Montreal, Quebec H3C 3J7, | North York, Ontario M3J 1P3, |
|   Canada |   Canada |
| | |
| Population Research Laboratory | |
| Department of Sociology | |
| University of Alberta | |
| Edmonton, Alberta T6G 2H4, | |
|   Canada | |

*Source:* Survey Research Laboratory, University of Illinois, 1987.

data collection activities have been national as well as local, with many of the studies related to health topics.

*Institute for Policy Research, University of Cincinnati.* In addition to local and state policy studies, this survey facility has conducted methodological work on the effects of question wording on responses to attitude questions.

### Commercial Market Research Organizations

The major function of the commercial research organizations is to provide marketing and management information to businesses, so that they can serve their markets better. Some of these firms offer syndicated services to many clients simultaneously; others offer custom research services on special assignments to a single client; still others offer both syndicated and custom services. Although there are far more custom than syndicated services, the syndicated services tend to be much larger and better known. We discuss some of these and then give a general discussion of custom services.

*A. C. Nielsen Company.* By far the largest and best known of all market research companies in the United States and the world is the A. C. Nielsen Company. Although the Nielsen Company does some custom research, it is especially known for two syndicated services: the measurement of television viewing and the measurement of product purchases through use of store audits. Since the store audits do not really involve any survey methods, we shall limit our discussion to the media measurement procedures.

For its national sample of television viewing, the Nielsen company selects households whose members agree to have their television sets wired with a device that records when the set is turned on and what channel is being viewed. This information is then automatically transmitted by telephone wire during the middle of the night to the Nielsen processing center in Florida, where reports are prepared. To obtain information on who in the household watched specific programs, Nielsen asks individual household members to report their viewing, either in written records or by pressing a button when they are viewing a program.

Nielsen and its major competitor, Arbitron, also measure viewing in local markets, with samples of about 300 households reporting in a specified week. These households use diaries to report viewing for the week, with some indication of viewing by individual household members. Arbitron uses the same procedure for reports of radio listening. As the technology improves and measuring devices become cheaper, more of this work is being done with electronics and less with diaries and more typical survey methods. Nielsen and several competitors are also attempting to combine viewing data with purchasing data obtained from store cash registers that automatically read the product codes on purchases.

*IMS International.* The second-largest research company, but one that is almost totally unknown to the general public, is IMS International, which specializes in studies on the prescribing and purchasing of prescription drugs. Most of the surveys conducted by IMS International are with physicians or pharmacies, and many of them are conducted by nurses or medical students.

*National Purchase Diary/Market Research Corporation of America.* These two competing firms use diaries filled in by household reporters to obtain continuing information on purchases of selected categories of products. MRCA, the older and smaller of the two, limits its reporting to grocery, drug, and textile products. NPD reports on these products but also has been successful with a service reporting on food eaten away from home and toy purchases. Both firms sell a menu census, which reports on how food is prepared and eaten within the home. The current NPD panel consists of 13,000 households, although not all report on all products. The MRCA panel consists of 7,500 households.

*Market Facts/National Family Opinion.* These two firms, in addition to their custom research, offer the availability of a group of about 100,000 households who have been prescreened and balanced on basic demographic characteristics and who have agreed to participate in mail surveys on individual products. Cooperation on individual surveys with these panels ranges around 70-80 percent; however, only 5-10 percent of those initially contacted agreed to participate in these panels. The panels are primarily used to test new products or promotions where the possible sample biases are not critical.

*Simmons Market Research.* Simmons and its competitors are primarily in the business of measuring magazine and newspaper readership. Their surveys are conducted with large samples who are asked about a large number of print media in an interview. Since there is some tendency for individuals to overreport reading, and since some of the estimates are made on small subsamples, the print media reports are frequently controversial. Such controversy is particularly sharp because both the quality of advertising and the rates that can be charged are based on readership as reported by surveys rather than subscription data.

*Custom Research.* Although there is actually a firm with this name, we use this term to refer to the thousands of firms, usually small, that conduct specialized research for individual clients. These firms are responsible mainly for designing the project, since subcontractors in data collection and data processing actually conduct the survey. For example, every city of any size will have one or more field supervisors who will hire, train, and supervise interviewers for any client. The quality of work of these field supervisors is highly variable. Custom research firms are used by businesses that do not wish to maintain large market research staffs of their own because these staffs would not be fully utilized. Even a very large firm such as Procter & Gamble, with a market research staff of several hundred persons, farms out a substantial part of its work when it needs to obtain specialized skills or when its permanent staff is fully occupied.

## Professional Associations in Survey Research

There is one major organization of commercial firms: the Council of American Survey Research Organizations (CASRO). A smaller group, the Council on Public Polls, consists of organizations whose polls are published in newspapers or magazines or presented on radio or television. This group sets standards on how poll data should be presented to the public.

Of the three major organizations of individuals engaged in survey research, the organization most directly involved with survey research in the United States is the American Association for Public Opinion Research (AAPOR), which includes both commercial and academic researchers in its membership. This organization, which appropriately has its headquarters in Princeton, New Jersey, publishes *Public Opinion Quarterly* and continues to stress methodological and ethical as well as mass communications and political issues at its annual conferences. Because the organization has only about 1,200 members and the annual meetings are held at relatively isolated settings, it is easy for new researchers to meet and talk with others in the field. In addition, AAPOR has active local chapters in New York, Washington, D.C., and other regions. The World Association of Public Opinion Research (WAPOR) plays the same role internationally.

The Survey Research Methods section within the American Statistical Association contains about 4,000 members, mainly from the ranks of government and academic statisticians interested in survey methodology. This section organizes a large number of sessions at the annual meetings of the American Statistical

Association and has also been responsible for special sections on survey methodology in the *Journal of the American Statistical Association.*

Market researchers are an important segment of the membership of the American Marketing Association, which has a vice-president of marketing research and features discussions of market research at its annual meetings and at special conferences. The American Marketing Association publishes the *Journal of Marketing Research,* which is one of the major journals on new data collection and analysis methods.

Many other organizations will have discussions on survey methods at their meetings or in their journals, but these relate primarily to the use of such methods for substantive studies in fields such as consumer behavior, political science, sociology, education, and evaluation research.

### Opinion Polling Abroad

Survey organizations are found in all developed countries and in many developing countries, regardless of their forms of government. There are polling organizations and continuing surveys in the Soviet Union, Poland, and even the People's Republic of China. While direct criticism of the form of government is unlikely, data on specific topics—such as satisfaction with housing—can be, and are, obtained even in totalitarian regimes.

In many ways, the structure of the polls, especially in developed countries, is similar to that in the United States. Media polls are important everywhere, although in some countries their activities just before and after elections are severely limited. Government surveys are very common, although there is more centralization in their execution than in the United States, mirroring the differences between the centralized parliamentary governments elsewhere and the decentralized federal government in the United States. That is, the state and regional polls found in the United States are rare elsewhere.

Commercial market research organizations are found everywhere, and it is much more common than in the United States for them also to do policy research for their governments. Academic survey organizations are far less common than in the United States, except in Australia. In many European countries, the social sciences still place much more emphasis on theoretical analyses than on data collection.

Opinion researchers around the world are in touch with one another through WAPOR, other international meetings, and some cross-national research. Currently, for example, there is an international General Social Survey with key questions replicated in the United States, Great Britain, West Germany, and Australia.

## Summary

In this chapter, we have tried to give a picture of the types of firms involved in survey research. We started with the media polls, then discussed other private polls, government surveys, policy researchers, university survey organizations, and commercial market research firms.

Despite the diversity of these organizations, most survey researchers belong to a small number of professional associations and work together with one another on common issues, such as legal restraints against surveys of all kinds. There are also many job switches by researchers among the different types of organizations. Those who are interested in survey research as a career will want to consider the broad range of job possibilities rather than limiting themselves to only one kind of organization.

## Additional Reading

The professional organizations are usually the best providers of information about sources of help on surveys or possible job opportunities. In addition to its membership directories, the American Association for Public Opinion Research publishes an annual "Blue Book" of agencies and organizations represented in AAPOR membership. AAPOR also publishes a pamphlet on *Careers in Survey Research.* The New York chapter of the American Marketing Association publishes an annual "Green Book" listing all commercial market research firms. A shorter list of commercial firms is also found at the front of the membership directory of the American Marketing Association.

# 5

# How Information
# Is Collected

We often read in a newspaper or hear on a news broadcast
that "The unemployment rate has remained unchanged this month
at 7.2 percent" or "Fifty-six percent of the American population
approved of the way the president is doing his job" or similar information containing statistics. Behind these numbers lies a complex
data collection process whereby a sampling plan is formulated, a
questionnaire is constructed, respondents are asked to answer the
questions, and the answers are converted into a form that can be
tabulated to produce these numerical statements. The validity of the
final results depends on the quality of the entire chain of events: from
the design of the survey through the data collection phase to the final
tabulation and interpretation of the data. If any of the links in the
chain is weak, the validity of the final result will be undermined. A
well-designed study that is poorly executed will have as bad results
as a poorly designed study that is well executed.

Survey interviews have been described as "conversations with
a purpose." This definition points to some of the essential features
of data collection and surveys. Above all, survey data consist of
answers to questions—questions that are posed by a researcher and
answered by respondents who have been selected according to some
sampling plan (see Chapter Six for a discussion of sampling). For
the most part, surveys require that individuals talk to one another

either face to face or on the telephone, although data for some surveys are collected by means of a self-administered questionnaire, where the interviewer is present only symbolically, in the form of the written questions.

Although survey interviews are sufficiently like ordinary conversations to partake of the social rules governing conversations, a fact that is used by interviewers to help secure respondent cooperation, the purpose of the survey interview gives it a specific form that sets it apart from ordinary social conversations. As distinct from ordinary conversation, one of the participants (the interviewer) guides the conversation in very specific ways. Respondents are constrained to talk about the topics that the interviewer introduces in the interview and most often are required to respond in a stylized language (for example, "not very often, fairly often, very often") that is not necessarily congenial to them. Both the widespread experience of people with survey inteviews and the artificiality of the particular conversational style that it imposes on people make it an ideal subject for cartoonists and social satirists.

Interviewing is labor intensive. The growing number of surveys and interviews has led to the concomitant growth of interviewing as an industry. Although some of the larger social research centers and market research firms have their own interviewing staffs, a large proportion of survey interviews is conducted by firms that provide only interviewing services. Thus, the interviewing component of the data collection process is often completely separated from the research design, questionnaire construction, and data-processing portions of the survey operation. Such a separation has some advantages in providing for professionalization of the interviewing link in the research chain, but it also has dangers in that too often the researcher is totally cut off from the actual interviewing process, and is unable to maintain quality control over the interviewing process, while the interviewer does not know the purpose of the research.

## The Organization of Interviewing

In most cartoons dealing with survey interviews, the interviewer is a man with a clipboard standing at the door and talking to the respondent. This image of the interview is entirely wrong. Interviewers are almost always women. Most interviews these days are conducted by telephone, rather than face to face; and when face-to-face interviews *are* conducted, they take place not at the front door but in the living room or at the kitchen table. Technological innovations may well modify these methods even further in the next decade.

Interviewing is usually a part-time job, with the amount of work varying considerably over time. When there is a tight deadline, an interviewer may need to work seven days a week and possibly both days and evenings. Flexibility is essential. While hourly rates for interviewers are higher than for most part-time jobs, they do not compare to salaries for full-time work by persons with similar skills.

Thus, a typical interviewer is a middle-aged, married woman who has some college education, but not a college degree, and obviously wants or needs to work part time but is not able or willing to work full time. The reason that the interviewer is middle-aged and married is that most younger women are working full time or caring for small children. Some older and retired women make excellent interviewers, but interviewing is a job that requires substantial energy, even on the telephone, and most older women find the work too tiring. Formal education is not required for interviewing, but the interviewer must be able to understand and perform complicated sampling and clerical tasks and these days to be comfortable with a computer terminal.

Personality traits are far more critical for interviewer success than are age or education, and these traits are difficult to measure. In a study of NORC interviewers conducted about twenty years ago, Sudman (1968) found that the most successful interviewers scored high in intelligence and in need for achievement, enjoyed interviewing activities, and did not regard interviewing as a stepping stone to another job or as a high-prestige part-time occupation. It is uncertain whether the same characteristics would be found in other organizations using other methods of data collection.

There has been a substantial decrease in the number of women who are interested in interviewing or in any part-time work as the opportunities for full-time work for women have increased sharply. As a result, both the quantity and the quality of the labor pool available for interviewing have declined, and the costs of interviewing and data collection have increased.

Since survey interviews resemble conversations in many respects and interviewers are constrained in their behavior, it is tempting to assume that interviewing is a job that can be done with little or no experience or training. Indeed, most interviewing staffs have had relatively little training, and turnover rates are high. There is, unfortunately, very little systematic research that assesses the effects of experience and training on the quality of interviewing. For two reasons, however, experienced interviewers should generally do better than new interviewers. First, interviewers who do not do well at the task are likely to quit or be fired, so that experienced interviewers are those who have survived this process. Second, because experienced interviewers have learned the necessary interviewing skills, they obtain higher levels of cooperation than new interviewers do.

There are two kinds of interviewer training: general and specific. Persons new to interviewing must be trained to read questions as they are worded, to engage in neutral probing, and to be nonjudgmental about the respondent. Specific interviewer training deals with the special features of a particular study. The importance of specific training is related to the complexity of the survey questionnaire and the sample design. Simple questionnaires with uncomplex formats and straightforward sample designs probably can be executed by minimally trained interviewers. Other types of surveys—for example, surveys with complex sample designs requiring the use of probability mechanisms to select respondents; surveys with complex questionnaires that attempt to measure respondents' behavior precisely; and surveys that require high completion rates—will need interviewers who are much more highly trained. Organizations (such as the U.S. Bureau of the Census) which conduct complex surveys that attempt to make precise estimates of such things as the unemployment rate, utilization of health care facilities, and expenditure patterns invest heavily in training their interviewers and attempt to maintain a staff of experienced interviewers.

Other survey organizations deliberately avoid hiring experienced interviewers because they believe that using experienced interviewers increases the cost of data collection with no evident increase in quality. If one considers dropout rate, training, and supervisory time, experienced interviewers are probably a better bargain. It has been found, however, that experience in other activities, such as selling, does not necessarily mean that a person will make a good interviewer.

While survey organizations disagree about the importance of experience and training for interviewers' performance, they all agree that interviewers must be adequately supervised. Supervision of interviewers who conduct face-to-face interviews has always been a difficult matter, because the interviewers work by themselves; in such cases, the supervisor must review interviewers' work soon after its completion, so that carelessness or systematic errors can be picked up quickly and the interviewer can be given feedback on her performance. In addition, the supervisor usually undertakes to validate a certain proportion of the interviewer's work; that is, the supervisor contacts the respondent (usually by telephone), repeats a few questions from the interview, and asks the respondent about the interviewer's behavior.

The supervisor must determine whether interviewers are working at the right pace and, particularly, whether they are encountering problems (such as a large number of refusals) that might cause low response rates. Interviewers will need special support and advice from supervisors if they are working in depressed areas, if the subject of the interview is sensitive, or if they have had an especially trying case. Because of the difficulties in supervising interviewers in face-to-face interviews, a supervisor can handle only about eight to ten interviewers at once. This relatively low supervisor-to-interviewer ratio helps to explain why face-to-face interviewing is expensive.

The total number of interviewers working at a given time for a survey organization is elusive, since interviewers may work for multiple organizations and not be available for a specific survey. Organizations that conduct national face-to-face studies usually recruit several hundred interviewers, although only about one hundred are used on a typical study. (There is a wide range, depending on the total sample size.) State and regional survey organizations have somewhat fewer interviewers, since their samples are smaller.

Telephone interviews conducted in central locations require smaller staffs than face-to-face interviews, since the interviewers do not have to travel and therefore can conduct more interviews. A typical survey might use twenty-five telephone interviewers, although the range would again be wide. Far fewer supervisors are needed for telephone interviewing, usually just one at any time period and two or three in total to cover the entire period during which interviews are conducted. Supervision in a telephone-interviewing center is a much easier matter, since the interviewers' behavior can be monitored directly by the supervisor. Most telephone-interviewing centers are equipped with supervisory stations, where supervisors can listen in on actual interviews and monitor the activities of interviewers directly. Supervisors can sample the work of a larger number of interviewers on an ongoing basis and provide additional training, if needed, or help with a particular problem. Thus, supervision can be more effective in centralized telephone facilities.

Because the probability of someone's being at home is much greater in the late afternoon and early evening, most telephone interviewing is done then or on weekends. These time constraints in turn mean that interviewers have to be available at those times—a fact that makes interviewing a part-time occupation for most interviewers and favors those whose regular occupations allow them freedom in the late afternoon and evenings (for example, teachers) or those who have periods of unemployment (such as actors), as well as those who only want to work part time (for example, housewives).

### Face-to-Face Versus Telephone Interviews

*Telephone-Interviewing Facilities.* Most telephone interviewing today is done in a centralized facility. Such facilities typically include a number of telephone-interviewing stations (twenty to one hundred or more) consisting of a telephone with a special headset that allows interviewers to listen and talk without having to hold the receiver, so that their hands will be free to operate a computer and record answers. Telephones are placed in soundproof cubicles with a small desk for the interviewer. The telephones are specially wired so that supervisors in a separate room can listen in on selected conversations and can identify which interviewer and instrument is being used.

Although many telephone interviewers still use printed questionnaires on which they record the respondents' answers, a large and increasing number of telephone facilities use computer-assisted telephone-interviewing (CATI) systems. CATI systems vary considerably in their degree of sophistication. Basically, they consist of a computer program in which each question on the question-naire is separately displayed on a cathode-ray terminal. The interviewer reads the question from the screen and records the respondent's answer, either verbatim or by entering a number that is indicated on the screen. Responses are entered from a keyboard. A CATI work station thus requires a computer terminal in addition to the telephone and work space mentioned above. More compli-cated CATI systems can produce a randomized telephone number, schedule calls, keep track of the outcomes of attempted calls, and maintain the file for scheduling callbacks of numbers where no one answered or the designated respondent was not home.

CATI systems have a number of advantages. Most notably, they automate a number of contingent decisions that the interviewer would have to make, thus reducing the probability of error in the administration of the questionnaire. For example, a questionnaire may contain a number of alternative questions. The choice of question to ask depends on the response to a previous question. When interviewers are working from printed documents, they sometimes become confused about what is the next question to be asked. In CATI systems, the next question appears automatically even if it is contingent on particular responses given to previous questions. If the system contains scheduling programs as well, much of the clerical work involved in scheduling callbacks is done automatically. In addition, the data are entered automatically into the computer as the responses are given, so that a separate data entry step is omitted. Data summaries can also be obtained at any point in the data collection process that one wants them. Such ability to get an almost continuous reading on the results of the data collection process enables the researcher to monitor the progress of

the study and allocate resources more effectively. Without the ability to monitor anything more than the overall completion rate, the researcher can only work on increasing the total completion rate. With the CATI system, however, one can monitor the completion rate for different subgroups and direct resources to the subgroups that might have a disproportionately low response rate. Some of the new non-CATI data management systems also permit this more specialized monitoring, but with substantially greater delays. In addition, CATI systems can enable researchers to use different versions of questionnaires, to alter the order of questions, to randomize questions across respondents or respondents across interviewers, and to employ other techniques that can reduce or measure errors in surveys.

CATI systems are not without their problems. They were initially developed to be run by one large central computer, with many work stations being served by the same computer. If the computer should malfunction during the interviewing time, the entire set of work stations hooked into that computer would become nonworking at the same time. As a result, interviews might be cut off in the middle, and interviewers would be left without knowing what questions to ask—an embarrassing situation in the middle of an interview. Also, if large numbers of interviews are going on simultaneously, the lapse in time before the next question appears on the screen introduces awkwardness into the flow of the conversation. With recent developments, these problems are being solved by the use of microcomputers as work stations, the questionnaires being programmed separately for each of the work stations.

The process of entering a questionnaire into a CATI system is both time-consuming and costly, although new computer software is making the process simpler. Because of the cost, CATI systems tend to be used primarily in larger, more complex surveys, where the investment in entering the questionnaire into the computer system—resulting in a better interviewing process and higher-quality data—is deemed worthwhile. Another disadvantage is that it is sometimes difficult to access data when a complex sample design has been used, such as one that involves multiple respondents in a household or multiple informants in a firm.

*Face-to-Face Interviewing.* Face-to-face interviewing, despite its costs, is still the method of choice for certain types of studies: studies that require complex reports of behavior; studies that have a particular interest in people who are difficult to interview by telephone (for example, the poor, minorities, and the aged); studies that require interviewers to make an inventory of purchases or an evaluation of housing or neighborhood conditions; and studies that require respondents to see materials as part of the data collection process, or to consult records, or to compare their records with previously reported data. All these studies require face-to-face interviews, although in some cases advance contact can be made by mail or telephone. Supervision problems are much greater for face-to-face interviews, because interviewers are working on their own at remote sites, and the results of their work typically are not known for some days after the completion of the interviews. Supervisors also must verify a fraction of all work conducted, to be sure that interviewers actually spoke to the designated respondent and recorded the data accurately.

*Advantages and Disadvantages of Both Methods.* On the telephone, interviewers have only their voices to convey an appeal to participate in the study, and they have no visual information about the characteristics of the household or the individual respondent—information that might enable them to shape a strategy for gaining cooperation. Interviewers in the face-to-face situation can both see respondents and their neighborhoods and can be seen by the respondent; they can also show identification material, if that is relevant. It is easier for people to hang up the telephone on an anonymous voice than it is to shut the door in the face of a person talking to them.

On the other hand, face-to-face interviewing has its own disadvantages. Interviewers are reluctant to go into rough neighborhoods, where they have fears for their safety, even if accompanied by another person. In many buildings, such as high rises with doormen, the interviewer cannot make contact with the respondent. Respondents in single-family dwelling units or small apartments sometimes are unwilling to open their doors. Finally, it is easier to make the initial contact by telephone, although the increased use of answering machines as a screening mechanism may be a problem in the future. In some cases, interviewers may be able to reach the respondent by telephone to make an appointment for a personal interview. In other cases, an initial personal interview is followed by a telephone call to correct an error or obtain additional information. That is, the use of joint methods is often more effective than any single procedure.

For those questions that are usable both on the telephone and in face-to-face interviews, there appear to be no consistent or important differences between the modes of interviewing in the validity of the data obtained. Responses to questions in telephone interviews tend to be somewhat shorter than in the face-to-face situation, and respondents are somewhat less likely to elaborate on their answers; but the small differences that have been observed do not appear to make either method more valid than the other. Because of the cost advantages, the advantages in supervision of interviewers, and the speed with which telephone surveys can be completed, telephone interviewing has become the predominant mode in survey research today. Most researchers are willing to pay the price in possible sample bias and a limitation on the type of question that can be asked in the telephone interview, in order to get the advantages of lower cost and more rapid execution of the survey.

## Mail Questionnaires

An alternate method of data collection is the self-administered mail questionnaire. Mail surveys, like personal interviews, use printed questionnaires with precoded response alternatives for each question. The difference, of course, is that no interviewer is present to explain things that the respondent might not understand or to motivate the respondent to answer all the questions. Mail questionnaires can be effectively used with respondents who have experience in dealing with written material and above-average motivation to participate in the survey. Surveys of organizational members are one of the most common types of mail surveys.

The principal problem in the design of mail questionnaires is making them clear and unambiguous, so that the respondent can answer easily and not have to puzzle over the meaning of the question. The questionnaire must be easy to fill out, and it also must *look* easy to fill out, so that respondents will not put it aside until they have more time to deal with it. Unless respondents are exceptionally highly motivated, it is also difficult to get high completion rates if mail questionnaires are very long. Dillman (1978) reports that mail questionnaires can be up to twelve pages in length without causing problems in response rates for motivated respondents. When they are longer than twelve pages, the response rate begins to erode seriously. For less motivated respondents, even shorter questionnaires are necessary.

The major problems in carrying out mail surveys are getting a good sample and an acceptable completion rate. There are no serious differences in completion rates between telephone and face-to-face interviews, particularly if adequate resources are given to follow-up procedures. It is extremely difficult, however, to get a high completion rate on mail questionnaires unless respondents are highly motivated to begin with and a good address list is available. Even a good, seemingly up-to-date list will contain a substantial proportion of incorrect addresses. Getting new addresses for people who have moved is often quite difficult and expensive.

A major factor in increasing motivation is the cover letter that describes the purposes and auspices of the study. People are much more likely to respond to a request from an organization they belong to or for a purpose they regard as important. Multiple mailings, usually three, increase the response rate substantially, since many people who are willing to cooperate put the mail questionnaire aside when it first arrives and need to be reminded. Finally, enclosing a small monetary gift, usually a dollar, increases cooperation, since respondents feel some obligation to return the questionnaire after taking the dollar.

When conducted with appropriate samples and question-naires, and when multiple mailings and some form of compensa-tion are provided, mail surveys can obtain cooperation rates as high as or only slightly lower than cooperation rates obtained by personal methods. There are many examples of carefully conducted mail surveys with cooperation rates in the 80–90 percent range. There are also many horrible examples of mail surveys with cooperation rates in the 10–20 percent range, or even lower. The biases in such studies are so great as to make the results almost meaningless. Studies where the response rate is too low, even when optimum mail methods are used, should be conducted by personal or combined methods.

In surveys conducted by mail, the desire to ensure respondents that their answers will be kept confidential conflicts with the need to keep track of who has responded, so that follow-up efforts can be made. Except in special circumstances, the bias that might result from identifying a questionnaire will be more than offset by the biases that occur from a low completion rate caused by the inability to make follow-up efforts when respondents return questionnaires anonymously. The usual method of identification is with a number stamped on the questionnaire. Some researchers have attempted to identify questionnaires by using secret methods, such as small pin holes or invisible ink. These methods are not only unethical but unnecessary. Hardly any respondents object to identifying the questionnaire if the reason for doing so (to follow up) is given in the cover letter.

Mail questionnaires are legitimate means of data collection and can produce valid results when used properly; unfortunately, however, they are open to severe abuse—mainly by organizations that use them in mass mailings as part of fund-raising efforts. For the most part, such questionnaires are recognized for what they are, both by potential respondents, who have the good sense not to respond (typically such questionnaires receive about a 1–2 percent response rate), and by their sponsors, who do not tabulate or report the results. Occasionally, however, an organization gets carried away with enthusiasm for its own ideals and reports the data from such a pseudo-survey as if it were a meaningful survey. In spite of vigorous protests by statistical and survey professional organizations and by many individual professional survey practitioners, organizations continue to send fund-raising questionnaires to their members or to those whom they would like to become contributors to their cause.

## Combinations of Methods

When the three different methods of data collection—face-to-face interviews, telephone interviews, and mail questionnaires—are combined, one can get the benefits of the method most appropriate to the problem at hand. In the Current Population Survey conducted by the Bureau of the Census, a mixture of face-to-face and telephone interviewing is used. In this survey, sample households are interviewed once a month for four months consecutively and then are reinterviewed another four months in the next year after an eight-month interval. Face-to-face interviewing is used in the first and fifth interviews, with telephone interviewing permitted in the other months if it is possible—that is, if the household has a telephone and the respondents are capable of responding on the telephone.

Another possible combination of methods occurs in the dual-frame design. In such a design, a large sample of telephone numbers is selected and becomes one sampling frame for a study. A smaller sample of households is taken in the regular manner for face-to-face interviewing. Results from the two independent frames are then merged into the final sample, with appropriate weighting for the households in the face-to-face frame that have telephones and, thus, could have fallen into both samples. The dual-frame design gains some of the cost advantages of telephone interviewing and at the same time avoids the sample bias inherent in telephone interviewing.

Another design that combines two methods is one in which a telephone sample is used to screen for unusual characteristics—for example, families with twins or three-generation households—and then a mail questionnaire is sent to the respondents who have agreed to participate in the survey. For those respondents who do not return the questionnaire or who have trouble filling it out, telephone or face-to-face interviews can be conducted. Such a design allows the researcher to combine the cost savings of the mail questionnaire with the advantages of the telephone contact (in locating a sample of individuals for whom there is no preexisting mailing list, in conducting follow-up interviews, and in encouraging participation). Alternatively, face-to-face interviews can be conducted after telephone screening.

The reverse of this procedure is to start with a mail questionnaire and to follow up a subsample of nonrespondents by telephone. As an example, NORC once conducted a study of physicians to determine whether they were smokers and whether they approved or disapproved of smoking. After three mailings, fewer than half of the sample had responded. There was concern (which was later confirmed) that those who did not respond were likely to be smokers. A follow-up study of approximately one-third of nonresponding physicians was conducted by telephone. The reasons why this was an optimum design are discussed in the next chapter.

Face-to-face interviewing also can be combined with self-administered questionnaires. In the course of surveying, for example, a sample of the adult population of the United States, a self-administered supplement might be left at the household for teenagers or some other member of the household. These questionnaires can then be picked up by interviewers in a subsequent trip to the neighborhood for other interviews in their assignment; or, alternatively, respondents can be given envelopes to mail questionnaires back to a central office. Having interviewers pick up the completed questionnaire tends to produce higher completion rates and gives more encouragement to the respondent to fill out the questionnaire.

## Relative Costs of Alternative Methods

A telephone survey—including all direct interviewing costs as well as supervision and telephone line charges—will cost about half as much as a face-to-face survey of the same length. This cost advantage explains the growth of telephone-interviewing procedures. Mail questionnaires cost about one-fifth of telephone methods and one-tenth of face-to-face methods. Researchers usually select the cheapest method that provides the quality of data needed.

## Future Technologies

Technological developments in communications and micro-computers may change the ways that surveys are conducted in the future. The spread of cable television and satellite transmission of information should make it possible for data to be transmitted directly from households to a central location. One can imagine an electronic face-to-face interview in which interviewers, either visually or through representation on a questionnaire, appear on a television screen, and respondents participate in the survey by means of a home computer terminal. Thus, some of the limitations of telephone interviewing are avoided, and some of the advantages of face-to-face interviewing are achieved; at the same time, interviewers no longer need to travel to respondents' homes.

A prototype of portions of such a system has already appeared in Columbus, Ohio. In that experiment, however, the survey designer did not have effective control over the sample because he could not monitor who was responding. The technology needed is essentially the same as that which is envisioned for the use of computers in bank transactions, home catalogue ordering, and other shopping-at-home electronic systems. While prototype systems have been around for some time, they have not met with much favorable customer response; and it is unlikely that such electronic interviewing will be a reality until all, or almost all, households have home computers that can be accessed.

One technology that is already available is the use of computers for face-to-face interviewing in locations such as hospitals or shopping malls. Some computers are sufficiently light, durable, and powerful to make it possible for interviewers to use them as they go door to door. All the advantages cited for CATI are available in CAPI (computer-assisted personal interviewing). To date, the major problem has been cost. CAPI is cost-effective only for large continuing studies, such as the Health Interview Survey. Future reductions in the cost of portable computer equipment will lead to a more extensive use of CAPI.

In the meantime, the cost-effectiveness of telephone interviewing is so great, particularly for those surveys that do not have high standards for the quality of data, that it has greatly expanded the use of surveys by firms and organizations. It remains to be seen whether this expansion in the numbers of surveys conducted will lead to greater resistance to surveys; that is, so many people may refuse to participate that the purpose of conducting surveys is defeated. There is some possibility that in the future telephone interviewing may be defeated by its own success.

## Additional Reading

There are two handbooks that readers who want more details on data collection may consult. *The Handbook of Survey Research* (Rossi, Wright, and Anderson, 1983) is mainly aimed at social science readers, while *The Handbook of Marketing Research* (Ferber, 1974) is intended for business readers.

A useful discussion of face-to-face survey methods can be found in *Survey Methods in Social Investigation* (Moser and Kalton, 1972). A good short discussion is found in *Survey Research Methods* (Fowler, 1984). Telephone procedures are extensively discussed in *Surveys by Telephone* (Groves and Kahn, 1979). A shorter discussion appears in *Telephone Survey Methods* (Lavrakas, 1987). The standard book on mail surveys is Dillman's (1978) *Mail and Telephone Surveys: The Total Design Method.* An older book by two experienced commercial researchers is *Professional Mail Surveys* (Erdos and Morgan, 1970). A short useful book is *Making Effective Use of Mailed Questionnaires* (Lockhart, 1984).

# 6

## How Respondents
## Are Selected

The science of statistics is fundamentally concerned with generalizing from samples to populations. By a population, we mean all the persons or units that are of interest—for example, all the registered voters in the United States, all households in New Jersey, all the physicians in the United States, or all public schools that teach children in grades 1 to 8. If everyone or every unit is included, then the survey is a census. Samples are merely parts (usually small) chosen to represent the total population. Carefully selected samples chosen from the same population will yield results that tend to approach population values as the samples increase in size. To determine the reliability of results, one can measure the variation between repeated samples chosen in the same way. (Other sources of unreliability, particularly question-wording errors, are discussed in Chapters Seven and Nine.)

In this chapter, we discuss what is meant by carefully selected samples, give some examples, describe the problems with the major polls, and warn of the serious problems that arise when loose procedures are used. The need for sampling comes from two major constraints in attempting to obtain opinions from the total population: time and money. The 1980 census cost over one billion dollars, even though it contained relatively few questions. It takes more than two years to process the census results, even though the most technically advanced equipment is used. Useful and timely public opinion information cannot be obtained in this fashion. Moreover, the census contains errors that inevitably result when such a massive operation is undertaken every ten years with large numbers of inexperienced staff. For some purposes, many statisticians believe that large, carefully controlled samples may provide more accurate data than are provided by the census.

## Defining the Population

Since a sample must be a sample of something, opinion researchers must first define the population that they intend to describe. Perhaps the most common population used in surveys in the United States is that of all persons eighteen years old or older. This definition does not exclude noncitizens, nonregistered voters, or nonvoters. In election studies, of course, only registered voters are included initially, and the major problem facing the researcher is to determine the likelihood that the person answering will vote.

Other limitations in the definition of the population may be introduced for cost reasons, because respondents are difficult or impossible to reach. For example, many studies exclude the states of Alaska and Hawaii; others exclude people living in institutions, such as prisons or mental hospitals. United States citizens living abroad, either as civilians or in the military, also are normally excluded.

For some purposes, special populations may be appropriate. For example, in studies of attitudes toward abortion, the population may be limited to women under the age of fifty. Studies of ethnic, racial, religious, or other groups require respondents to tell the interviewer whether or not they are members of the population. Other special populations might be composed of members of a particular occupation—for instance, physicians, business executives, or steelworkers.

Although most populations consist of individual persons, it is not at all unusual, particularly in market research, for the population to consist of households or families. Thus, if one wished to measure usage of a product—such as paper towels, frozen orange juice, or refrigerators—households would probably be the appropriate population. A knowledgeable household member would be asked to provide the information, but the information would be about the household, not about the person. Similarly, the family might be the appropriate unit if one wished to study child-rearing practices. Some populations are composed of institutions, such as schools, hospitals, or businesses—although, again, one or more persons may report on the behavior of these institutions.

Any careful sampling starts with a detailed definition of the population. In judging the value of a poll, the user can then determine whether that population is appropriate for the purpose of the study. Psychology students at universities may be a highly appropriate population if one wishes to measure college students' attitudes toward psychology teaching, but they may be totally inappropriate if one wishes to measure the general population's attitudes toward education.

### Probability Sampling

Careful sampling from populations requires that every member of the population have a known, but not necessarily equal, chance of being selected. In most opinion polls of individuals, it is convenient to give each person in the population an equal chance of selection. Such a sample is self-weighting; that is, each person in the sample represents exactly the same number of persons in the population as every other sample member. Thus, the sample will contain about the same proportion of people with certain charac-teristics (for example, high school graduates) as there is in the population.

For some purposes, however, equal-probability-of-selection methods may not produce a large enough sample of people with a desired characteristic for adequate analysis. For example, if the unemployment rate is 7 percent, a sample of one thousand people drawn with equal probability from the adult labor force in the United States will contain about seventy unemployed persons. If a researcher wants to do some special analyses of the unemployed, she would not have enough cases to analyze. In order to produce a larger number of unemployed in the sample, oversampling (or a dispro-portionate sample) must be used; that is, unemployed persons are sampled at two or three (or more) times the rate at which they actually appear in the population.

When different members of the population have different chances of selection, it is necessary to weight the results to make correct estimates of characteristics of the population. The simplest weights are the reciprocals of the probabilities of selection. If one group is sampled at twice the rate of the rest of the sample, that group will be weighted by one-half.

A variety of methods are used to ensure that every person in a population has a specified chance of selection. We describe these methods in detail when we discuss the specific polls. All procedures use variations of methods that are like drawing names out of a hat. The actual process of selecting names from a hat does not give every person an equal chance of selection, since it is difficult to shuffle names well in any kind of container. Instead of manual methods, researchers currently use computers to make selections, or they may use printed tables of random numbers generated by electronic processes that ensure that each number has the same chance of selection.

The final selection of sample members must be determined by chance if one wishes to generalize to a larger population. If the final selection is made by the researcher, for convenience or for some other reason, then the researcher cannot use mathematical theory to generalize to the total population. Repeated studies show that people do not do a good job of selecting a sample. If asked to select a sample of colleges and universities, for example, people will always oversample the best-known ones, since these schools come most readily to mind. They may also deliberately omit unusual units because they are not "representative"—thereby distorting the estimates of population variability. Ultimately, people—even researchers—just do not know enough to be able to select an appropriate sample and therefore must use chance procedures. Note that the omission of unusual units or the overrepresentation of common or well-known units, which often occurs when selection is made purposefully by the researcher, will not make repeated samples identical to a census, because units are left out or appear too frequently. In such cases, estimates of the variance will be distorted or "biased." (See Chapter Nine for further discussion of sample biases.)

## Sampling Variance

It is sometimes observed that two public opinion polls using the same question and methods and taken at the same time have results that disagree. The differences are usually small, but sometimes they are substantial. On the average, however, repeated samples selected in the same way will give results identical to those from a census of the entire population, although no single sample will be identical to the census results.

The variation between these repeated samples is called sampling variance. What can be demonstrated mathematically is that, as the size of these repeated samples is increased, the variation between them becomes smaller and smaller. That is why we say the sample results can be generalized to the population with known error.

Methods have been discovered that minimize this variation between samples for given sample sizes. We discuss these efficient procedures later in this chapter. Although the concept of variance relates to repeated samples, statisticians are able to estimate sampling variances for a single sample. Sometimes, instead of variance, the square root of variance is estimated. This is called sampling error or the margin of error in media accounts.

## Simple Random Samples: The Use of Lists

In sampling members of an organization, the researcher usually has access to a list (either on computer or printed). She can then select a specified number of members from the list, using random numbers or taking every nth member after a random start. This latter method, known as systematic sampling, is generally the same as random sampling.

The major problem with list sampling is that, for many populations, no list is available. There is no list of all households or individuals in the United States. Although this information is obtained every ten years by the Census Bureau, it is never divulged to outsiders. Nor are there lists of all the residents of a state. Many cities have directories that list all housing units and the name of the occupants, but some of these directories will be out of date at the time that the sample is being selected. Lists of business establishments are available from Dun and Bradstreet; and many other lists—such as lists of shopping centers, participants in legal cases, and magazine subscribers—are also available.

No list is perfect, but methods have been developed for dealing with list deficiencies. For example, some lists may contain elements that really do not belong there (such as persons who have moved or died, firms that have gone out of business, or organizations that are included in a list of individuals or households). The solution is simply to recognize in advance that not all units selected will be eligible and to oversample enough so that an adequate sample will remain after ineligible units are discarded. The naive approach of taking the next unit on the list if a selected unit is ineligible often leads to biased samples, since it gives business and professional people, with both office and home listings, multiple chances of selection.

A second problem with lists is that some units may be on the list multiple times. For example, a master list of social scientists might be made up of the individual lists of half a dozen social science organizations. A person belonging to multiple organizations has multiple chances of selection. Similarly, the Dun and Bradstreet lists include separate listings for each facility; therefore, firms with many different locations will be listed many times. Obviously, units that are listed many times on a list have a higher probability of selection than units listed only once. If every unit is to have the same probability of selection, either all duplicates must be purged from the list (which is usually expensive and tedious) or the units with multiple chances of selection must be subsampled inversely to the number of times they are listed. Thus, one would take half of all units with two listings, one-third of units with three listings, and in general $1/n$ of units with $n$ listings.

By far the most serious problem with lists are omissions, units in the population that are not on the lists. Usually, one can estimate the completeness of a list by comparing the total number of units on it with census or other independent estimates. There are three alternatives for handling omissions. First, one can simply ignore these omissions, since no list is perfect. Except for the most important policy studies, many scientists will use lists that are 90 percent or more complete; for difficult populations, they may even use lists that are 80 percent or more complete. On the other hand, some lists may be so biased and incomplete that one is better off not using the list at all and trying some other method. For example, a study of teenage drug use would result in very biased results if the teenagers were selected from the list of the Boy Scouts of America.

The most complicated, although frequently the best, procedure with an incomplete list is to use the list but to supplement it with another sample, so as to remove biases. This procedure is no longer simple random sampling and requires skill in sampling and making estimates from the dual frames. The combining of dual-frame samples is currently an important research topic of survey statisticians.

### Random Digit Dialing

The most common example of simple random sampling where there are no lists is telephone sampling with random digit dialing. No directories are used, and telephone numbers are simply selected at random from known working exchanges and area codes. The advantage of this method for a national study is that it does not require obtaining hundreds of telephone directories that are continuously going out of date. Even more important, it enables the interviewer to reach households with unlisted numbers. In large cities such as New York, Chicago, and Washington, D.C., more than half of all households have unlisted numbers. Although the fraction of unlisted numbers is lower in the suburbs and is 10 percent or less in smaller cities and nonmetropolitan areas, even careful directory samples are seriously biased.

The disadvantage of random digit dialing is that 80 percent of the numbers dialed are either nonworking numbers or ineligible businesses and organizations. In the past few years, a procedure known as "clustering" has made random digit dialing more efficient in this respect.

## Clustering

Clusters are groups of units found in the same location or area: people in a household, children in a classroom, workers in a plant, patients in a hospital. Many studies obtain samples in two stages. In the first stage, a sample of clusters is chosen; that is, a number of units—such as colleges, hospitals, or geographical areas (cities, counties)—are chosen with known probabilities. Each of these units contains a number of individuals who are now eligible for the sample, while those in the units not chosen are no longer eligible to be picked in the sample. In the second stage, individuals within the units chosen in the first stage are chosen with known probabilities to be in the sample. A study might, for example, obtain a sample of college students by first selecting a sample of colleges and then a sample of students from each selected college. Similarly, for a study of hospital patients, a researcher might select a sample of hospitals and then a sample of patients from the selected hospitals. For a national sample of households or businesses, the researcher might first select a sample of geographical locations, usually metropolitan areas and counties. Then, within the selected areas, lists are used if available; if lists are unavailable, new lists are prepared for each selected site. Through such procedures, one can obtain sample lists at moderate expense when complete lists would be prohibitively expensive.

Another form of clustering is used in telephone random digit dialing. As noted above, many series of telephone numbers in working exchanges are not in use or are used only for business or nonhousehold purposes. A procedure whereby these series can be identified rapidly and omitted—thus reducing the number of wasted screening calls from 80 to 50 percent, a major cost saving—was developed by Waksberg (1978) and Mitofsky. Telephone numbers are grouped into clusters of one hundred consecutive numbers, and one is sampled. For example, consider the bank of numbers (217) 555-2300 to 2399. Suppose the number (217) 555-2326 is selected by chance. If it is not a working number, no additional numbers are chosen from that cluster. If it is a working number, additional calls are made in the cluster until a prespecified number of households (usually five to ten) are reached.

Aside from sampling costs, clustering saves interviewer training and travel costs in face-to-face interviewing. These costs are substantial and may account for the majority of costs in a national study, even if clustering is used. Obviously, clustering has no effect on costs of mail surveys or telephone surveys from a central location once the sample has been selected.

Given the major cost savings from cluster sampling, the temptation is always to have as few clusters as possible. From the cost perspective only, one or a few clusters are much more efficient than many hundreds of clusters. There is a negative effect of clustering, however. Generally, clustering increases the sampling variance of the results. That is, with the same population and sample size, a simple random sample will have a sampling error that is smaller, sometimes much smaller, than a cluster sample. Why is this so? It is because, on some variables, members of a cluster are similar to each other; that is, birds of a feather flock together. For example, two members within a household cluster tend to be more alike in their political view than are two individuals chosen at random from the United States population. Also, consumption of groceries in two households on a given block is more similar than consumption of two random households selected anywhere in the United States, because households on the same block tend to have similar incomes as well as the same outlets from which to shop. To the extent that members of a cluster are similar, the information obtained is not as useful as information obtained from completely independent observations. The increase in sampling variance is a function of the similarity within clusters and the size of the cluster selected.

To obtain an optimum number of clusters and number of units within each cluster, one must simultaneously consider both costs and variances and must understand the cost functions involved in data collection—that is, the relative costs of different aspects of the data collection process. For some standard cost functions, optimum solutions were given by Hansen, Hurwitz, and Madow (1953). These solutions are reflected in the examples presented later in this chapter.

## Stratified Samples

The other major method for improving sampling efficiency is stratification, in some ways the opposite of clustering. Here a heterogeneous population is subdivided into more homogeneous subparts (strata). For example, in a study of health care, the total population of adults may be divided into those who have and have not been hospitalized; or, in a study of pension plans, manufacturing plants may be divided into groups on the basis of total number of employees.

The purpose of stratification is to reduce to a minimum the sampling variance of the estimates within a fixed budget, and thus to maximize the amount of information obtained. There are three major situations where stratified sampling greatly improves efficiency.

First, stratification is useful when the strata are of primary interest. In some situations, one is less interested in total estimates than in comparisons of subgroups (strata) within the population. Thus, one might want to compare different age groups, different races, or the two genders. For these comparisons, an optimum design is to have the same sample sizes for each of the groups being compared. If the groups are not naturally the same size—for instance, if a researcher is comparing the 7 percent of the work force who are unemployed with the 93 percent who are employed—the unemployed will need to be oversampled while the employed are undersampled. Before such oversampling can be attempted, the researcher must do a short interview, called a screening interview, with a large enough sample to yield the required number of unemployed. For example, if she wants to interview 100 unemployed persons, and if they constitute 7 percent of the work force, she will need to screen 1,429 households that have someone in the work force in order to find 100 unemployed ($1,429 \times .07 \cong 100$), assuming that she is not going to interview more than one person from each household. But if she wants only 100 employed persons for comparison, she will take only every thirteenth employed person out of the remaining 1,329 households ($1/13 \times 1,329 = 102$, or approximately 100). In practice, of course, not every household contains someone who is in the work force, so the researcher would have to screen more than 1,429 households to find the 100 unemployed.

Sometimes one wants to have both total and subgroup estimates of some characteristic—for example, the proportion of both employed and unemployed persons who are high school graduates. There is then no perfect sample to achieve minimum variances for both of these estimates simultaneously, since total estimates will have a minimum sampling variance when the sample is self-weighting. If disproportionate samples are used and a total estimate is required, the sample will need to be weighted to account for the differential sampling.

Second, stratified sampling improves efficiency when variances differ between strata. Differences in variances between strata are most often observed in studies dealing with organizations such as businesses, schools, and hospitals. There it is observed that a key variable is the size of the organization. Small organizations tend to be more similar to each other for almost every variable than large organizations are to other large organizations. Therefore, minimum sampling variances in studies of organizations are obtained by heavy oversamples of larger organizations (Neyman, 1934). Neyman showed that the optimum design was to allocate the samples to strata on the basis of their size measures (total sales, students, or patients) rather than on the basis of number of organizations. In many cases, the most efficient designs involve a complete census of all the largest organizations. This procedure is used by the Census Bureau in its surveys of business and manufacturing. The 2,000 largest establishments are included in each monthly survey, while samples of smaller establishments are rotated. Such methods may often reduce sampling variances by half.

Third, stratification is a method of choice when costs differ by strata. When combined methods—such as mail and telephone or telephone and face-to-face interviewing—are used, the minimum sampling variance is obtained when the cheaper strata are sampled more heavily than the more expensive strata, proportional to the square root of the ratio of costs. In a survey of physicians, for example, a mail survey with follow-ups might be sent to a sample of physicians. If about half of the physicians respond, only one-third of the remaining half would be contacted by telephone. (Telephone charges are about nine times as costly as mail charges.)

When a sample is self-weighting, such as a national sample of individuals, elaborate and costly efforts at stratification may not be worthwhile. Naive researchers with high anxiety levels may fear that a sample obtained by probability methods will yield strange results—a large oversampling of men, an undersampling of middle-aged persons, distorted income distributions, or other catastrophes. They therefore insist that the sample be stratified, so that age, race, sex, occupation, income, education, household size, and other variables are guaranteed to be perfectly represented.

If one takes such a request literally, there is no way to comply with it. The census data that would be needed for strata controls would not be available in such detail, since the privacy of individual households must be preserved. Even if one could estimate strata totals, the cost of matching them perfectly in the field would be prohibitive, since hundreds of additional screening interviews would be required. Finally, the effects on the data of this tortuous process would probably be undetectable.

The reader may wonder whether it is ever appropriate to stratify a sample if the strata are to be sampled proportionately. Under some circumstances, stratification will be inexpensive and some gains can be expected. For example, a researcher may want to stratify primary sampling units (PSUs)—such as states, counties, and metropolitan areas—for a national survey and not by households. Since census data of such geographical areas are already available, PSUs can be stratified during the normal sample selection process without additional field costs. The PSUs would be grouped by relevant variables, rather than arranged in alphabetical order or in haphazard fashion. The variables usually used are region of the country, degree of urbanization, proportion nonwhite, and some socioeconomic measure, such as income or education.

The effects of such stratification are moderate. Sampling errors are generally less than 10 percent smaller than they would have been without stratification; but, unless much time and expense have been devoted to agonizing over how to stratify, it is worthwhile to obtain this small improvement.

### Estimating Sampling Variances

The estimation of sampling variances is easy when one uses simple random sampling. The formulas are given in elementary statistics books, and many computer programs are available to do the computations. However, when one uses the more complex clustered or stratified samples, these basic formulas no longer apply. More complex computations are needed. There are now several sophisticated computer programs to compute variances from complex samples. The two major errors that are made in reporting or using sampling variances is to assume simple random sampling when a more complex design was used and, even more seriously, to assume that the only possible errors in the survey are sampling variances. In most surveys, errors caused by sample biases (discussed in the next section) and the effects of question wording (discussed in Chapter Seven) are substantially larger than sampling variances.

### Sample Execution

The careful design of a sample is insufficient to ensure its quality. The sample also must be carefully executed in the field. The standard way of measuring sample execution is as a cooperation rate, usually defined as the percentage of eligible units participating. Although it is impossible to locate and persuade all members of a population to cooperate in a survey, the final cooperation rate depends heavily on the efforts made by the survey organization. For personal interviews, a major problem is finding the correct respondent at home (or work) when the interviewer calls. Cooperation rates are increased when the number of callbacks is increased, although callbacks also increase cost and time required. The highest-quality face-to-face interviewers make three or more calls to find the respondent. Many more calls, ten or more, can be made by telephone, since there are no travel charges and phone charges are minimal if no one is home. Many surveys do no callbacks, even on telephone, and thus are certain to miss persons at work or otherwise away from home.

Once the eligible respondent is located, it is still necessary to obtain an interview or a self-administered survey form from that respondent. Here experience and effort help. Experienced interviewers obtain substantially higher cooperation rates than do inexperienced interviewers, either paid or volunteers. In addition, some refusals can be converted if one of the best interviewers or a supervisor makes another effort. Of course, such efforts add to the cost. For mail surveys, cooperation is increased by additional mailings.

People often wonder what levels of cooperation can be obtained if the survey is well conducted. The Census Bureau obtains cooperation rates of about 97 percent on the Current Population Survey (see below) and rates above 90 percent on many household surveys. Higher cooperation rates are possible in household surveys, where any knowledgeable adult can be the respondent. Other high-quality organizations achieve cooperation rates of 80 percent of households and 70 percent of individuals. Many users of market research surveys are willing to settle for cooperation rates at 60 percent to reduce costs. Panel studies (studies in which the same individuals are interviewed more than once) face special problems, since they require continuing cooperation. Here rates of 50 percent or less are common.

Well-run mail surveys can achieve the same levels of cooperation as personal interviews. Surveys of organization members usually have cooperation rates above 70 percent if follow-ups are conducted. Cooperation rates well below 50 percent are found when inexperienced researchers are doing the work or even in some commercial research where resources are limited and the work is in an exploratory stage. Mail surveys of inappropriate groups with a difficult questionnaire and no follow-up activity often result in cooperation rates of 20 percent or less.

Of course, a low cooperation rate need not necessarily mean a biased sample if the noncooperators are no different from the cooperators. In the absence of proof that there are no such differences, the researcher is better off to assume that there are differences and attempt to reduce potential problems by increasing cooperation rates.

The user of polls and surveys should be aware that sometimes the definition of cooperation is shifted to make results appear to be better than they are. Cooperation is properly defined as the percentage of all eligible units that ultimately provide complete (or almost complete) information. Thus, all units that cannot be located and those that cannot be interviewed because the respondent is too ill or does not speak English, as well as units that refuse to cooperate, should be included in the denominator. Instead, cooperation sometimes is defined as the ratio of those who give an interview divided by the number of units located, or those located divided by units attempted, or those interviewed after an initial screening interview is completed divided by the number of successful screenings. All these estimates incorrectly make the cooperation rate appear to be higher than it would be if it were computed correctly.

Finally, even respondents who go through an entire interview may not answer specific questions, either because they do not know the answer or because the question is threatening. In practice, nonresponse to most questions is low except for household income, where nonresponse ranges from 10 to 25 percent, depending on how much detail is wanted.

### Determining Sample Size

Unsophisticated researchers often ask, "what percentage of the total population should I sample?" This question is usually not meaningful unless the population is very small. Then the answer would probably be to take everyone. For populations of any size, from towns to nations, the question to ask is "How many units should be sampled?" since the sampling variance is primarily a function of the sample size and not the percentage of the population.

There are several ways of approaching this problem. The easiest is an empirical approach; that is, one can simply use sample sizes that others with similar problems have used. Tables 5 and 6 present actual sample sizes used in a large number of studies. Note that sample sizes for regional and special populations tend to be somewhat smaller than sample sizes for national studies. That is because those who conduct the surveys believe that regional and special studies are less important than national studies are.

A more formal approach, called Bayesian analysis (not developed here), emphasizes the need to balance the value of

**Table 5. Most Common Sample Sizes Used for National and Regional Studies, by Subject Matter.**

| Subject matter | National | | | Regional | | |
|---|---|---|---|---|---|---|
| | Mode | $Q_3$ | $Q_1$ | Mode | $Q_3$ | $Q_1$ |
| Financial | 1,000+ | —— | —— | 100 | 400 | 50 |
| Medical | 1,000+ | 1,000+ | 500 | 1,000+ | 1,000+ | 250 |
| Other behavior | 1,000+ | —— | —— | 700 | 1,000 | 300 |
| Attitudes | 1,000+ | 1,000+ | 500 | 700 | 1,000 | 400 |
| Laboratory experiments | —— | —— | —— | 100 | 200 | 50 |

*Note:* $Q_3$ = Third Quartile; $Q_1$ = First Quartile.

**Table 6. Typical Sample Sizes for Studies of Human and Institutional Populations.**

| Number of subgroup analyses | People or households | | Institutions | |
|---|---|---|---|---|
| | National | Regional or special | National | Regional or special |
| None or few | 1,000–1,500 | 200–500 | 200–500 | 50–200 |
| Average | 1,500–2,500 | 500–1,000 | 500–1,000 | 200–500 |
| Many | 2,500+ | 1,000+ | 1,000+ | 500+ |

increased information with the costs of gathering the data. The problem may be considered from the viewpoints of both the designer of the study and the funding organization. The designer of a study must recognize that the organization funding the study will ultimately make the decision on sample size. Although the precise benefits of most basic social science research cannot be well specified, an optimum sample size can be determined in business and policy applications if gains and losses of alternative decisions are known.

One important question that is frequently overlooked entirely is whether or not new sample information should be gathered at all. The decision depends on both the cost and the value of the new information. If the fixed costs of the study exceed the value, no new sampling is justified. The value of information depends on what is already known and is, thus, best determined by the Bayesian approach rather than the classical statistics with which most readers are familiar. For additional discussion of the formal Bayesian approach, see Schlaifer (1959) and Sudman (1976a, chap. 5).

## Samples Used in Typical Polls

*Newspaper and Network Polls.* The polls that most readers will be familiar with are either published in newspapers or reported by the major networks. These include the Gallup poll, the CBS/ *New York Times* poll, the NBC/*Wall Street Journal* poll, and the ABC/*Washington Post* poll. All these polls except the Gallup poll are conducted by telephone in the continental United States, excluding Alaska and Hawaii. Telephone polling is now the most widely used procedure because face-to-face interviewing has become very expensive and because about 95 percent of all households now have telephones. While the universe of all persons in a household with a telephone is not identical to the universe of all persons, the differences are small and have usually been ignored.

Typically, the selection of persons to be sampled proceeds in several stages. At the first stage, an area code and exchange is selected by chance from a list of all working exchanges. This list of working exchanges is available from the long-lines division of the American Bell Company, and its use prevents the dialing of nonoperating exchanges.

Once an exchange is selected, a four-digit number within that exchange is selected and that number is dialed. This method ensures that even households with numbers not listed in current telephone directories have the same chance of selection as other telephone households. The problem with this method is that only about one number in five chosen this way is a working household number. The other numbers either are not in operation or are used for businesses, schools, and other nonhouseholds. To reduce the number of wasted calls, researchers have attempted to identify banks of numbers that are not in operation. A major sampling service used by the ABC/*Washington Post* poll has a computerized file of all the listed numbers in published directories. The pollsters then can exclude groups of numbers for which not a single listing exists and be almost certain that they are nonworking numbers. Business listings also can be excluded.

Other researchers, including the CBS/*New York Times* poll, use the Mitofsky/Waksberg method discussed earlier in the chapter. A widely used method is to select numbers from a telephone directory and simply add 1 to the last digit (for instance, the number (206) 468-2201 would become (206) 468-2202), to give unlisted numbers a chance of selection. This procedure, however, is slightly biased because it omits all banks of ten numbers that were not in operation or were all unlisted when the directory was printed. This method also oversamples banks of numbers that have a higher fraction of listed numbers and undersamples banks of numbers that have a higher fraction of unlisted numbers.

At the final stage, a respondent must be selected from within the household, since not all household members are equally likely to answer the phone. Women are three times more likely to answer than men, and older household members are more likely to answer than younger adults. We exclude teenage phone conversations from this generalization. A simple, widely used method to obtain a random household respondent is to ask for the person who had the most recent birthday. But this method will usually result in a small undersampling of males because men are more likely to refuse to be interviewed. Therefore, to obtain samples with about equal numbers of men and women, the interviewer can ask first to speak to a male; if no male is present, a female can be interviewed. Or, after the interviewer has reached a specified number of one sex (usually women), the interviewer continues to call but conducts interviews only if a man is available. Still another method is to give each person in the household a chance of being selected but to give men a greater chance, since they are harder to find.

The greatest problem with telephone surveys, as with all forms of opinion polling, is that some individuals refuse to participate. Opinion surveys can only report information from respondents who are willing to give their views when contacted. Actual refusals after contact are typically about 5 percent lower if the contact is made face to face than if it is made by telephone. On the other hand, it is possible on the phone to contact people who would refuse to open their doors to strangers. Thus, overall, one does not see differences in cooperation between face-to-face and telephone procedures.

The content and length of the interview would be expected to have some impact on cooperation, and they do. The more salient the topic to the respondent, the higher the cooperation rate. Studies dealing with health and family get better cooperation than studies dealing with foreign policy. Unfortunately, many of the poll questions in newspaper and network polls deal with foreign policy issues. Very long interviews, unless on highly salient topics, would probably reduce cooperation; but most polls are fairly short.

A major cost advantage of telephone procedures over face-to-face methods is that it costs very little on the telephone to call a number if no one is home; for this reason, it is possible to make repeated calls to a telephone number until someone is contacted. One limitation to the number of calls that can be made is the time period allotted for the survey. If only three or four days are provided, households where no one is home, because of vacation or business, will be missed. These households tend to have younger persons living in them; therefore, telephone surveys conducted in short periods usually have too few younger adults and too many retired persons as respondents. However, as was demonstrated in 1948, for election studies and other rapidly breaking events, it is better to have current information, even if the sample is slightly biased, than to have unbiased information that is out of date.

Even in households where someone is home, older members are more likely to be available for interviewing than are younger adults. An interviewer can correct for this imbalance by making appointments and calling back to reach these less available household members, but that is not typically done in the newspaper and network polls. In any event, for many kinds of questions, the adults in a household will have similar views, so that no major errors are introduced if not everyone in the household has exactly the same chance of selection.

In actual fact, the telephone samples described here are not self-weighting, even if every effort is made to select the respondent within the household strictly by chance. It is standard practice for only one interview to be conducted at a given number, so that the time required of any family will not be too great and so that members of a household do not consult with each other before responding. Thus, an individual's chance of being selected is inversely related to the number of eligible adults in the household. In a household with only one adult, that adult must be interviewed. In households with four adults, the chance of any person's being selected is one in four. To correct for this bias, the simplest procedure would be to weight by household size. Some polls also weight by additional variables, to correct for sample cooperation and location problems. As an example, the CBS/*New York Times* poll also weights by region, race, sex, age, and education. However, if there are systematic differences on variables of interest between those who do and do not answer, and if these differences are unrelated to the weighting variables, then weighting will not correct all sample biases. Since one usually does not know what the biases and their causes are, one cannot assume that weighted data are unbiased but must expect that some biases remain.

The sample sizes used in the national newspaper and network polls are in the range of 1,200–1,500. The effective sample sizes are slightly lower than this because the procedures used result in some geographical grouping of telephone numbers. Nevertheless, the samples are large enough so that repeated samples drawn in the same way would be very unlikely to differ by more than three or four percentage points from those of any particular sample. It is difficult to know the magnitude of the effects of not locating respondents and of sample biases. Past experience suggests that for some questions the effects could be zero, while for others they might be as high as ten percentage points or more. Overall, these sample biases would usually be two or three times larger than the variance between samples.

It might be argued that noncooperators can be ignored because they are less likely to be informed or to hold views on public issues and are less likely to vote. Nevertheless, some noncooperators do vote and may be responsible when the polls go wrong, as they do once in a while. The *New York Times*, when it publishes poll results including a measure of variation between samples, adds the following disclaimer: "Theoretical errors do not take into account a margin of additional error resulting from the various practical difficulties in taking any survey of public opinion."

As discussed above, the "practical difficulties" may account for substantially more error than sampling does. In our judgment, however, these practical difficulties do not detract from the usefulness of the data, once their limitations are recognized.

*The Best United States Survey.* Most people may not realize that, in addition to conducting a complete census of the population every ten years, the United States Census Bureau conducts a continuing survey of the population, to measure the unemployment rate and other characteristics of the population. In this monthly survey, called the Current Population Survey, more than 52,000 households are interviewed each month. The initial contact with all households is from a face-to-face interview. Households are interviewed a total of eight times, and later interviews are conducted on the telephone if that is possible.

The households are selected by a probability sampling method called area probability sampling. First, a sample of dwelling units is obtained; then, in those dwelling units that are occupied, information is obtained about all persons in the unit. Area sampling procedures are much more expensive than telephone procedures because interviewers must be hired in many locations rather than working from a central office as they do for telephone surveys. Interviewers must also be paid for the time they spend traveling to the selected dwellings as well as for car expenses. These travel costs account for about half of all interviewing costs and thus make face-to-face interviewing at least twice as expensive as telephone interviewing.

To reduce some of the costs of face-to-face interviewing, the sample is clustered by geography into a limited number of locations. The Current Population Survey is conducted in 449 sample areas comprising 863 counties and independent cities out of a total of slightly more than 3,000 in the entire United States. These sample areas are selected by chance, with the different-sized populations in the areas taken into account. The largest metropolitan areas in the country—such as New York, Los Angeles, and Chicago—are included not only in this sample but in every large national area probability sample of the United States.

There are several additional stages of selection of subareas within the selected sample areas. At the penultimate stage, blocks or other small geographical segments are selected by chance, again with their sizes taken into account. At the final stage, dwelling units are selected by chance from each block. The sample is designed so that every dwelling unit has an equal chance of selection.

The design yields a sample of about 60,000 dwellings, but about 10 percent of these are unoccupied. In the occupied dwellings, information is obtained from a knowledgeable person about the employment status and other characteristics of all household members. The cooperation rate on this survey is very high, averaging about 97 percent. No nongovernment survey organization achieves levels of cooperation this high. In part, this level of cooperation is achieved because of the government sponsorship of the survey, but it is also the result of the high quality of Census Bureau interviewers and the training they receive.

Not only is the Current Population Survey the best of continuing surveys; it is also the most expensive. Current annual costs of the CPS exceed twenty million dollars, but the data are so important in determining national economic policy that there is no significant political opposition to this expenditure. Because of the large sample size, sampling variation between repeated samples is only about one-tenth of 1 percent; therefore, policy makers are assured that changes of more than one-tenth of 1 percent up or down reflect real changes in the economy and are not caused by sampling. The cooperation rate of the CPS is so high that no one is concerned about sample biases. The major concern raised about the unemployment statistics is that they may reflect a definition of unemployment that not all economists agree with, because it depends partially on the subjective report that the respondent is "looking for work."

*Typical Face-to-Face Surveys.* As with telephone surveys, the typical sample size for a national face-to-face survey is about 1,500 persons. The same area probability procedures used in the Current Population Survey are used for the typical face-to-face survey, but on a smaller scale. Usually, between 100 and 200 initial sample areas are selected, and the number of subareas and blocks is proportionately smaller than in the CPS. The number of dwelling units selected from each block, however, is approximately the same as in the larger CPS.

Typically, survey organizations obtain cooperation of about 80 to 90 percent of all households contacted, depending on the subject of the study and the intensity of effort. There is an additional loss of about 10 percent if a specific respondent in a household is required. Some of this noncooperation is caused by the unavailability of the selected respondent during the interviewing period. It is now harder to find people at home than it was two or three decades ago—mainly because of the increase in employment of women but also because of the increase in meals eaten away from home and other factors.

As we pointed out earlier, overall levels of cooperation do not differ much between telephone and face-to-face interviewing, nor is the small percentage of households without telephones very important in a typical survey (although it is to the Census Bureau). Why, then, is the substantial extra money spent to do face-to-face interviews? The prime reason is that the questions asked require some visual cues or other forms of questions that cannot be handled well on the telephone. For example, in face-to-face interviews, respondents can sort cards indicating both how strongly they agree with certain political outcomes and how strongly they believe that these events are likely to occur. They can read statements from a long list and choose the one with which they agree most. Face-to-face interviews provide the greatest flexibility in how questions can be asked and answered. However, as telephone procedures have become more widespread, new procedures for asking questions on the telephone have been developed, so that most questions asked face to face can also be asked in some modified form on the telephone. For special populations, such as Hispanics, the poor, or the aged, difficulties in communicating on the telephone as well as lower-than-average phone coverage may require that all or some of the interviews be face to face.

*Mail Surveys.* By far the cheapest way of collecting information is to eliminate all personal contact and to use mail surveys. While mail surveys are widely used for special purposes, they also have severe limitations that prevent their use for most opinion surveys. It is sometimes possible to take advantage of the efficiency of mail and to avoid the limitations by combining mail with telephone surveys.

Let us first describe an appropriate use of a mail survey. Suppose the publisher of *Time* magazine wants to determine the characteristics of the magazine's subscribers, their purchasing of various products, and their attitudes toward *Time*. The persons conducting the survey can easily select a sample from *Time*'s subscription lists, using chance to determine the 10,000 readers who are selected. They send out by first-class mail a four-page questionnaire to those selected, along with a self-addressed return envelope, and either enclose a dollar or offer to send a dollar to the respondents' favorite charity if the questionnaire is returned.

Approximately 40–50 percent of all subscribers return the questionnaire. In two weeks, an additional mailing is sent to those who have not responded, and a final mailing is sent to those who did not respond to the second mailing. After these three mailings, about 70–80 percent of all those selected have returned the questionnaires, which is about as high as could have been reached with personal procedures. The publisher uses the results to help sell advertising by providing the advertiser with the characteristics of the *Time* audience; and the editors may use the information to add or delete features.

It may not be obvious why this example is special and why mail surveys cannot be used for general population samples. The special features of this survey are these:

1. *Time* has a list containing the names and addresses of its subscribers. No such list is available for the general population. Note, however, that *Time* does not know the names of people who buy or read individual copies but are not subscribers.
2. The educational level for subscribers of *Time* is significantly higher than the educational level in the general population. Therefore, *Time* readers probably are more willing and better able to respond to a mail survey.
3. *Time* subscribers probably feel some loyalty to the magazine and are more willing to respond than nonsubscribers would be.

Let us elaborate on these points, since they determine when mail samples are appropriate. First, the persons conducting a mail survey must have a list of names and addresses of the population. Many such lists are available, including lists of physicians, dentists, other professionals, businesses, hospitals, and other special groups. A list of the general population of the United States does not exist, although some people have used lists that are approximations. The most widely used lists of the general population are lists of licensed automobile drivers, which are available from each state. The major omissions on these lists are persons who do not have a driver's license and persons who have moved since the license was issued and cannot be located. These omissions could account for as many as 20 percent of all adults. Other lists have similar omissions. Lists of registered voters exclude the third of the population that is not registered and also tend to contain out-of-date addresses. The file of all listed telephone numbers excludes not only households without phones but households with unlisted numbers—a severe limitation in large cities, where up to half of all telephones are unlisted.

A good deal is known about the characteristics of people who will respond to mail surveys. In the first place, they are likely to be well-educated persons, since mail questionnaires require that a respondent be able to read and follow instructions; of course, the more complicated the survey, the more education will play a role. Even though there has been an increase in the years of formal schooling of the general public, a large number of people still are not comfortable with mail surveys.

Aside from ability to understand a mail survey, the other key factor is motivation. In general, people who feel strongly about the topic of the survey, either pro or con, are more likely to respond than are those who are neutral or have given little thought to the topic. Thus, if one took a mail survey at face value, one might overestimate the public's knowledge of and interest in a topic.

Finally, the sponsorship of a survey also has an effect on cooperation. If people have positive feelings about the person or organization conducting the survey, they will be more likely to respond. But, although the quality of surveys of *Time* subscribers or members of professional organizations is improved by the friendly feelings of respondents, surveys conducted by politicians can run into trouble. For example, a congressman who conducts surveys of constituents to find out how they feel about public issues is likely to receive responses mainly from those who support the congressman; therefore, these surveys usually simply confirm the congressman in the views that he holds.

*Shopping-Center Sampling.* For many market research purposes, shopping-center sampling has become a popular procedure. The procedure has two major advantages. First, it is very inexpensive, since the interviewer does not spend time traveling to locate respondents but merely intercepts them as they pass through the shopping center. Second, the facilities at the shopping center can be arranged for all kinds of product tests. People can be asked to taste various foods, look at various product designs and colors of home appliances, react to print or television advertisements, and do many other tasks that require them to be in personal contact with the product and the interviewer.

Because most shopping-center studies have substantial biases, this method is inappropriate for measuring public opinion, although it may be appropriate for product tests. These biases are caused by the selection of the shopping centers and by the selection of the visitors to the shopping centers. Since there are lists of almost all shopping centers, a researcher could easily select a probability sample of shopping centers by using the same kind of chance procedures that are used for area samples. Instead, shopping-center studies are conducted in a limited number of locations that have been selected, at least partially, because the operator of the center was willing to rent space and permit interviewing. Most of these centers are in high-income suburban areas; only a few are located in cities or nonmetropolitan areas. This disparity is not a problem for manufacturers, since suburban customers may account for a very large part of their sales; but these customers cannot represent the entire population on an attitude survey.

The major problem with the selection of visitors to the shopping center is that not all people shop with equal frequency or at the same time. Although more than 90 percent of all households visit at least one shopping center in a year, younger people, women, and higher-income families are likely to shop more frequently, and thus to form a disproportionately high fraction of a shopping-center sample. A study that does not control for this disparity by weighting respondents inversely by frequency of visit will be seriously flawed. Also, different types of people shop on different days and at different times. A study that does not include people who visit shopping centers at night and on weekends will miss most employed persons.

Finally, it should be noted that about half of all people who are asked to participate in shopping-center sampling refuse because they have limited time and the interview interferes with their shopping needs. In turn, the interviewer may deliberately avoid certain people, such as the mother with the crying baby in her arms, because they look unlikely to cooperate.

There is really no objection to the use of shopping-center sampling for product testing, since sophisticated manufacturers have experience with other product studies and are aware of the data limitations and take them into account when making decisions. However, when this method is used to measure public knowledge and attitudes, the results can be unfortunate. In one such study, a shopping-center sample was used to measure public comprehension of the labels of over-the-counter drugs. People were stopped in shopping centers and asked to read and interpret some proposed labels. Unfortunately, the ability to read labels depends on age and education. Those persons most likely to be confused or misled by labels are the old and the poor, and it is just this group that is least likely to be found in shopping centers.

*Street-Corner Quota Sampling.* In the 1930s, the standard polling procedure was to stop people at street corners to obtain interviews. Interviewers were free to select where they would go, but they were required to obtain certain quotas of men and women and people in specified groups and income brackets. Since interviewers were mainly middle class, samples chosen in this way also were mainly middle class; both poor people and high-income people were largely excluded. Virtually no opinion research is done in this way anymore.

Until recently, the *Chicago Sun-Times* used street-corner polls to predict election results for a variety of races in Illinois. These polls generally proved to have about the same levels of accuracy as the polls conducted by telephone. One might wonder how this was possible given the loose procedures involved. There seem to be two explanations. One is that interviewing was very widely conducted, within every ward in Chicago and in most downstate counties. Second, the choice of locations was based on analyses of earlier election results and thus reflected past behavior. Although this was not really a probability method and there was no way of knowing how to measure the variation between repeated samples, the election predictions would be expected to be close if there was no great change in voting behavior from previous periods.

Of course, street-corner sampling reaches people who are out and shopping more often. Thus, older people and those who are ill or handicapped are less likely to vote in a street-corner poll. However, such people also are less likely to vote in the actual election. To the extent that the relative probability of voting in a street-corner sample is approximately the same as the relative probability of voting in an actual election, street-corner polling will approximate election results. The difficulties and uncertainties of street-corner polling prevent its use for other purposes, and one suspects that the method would be abandoned if it produced a large error for any reason.

*Really Terrible Sampling.* Sampling methods that depend on the respondent to volunteer will greatly increase the errors that were discussed earlier with mail questionnaires. Respondents are likely to be those with axes to grind and those who support the view of the organizations asking for the response. The best-known examples of volunteer respondents are those who clip out and return a questionnaire found in a newspaper or magazine. When people are required to use their own envelopes, to address those envelopes, and to affix a stamp, the cooperation rate can be as low as 1 to 3 percent of all readers.

A new version of the same procedures is the use of telephone call-ins to express a "yes" or "no" vote on an issue that is proposed in a newspaper or on television. Again, the requirement of having to make, as well as pay for, the call creates a substantial economic bias; and the responses will generally come from those most committed to an issue. Indeed, on these types of surveys, people can stuff the ballot box by making multiple calls or sending in multiple ballots supporting their position.

When results from volunteer surveys have been compared with those of carefully conducted telephone surveys, in a few cases the results have been the same, but in many other cases there have been substantial differences.

The newest developments in electronics make it possible for cable television subscribers to respond with answers to questions being presented at that moment on a program. Such systems are available in a limited number of cities and for small subgroups of the population in those cities. Thus, the results obtained by this method cannot be generalized to the total population and are not substantially better than the volunteer surveys that we have just decried. If all communities and all or most television sets were wired for two-way cable, and if all selected households cooperated, this procedure could become a valid sampling method, although it would still be limited to asking fairly simple questions.

### Summary

We have briefly described basic sampling ideas and the methods used by the best-known public polls and by a variety of other special polls for selecting respondents. In the most carefully conducted polls, respondents are selected from listed or unlisted telephone numbers; from addresses, using area sampling methods; or from a complete list of the population to be sampled, if such a list exists. In all careful samples, probability sampling methods are used. That is, the ultimate selection is made by chance, with the use of computer-generated or other selection methods that give each person in the population a known (and often equal) chance of selection.

From such samples, it is possible to know that repeated samples chosen in the same way will yield results that differ by a specified amount from each other. The differences between samples will depend on the sample size and actual design used.

Even if a sample is well designed, it must be carefully executed if it is to produce reliable results; that is, the selected persons must be located and persuaded to cooperate. Normally, finding respondents is simply a function of making enough effort at different times. Large numbers of respondents will remain unlocated if too few attempts are made or if the time period allotted is too short. Obtaining cooperation depends on the skill and experience of the interviewer as well as the topic and length of the interview. Ultimately, however, cooperation depends on the general public's understanding of and belief in public opinion polls.

## Additional Reading

Much fuller discussions of sampling are found in several sampling texts. The following six are suggested for readers with varying levels of interest and mathematical sophistication: *Sampling Techniques* (Cochran, 1963), *Sample Design in Business Research* (Deming, 1960), *Sample Survey Methods and Theory* (Hansen, Hurwitz, and Madow, 1953), *Survey Sampling* (Kish, 1965), *Sampling Opinions* (Stephan and McCarthy, 1958), and *Applied Sampling* (Sudman, 1976a).

The Sudman book is written at a simple level, in the same style as this chapter, and provides many examples. The Cochran text is the most mathematically sophisticated but is still clear and readable for those with good mathematical foundations. The other books combine practical applications and mathematical derivations. The Kish book deals mainly with the kinds of problems encountered at a large survey organization, such as the Survey Research Center at the University of Michigan. The examples given in the Hansen, Hurwitz, and Madow volume are taken primarily from their U.S. Census Bureau experience, whereas Deming, as indicated in his title, uses business examples. Finally, Stephan and McCarthy deal with field problems of respondent availability, cooperation, and the general topic of sample biases.

# 7

# Asking the Question: How Wording Affects Response

"Ask a silly question, and you get a silly answer" is an old saying, but one that has profound implications for survey research. Surveys ask a series of questions of a sample of respondents and use the answers to make generalizations about the larger population from which the sample was drawn. Although the sampling may be impeccably done and the analysis conducted with the most sophisticated methods, the results may still be worthless if the wrong questions are asked. The term *wrong question* is used here in two senses: wrong in the sense that the question did not ask what the researcher wanted to know and wrong in the sense that the wording of the question biased the results.

There are many ways in which the wording of questions can influence respondents' answers, some of which we will consider later in this chapter. No matter how good a question is from a technical point of view, however, it is still a bad question if it does not elicit the kind of response that researchers or policy makers require to meet their objectives. For example, if researchers are interested in finding out about intention to vote for particular candidates, they might ask: "Which candidate do you like best?" or "Which candidate do you think would do the best job?" Although the answers to each of these questions will no doubt be highly correlated with vote intention, they will not produce the same responses as a direct question: "If the election were being held today, which candidate would you vote for?" Which question is the right one to ask depends on the researcher's purpose in undertaking the survey. That is, the appropriateness of the questions for the survey is something that must be decided by the researcher in the light of the project's goals. The only general rule for the appropriateness of questions is "Ask what you want to know, not something else."

Questioning is a familiar activity. We engage in it every day in the course of our ordinary conversations. Since we are all experienced question askers, why should it be difficult to formulate questions for a survey? The answer is that conversations differ from surveys in several important respects. In conversations, we get immediate feedback about whether the other person has understood the question in the manner that we intended. If we perceive that a question has not been understood as we intended, we can reformulate it to make it clearer. Also, our conversational questions are usually open-ended, and the person who is asked a question can easily avoid giving a direct answer. We are not usually interested in pinning down the person we are talking to, because we do not need to record a specific answer. If the answers to our questions are irrelevant, incomplete, and evasive, we can simply formulate more specific probing questions.

Since the process of interaction in ordinary conversations goes on smoothly, we often are not aware of how much refinement has occurred in the question-and-answer sequence. In surveys, however, questions are formulated independently of the actual interview. They must be standardized for all respondents, and interviewers are not permitted to alter the wording of questions for different respondents. If interviewers are allowed to change the wording of a question to make it more easily understood, they run the risk of changing its meaning so that it no longer measures what it was intended to measure.

Good questionnaire development requires a great deal of pretesting—that is, trying out questions on small samples, often with follow-up questions to understand how respondents are interpreting the question. In the process of revising questions, the researcher continually refers to the purposes of the survey, in order to make choices among alternative wordings of questions. Unfortunately, in polling practice, questionnaires often are put together hurriedly, with little or no pretesting and inadequate attention to the goals of the research. Good questionnaire development is expensive because it takes the time of the professionals who are writing the questions and pretesting. Too often, the clients who pay for the research are not willing to invest funds in this aspect of the survey process.

Since the exact wording of questions is often left out of reports of survey results, the limitations on the data caused by the wording of the questions may not be apparent to the consumers of survey research, both those who commission the surveys and those who see the results in the media. Although some publications now recognize the importance of including the exact wording of questions (*Public Opinion Quarterly* requires that question wording be included in the article), limitations of space or time often mean that question wording, if produced at all, is put in a box with small print or is banished to an appendix, where it may not be noted by readers.

## Types of Questions Asked in Polls

Surveys are so widely used today that scarcely any topic has escaped the pollsters' interest. In general, the questions asked can be divided into two categories: factual questions and opinion questions.

*Factual Questions.* Factual questions are those that can be, in principle, verified by records or observation: "Did you vote in the last election?" "How tall is the Washington Monument?" "In what year were you born?" Although such questions could be verified by external observations, often—for practical, legal, or ethical reasons—it is not actually possible to verify them. For example, although it would be possible to observe how a person votes, it is illegal to do so. Therefore, we must depend on voters' reports of how they voted, rather than observing them directly. We could, of course, check on the truthfulness of groups of respondents by comparing the actual voting results with their reports of voting, but we could not match individual votes with individual voters. Questions about voting behavior (factual) are fundamentally different from questions about voting intentions (opinion), since there is no way to verify a voting intention apart from persons' reports of their intentions. Voters can (and often do) change their minds at the last minute. The fact that voters change their minds does not falsify their reported intentions.

Factual questions may be autobiographical ("How many times did you go to the doctor in the last week?" "What is the highest grade you completed in school?"), or they may be about the behavior of others ("How many of your friends smoke marijuana?") or about knowledge of public events ("What team won the World Series in 1985?"). Many of the government surveys—such as the decennial census, the Current Population Survey, the Survey of Income and Program Participation, and a number of health surveys discussed in Chapter Three—consist virtually entirely of questions about the behavior of respondents and other family members. Important commercial surveys, such as those used for television ratings and readership of magazines and newspapers, also depend on behavioral reports.

The growing importance of surveys involving autobiographical data for planning purposes and governmental programs has led to a growing interest in research on problems of memory in answering survey questions about personal behavior. Such research combines traditional survey and methodological studies on question formulation with psychological studies on memory and information processing. This research will provide a better understanding of the many ways in which autobiographical behavioral reports may be distorted. It should lead to improved ways of formulating questions to produce more accurate behavioral reports (see Bradburn, Rips, and Shevell, 1987).

Another important potential source of error in reporting about factual data is the social desirability or embarrassment of answering certain types of questions. For example, we conducted a methodological experiment to study ways to improve questions about socially undesirable, embarrassing, or personally sensitive behaviors, such as gambling, drug use, alcohol consumption, and sexual behavior (Bradburn, Sudman, and Associates, 1979). We asked respondents whether they might be reluctant to answer such questions truthfully and also whether, in their opinion, other people would give truthful answers. Very few respondents were willing to admit that they themselves would not answer questions about drug use, alcohol consumption, or sexual behavior. However, many of these respondents did say that, in their opinion, most people would find it difficult to answer such questions truthfully. An analysis of the data suggested that these respondents—those who denied that they themselves would have any trouble with such questions but thought that most others would—did have consistently lower reports of drug and alcohol use and lower reported frequency of different types of sexual behavior than did those who thought that most people would not have trouble answering such questions. Respondents' reported beliefs about other people's behaviors, of course, are based on indirect evidence and must be confirmed by extensive analysis of the data. Researchers making such indirect use of responses to questions must specify the types of inferences they are making and give some evidence that such inferences are legitimate.

*Opinion Questions.* Opinion questions are those whose answers are expressions of the respondent's psychological state and cannot be verified by external observation: "If an election for president were held tomorrow, whom would you vote for?" "Do you approve or disapprove of the Strategic Defense Initiative?" "How often in the last week did you feel bored?" Opinion questions are often divided into three types: evaluative questions (those that ask people whether they like or dislike something, approve or disapprove of something, or think that something is good or bad); cognitive questions (questions that ask respondents what they believe about a particular situation or policy or psychological state); and questions about action intentions (questions that ask what people intend to do).

A large proportion of questions in public opinion polls concern evaluations. Polls are frequently conducted to discover what people think about the behavior of prominent politicians, whether they approve or disapprove of various policies being considered by government, and whether they like or dislike certain products or attributes of products or services. In political campaigns, cognitive questions are widely used to study the image of candidates—that is, how people perceive different candidates and their policy positions. And, of course, behavioral intention questions, such as intention to vote for a candidate, are also used. All these types of questions have their proper place in surveys, and all are widely used. However, each type of question is prompting a different type of information. Thus, the survey designer must make sure that the type of information provided by the question is the appropriate information for the research question at hand.

Liking something, believing positive things about it, and acting positively toward it are not exactly the same things. Therefore, respondents who say that they like a particular politician may not endorse that politician's policy views and may not intend to vote for him or her. In a study of attitudes toward year-round daylight saving time conducted during the energy crisis (Murray and others, 1974), there was evidence of a considerable overlap between those who liked year-round daylight saving time and those who approved of Congress's proposal to enact such a law; however, a substantial minority liked year-round daylight saving time but disapproved of it as a policy, and some people approved of it as a policy but did not, in fact, like it.

Sometimes researchers deliberately use cognitive questions (projective questions) to make inferences about respondents' own psychological states. That is, the researcher may believe that respondents will not truthfully answer questions about socially undesirable, embarrassing, or personally sensitive behavior. In such instances, the researcher may ask respondents what they think about some behavior or beliefs of other people. The answers are interpreted as statements about the respondents' own beliefs or evaluations, rather than as the literal answers to the questions.

## Effects of Question Wording on Answers

Surveys may involve both factual questions and opinion questions and may use different types of each. In evaluating the results of surveys, a user must determine whether the type of question is appropriate to the subject of the survey and whether the inferences drawn from the responses to the questions are reasonable in light of the actual questions asked. In order to make this evaluation, one must pay careful attention to the exact wording of the question and consider its relation to the conclusions drawn. Without access to the exact text of the question, one cannot be sure that the inferences are reasonable—especially when the "results" of a survey are summarized in a brief headline or a sentence read by a newscaster: "A recent poll shows that . . ." Given the ambiguities of language and the frequent haste with which questionnaires are put together, the relationship between the questions being asked and the conclusions drawn from the answers is frequently less clear than the report of the data might indicate.

One of the charges commonly leveled against pollsters, particularly by those who do not like the results of a particular poll, is that the pollster—by formulating the question in a certain way— has deliberately biased the results in favor of one position or another. Although obviously biased questions rarely appear in polls conducted by professional, experienced survey practitioners, there have been enough studies of the effects of question wording on responses to make even the most skilled practitioner worry about potential biases. Heavily biased questions (such as the examples in Chapter Three, in the section headed "Using Polls to Persuade") are most commonly found in pseudo-surveys conducted by advocacy groups that are strongly committed to one particular policy position. True believers in such groups typically do not consider their questions biased, since, from their point of view, the questions are merely a statement of their beliefs.

Even when there is no evidence of deliberate bias, two polls taken at the same time on the same topic sometimes will produce results that appear to differ, perhaps substantially. Such results often lead commentators to question polling procedures even if the organizations conducting the polls are neutral and well qualified and utilize identical or nearly identical sampling and interviewing procedures. An examination of the data usually reveals differences in questionnaire wording that do not seem very large but are influencing the responses. We are not talking about deliberately biased wording but, rather, of differences in meaning that the alternative questions are communicating.

*Open Versus Closed Questions.* One of the most debated topics in survey research is the relative merits of open and closed questions. An "open" question is one that respondents are allowed to answer in their own words; the responses are later turned into categories that can be quantified through a process of coding. "Closed" or precoded questions are those that constrain the respondents' answers by giving them response categories from which they choose an answer—for example, "agree strongly, agree, disagree, disagree strongly."

In our review of methodological studies (Sudman and Bradburn, 1974), we did not find any overall superiority for either open or closed questions. Most experienced survey researchers, however, believe that closed questions produce more relevant and comparable responses, because they specify the dimensions along which the respondents are supposed to answer the question; on the other hand, open questions produce fuller and deeper responses reflecting differences in opinions and attitudes that are missed by the constraints of the precoded categories. The expense and practical difficulties in achieving good coder reliability for open-ended questions have inhibited their use in many surveys. Today open-ended questions are used most widely in pretests and exploratory studies where investigators are trying to discover various possible differences in opinions and attitudes, in order to formulate coding categories that might then be used later as precoded categories.

While there is no evidence that one form of the question or another is best for all purposes, research by Schuman and Presser (1981) indicates that the two formats—even when the same question is asked—elicit quite different responses. Therefore, a researcher might draw different conclusions about such things as "the most important problems facing the nation" or desirable aspects of jobs, depending on which form of the question was used. It is not possible on a priori grounds to say that one of these versions is correct and the other one not. The choice of question format would depend on the purposes of the study.

The open-ended format does seem to produce more accurate answers to quantitative behavioral questions, such as "How much do you smoke?" or "How often do you go to the movies?" When respondents are permitted to answer such questions in their own terms rather than selecting a precoded quantity, response error is reduced. Research suggests that respondents given precoded categories use these categories as clues to what is normal in the population. If respondents' behavior is at the high or low end of the distribution, they tend to move toward the center and, thus, to underreport socially undesirable and overreport socially desirable behavior.

*Double-Barreled Questions.* There are a number of ways in which the wording of a question can affect the distribution of answers to questions, some of them more obvious than others. One of the best known and most obvious is the double-barreled question. For example, "Are you in favor of economic sanctions against South Africa in order to end apartheid, or do you oppose economic sanctions against South Africa even though this means the perpetuation of apartheid?" In the typical double-barreled question, a policy means (economic sanctions) is coupled with a goal (end apartheid).

The question is structured so that approval signifies approval of both the ends and the means, and disapproval implies disapproval of both the ends and the means. Respondents who approve of the ends but not the means, or vice versa, are in a quandary about how to answer the question. If they feel more strongly about the means or the ends, they may answer the part of the question they feel more strongly about, or they may refuse to answer such a double-barreled question altogether. If respondents oppose apartheid but have not thought much about the question of sanctions, they may assume that sanctions are the only way to oppose apartheid and thus may endorse sanctions. This, of course, is what the authors of such a question would want to happen if they were trying to bias the results deliberately.

*Response Categories.* Another and subtler form of joining questions is what we have called the one-and-a-half-barreled question (Sudman and Bradburn, 1982). In the one-and-a-half-barreled question, qualifications put into one portion of the question or into the response categories pull responses toward a particular response category. Take the following example:

> The United States is now negotiating a strategic arms agreement with the Soviet Union in what is known as SALT II. Which of the following statements is closest to your opinion on these negotiations?
>
> 1.  I strongly support SALT II.
> 2.  SALT II is somewhat disappointing but on balance I have to support it.
> 3.  I would like to see more protection for the United States before I would be ready to support SALT II.
> 4.  I strongly oppose the SALT II arms negotiation with the Russians.
> 5.  I don't know enough about SALT II to have an opinion yet.

Response categories are ordered from strong support to strong opposition. They are not, however, symmetrical, since the response categories indicating opposition to SALT II invoke other references that are not present in the alternatives for support. In particular, response category 3 links SALT II with a particular goal (national defense) that is not present in the other alternatives. Finally, alternative 4 reminds the respondent that the agreement is "with the Russians," a reference that was omitted in the two alternatives indicating support for the treaty. A survey in which this form of the question was used produced lower support for the SALT treaty than other questions that presented more symmetrical response categories.

This example illustrates the importance of response alternatives for interpreting the meaning of questions. There is a good deal of debate in the literature concerning whether or not to offer explicit alternatives to respondents. For example, one could simply ask: "On balance do you support or oppose the SALT II treaty?" An example of the effect of using an explicit alternative is provided by Noelle-Neumann (1970) in a study in West Germany conducted by the Institut für Demoskopie/Allensbach. One question asked of nonworking housewives was used in two versions, each version being used on half of the sample. The first version was "Would you like to have a job, if this were possible?" The second version was "Would you prefer to have a job, or do you prefer to do just your housework?" In the first version, without a stated alternative, 19 percent of the nonworking housewives replied that they would not like to have a job; in the second version, with the stated alternative, "do you prefer to do just your housework," 68 percent reported that they would not like to have a job. A possible explanation of this effect is that the stated alternative provided a context for interpreting the question, which changed the way respondents answered it.

Unfortunately, the phrase "if this were possible" was omitted from the second form of the question, so that the two versions were not exactly comparable. To make sure that the effect was attributable to the alternative rather than to the phrase "if this were possible," the person constructing the second question should have worded it "Would you like to have a job, if this were possible, or would you prefer to do just your housework?"

An especially important example of the importance of response categories relates to questions dealing with public approval of government social welfare programs. Here it is found consistently that much higher approval is given to welfare programs when there is no explicit mention of costs or taxes necessary to fund such programs. Thus, in a May–June 1945 survey, Gallup found that 63 percent of respondents said "yes" to the first question below, but only 34 percent said "yes" to the second question:

1. Do you think the government should give money to workers who are unemployed for a limited length of time until they can find another job?
2. Would you be willing to pay higher taxes to give unemployed persons up to $25 a week for 26 weeks if they fail to find satisfactory jobs?

Methodological studies on question formulation do not make clear whether it is always better to give alternatives or not to give alternatives. What seems clear is that the explicit specification of alternatives standardizes the meaning of questions for respondents and indicates to the respondents the dimensions of response that the researcher wishes them to use in reporting their opinions. Thus, the particular alternatives selected by the question writer must provide the frame of reference for the respondents that the researcher wants them to use in answering the question. Much can be learned from previous methodological studies investigating response alternatives, and not every possibility needs to be tested equally. However, in order to ensure that a degree of uniformity is achieved, question writers need to do extensive pretesting and experimental work with alternative question wordings. Only through the empirical testing of different versions can the researcher determine how different alternatives will affect the responses to questions.

Even subtler forms of the one-and-a-half-barreled question are possible. For example, when an action is attributed to an admired person or group, such as the president or the Supreme Court, responses favorable to that activity are increased. In the following two versions of a question on abortion, more respondents favor abortion when the Supreme Court is mentioned:

1. Would you favor or oppose a law that would permit a woman to go to a doctor to end pregnancy at any time during the first three months?
2. The U.S. Supreme Court has ruled that a woman may go to a doctor to end pregnancy at any time during the first three months of pregnancy. Do you favor or oppose this ruling?

Conversely, an action of a disliked group is more likely to be opposed or an action against such a group is more likely to be favored. More Americans will favor an activity if it is claimed that this activity will oppose communism, as in these two questions:

1. Do you think the United States made a mistake in deciding to defend Korea, or not?
2. Do you think the United States was right or

wrong in sending American troops to stop the
Communist invasion of South Korea?

Also, it is sometimes difficult to obtain direct opposites for
words used in attitude scales. The words *agree* and *disagree* are good
opposites, but the words *allow* and *forbid* are not, since *forbid* is
regarded as a much stronger word. Therefore, in the following two
questions, more people are likely to answer that homosexuals
"should not be allowed" than "should be forbidden":

1.  Should a homosexual teacher be allowed or not
    allowed to teach in a public school?
2.  Should a homosexual teacher be forbidden or not
    forbidden to teach in a public school?

In some instances, the wording of questions may be so
sensitive to the particular positions of different advocacy groups
that it is nearly impossible to find a satisfactory wording that does
not appear to bias the answers to the question. Such a situation is
particularly apt to occur in attitude questions involving highly
polarized opinions and strong feelings on both sides of an issue.
Schuman (1986) gives a good example of such a problem in
conducting a survey about attitudes toward the use of animals in
biological research. The question dealt directly with the release of
pound animals to laboratories. The sponsor of the research wanted
the question to include reference to the fact that animals to be
released would otherwise be killed by the pound. The critics of the
survey, however, rejected this assumption, arguing that such
arrangements between pounds and laboratories reduced the
incentive for pounds to solve the surplus animal problem by
nonlethal means. Clearly, both sides believed that the addition or
omission of the disputed reference to what would happen to the
animals if they did not go to the laboratories altered the response
to the question. When both versions were actually used, however,
it turned out that there were no differences in responses to the two
versions.

When it is impossible to resolve differences in wording
between contending parties, an excellent alternative to omitting the

question altogether is to use alternative versions of the question on randomly selected parts of the sample. The technique, often called a "split ballot," is extremely useful for testing the effects of question wording on responses. Unfortunately, it is not widely used, although its origins go back to the earlier Gallup polls. When it is used, it demonstrates that serious thought has been given to alternative formulations of questions.

*Order Effects.* Responses to questions also can be influenced by the order in which questions are asked or response categories are given. Order effects are most likely to occur among issues about which there is no strongly developed opinion and among respondents who do not have well-formulated opinions about a particular topic under study. Other questions in the questionnaire form a context for succeeding questions. Respondents with no clear opinions about a topic may use this context to interpret the meaning of questions. As with explicit alternatives, which may provide a specific interpretive context, the preceding questions in a questionnaire provide a background of meaning against which respondents who know or have thought little about a particular topic interpret and react to questions. (A more detailed discussion of order effects is given in Chapter Nine.)

Since surveys are often used in the early stages of development of policy debates or, in marketing, to obtain reactions to new items or new products, the potential for order effects as biasing mechanisms needs to be taken seriously. Again, the way to sort out the effects is to use experimentation with alternate forms of question order. The existence or absence of such effects needs to be demonstrated empirically before one can have much confidence in survey results about topics that are not very salient or highly developed in public discussion. One clue to the possibility that order effects may need to be investigated is the existence of a substantial proportion of "don't know" answers to attitude questions. Since surveys are conducted on such a wide variety of topics, many respondents, particularly if they are a sample of the general population, will have only very vague ideas about the topic under investigation or may not have thought about it at all. Thus, the "don't know" or "no opinion" responses may at times be quite high.

*"Don't Know" and "No Opinion" Answers.* There are two opposite kinds of errors that pollsters may make with "don't know" answers. First, they may be too hasty in accepting such answers. Some respondents use a "don't know" answer to temporize while they are searching their memories and will give an answer if the interviewer probes or simply waits a bit longer. The opposite error is to force an answer from a respondent who truly does not know. Which error is more likely depends on the topic of the study as well as the respondent. Certainly, for newly developing public policy issues, many people will not yet be aware of the arguments and may not have an opinion.

When an explicit "don't know" or "no opinion" option is provided, the number of "don't know" responses automatically increases; often as much as 20 percent of the sample will give such responses. There has been relatively little study of these "floaters"— that is, people who will give a substantive response to an attitude question when there is no explicit "don't know" category but will select the "don't know" option if it is given explicitly. From what we do know about such people (see Schuman and Presser, 1981), it appears that they are different in some respects from those who give substantive answers without the explicit "don't know" category. Their answers may affect the conclusions one might draw from surveys.

Many pollsters believe that people who do not have clearly formulated opinions still lean in one direction or another. They wish to encourage people to give a substantive response by omitting an explicit "don't know" category. Again, extensive pretesting of alternative versions of the question could determine whether an exclusion of a specific "don't know" category makes any substantive difference. "Floaters" appear to be people who are most susceptible to the potential biasing effects of things such as question order and question wording. Researchers need to understand fully the effects of their question wording in order to make valid conclusions from their data.

## Summary

The most critical element in surveys—and, unfortunately, often the weakest link—is the formulation of the questions that make up the survey instrument. In this chapter, we have reviewed some of the principal considerations that affect the questionnaire design and pointed out some of the dilemmas that face survey researchers and users in putting together a good questionnaire. We have also pointed out some of the indicators of careful question formulation. Bad questions can undo all the good of careful sampling, interviewing, and statistical analysis. Good questions are the indispensable ingredient of a good survey.

## Additional Reading

Readers of this book who want more information on how to design a questionnaire may wish to consult our book *Asking Questions* (Sudman and Bradburn, 1982). An earlier book that still contains useful suggestions on questionnaire construction is Stanley Payne's 1951 classic, *The Art of Asking Questions*. A short book with much good advice is Converse and Presser's (1986) *Survey Questions*.

In addition, any reasonable study will contain a copy of the questionnaire, so that the user will know both the question wordings for individual questions and the context in which those questions appeared. Anyone designing a questionnaire should certainly become familiar with many other questionnaires and specifically with questionnaires from other studies on the same subject.

# 8

# *What Do the Answers Mean?*

The analysis of survey data takes on many forms, depending on the uses for which the survey is intended. At its simplest, the analysis may merely indicate how many people act or think in a certain way. Even here, the user of the results may need to take into account certain decisions that the researcher has made: the development of scales or indices, the treatment of no answers or uninformed respondents, and the discussions of statistical variation. A user of such data is likely to believe that conclusions based on them have high validity, but we shall show that it is possible to lie or make mistakes with statistics.

At a slightly higher level of complexity, survey data are used to show the differences between individuals or groups. Again, there are issues of analysis and presentation that we shall discuss. At their most complex, surveys attempt to *explain* what is happening and why people behave or feel as they do. These explanations are heavily dependent on the researcher's using the correct explanatory variables. If important variables are ignored, no analysis, not even the most mathematically powerful, can give a good explanation of what is happening. Even if the important variables are included and a relationship is found between them and the behavior or attitude to be explained, it is often difficult to make statements about causality without also making some implicit assumptions that are themselves uncertain. Researchers will often have strong prior views about the potential outcomes and may analyze the data to confirm these views. The user of such data must be aware that complex analyses may be driven by prior expectations.

We present some examples of controversial data analysis to alert readers to some of the issues. The intent of this chapter is not to arouse suspicions about all survey research analysis. Much of what is done is straightforward and noncontroversial. When survey research is used for advocacy, however, one must be cautious of the analyses presented, as well as all the other aspects of the survey. We must also make it clear that nothing we say here is new or technically sophisticated. All this material and much more will be found in many readily available elementary statistics texts. We believe, however, that it is useful to draw attention to some of the most common issues in using survey research results, since these are often missed or given only very brief mention in elementary courses.

### Omission of Results

The simplest form of analysis is to report the percentages of the total population who are for or against some government activity or who do or do not engage in a given behavior. Even here, the researcher's decisions about what to present can mislead the user. One way to slant results is by selective omission. A researcher who wishes to make a point for advocacy reasons may succumb to the temptation to omit unfavorable results. The Panel on Survey Measurement of Subjective Phenomena gives a vivid example of deceptive analysis of poll results by the Union Carbide Company (Turner and Martin, 1984, Vol. 1, pp. 84–86; see also Kinsley, 1981).

> Union Carbide reported survey results that purported, among other things, to show that "sixty-nine percent of the public would favor tax cuts [for business] if business said that some of the money saved would be used to buy new equipment and create additional jobs. Sixty-nine percent also favored increased tax credits for new capital investments, and 57 percent favored larger tax deductions for prior

investments by valuing equipment at replacement—
rather than historical—cost. . . . By more than two to
one, the public favored the reduction of restrictions
which prohibit companies from joint development of
export markets and R&D projects."

Union Carbide concluded that the results
showed that "Government is seen as being wasteful,
bloated, inefficient, and costly and as an inherently
negative factor in economic growth. Americans
believe that government programs should be cut
back."

However, the survey results that were *not* reported in the
advertisements revealed a somewhat different picture: 66 percent of
the respondents in the first survey thought that "businessmen are
more afraid to take risks than they used to be," and 60 percent also
thought that "a few big companies divide up business between
them." A substantial majority of respondents believed that both of
these factors were responsible for slowing growth. Furthermore,
more than 66 percent of the respondents agreed with each of the
following statements.

When the economy is booming, most of the
increase is kept by business in the form of higher
profits, higher executive salaries, and fat expense
accounts. The average person does not benefit much.

When the economy goes down, business keeps
its profits high and cuts jobs and wages.

All companies need to make some profits to
stay in business. But the profits that businesses are
making today are much higher than they need to be.

Far from disapproving of government regulatory activity, the
surveys seemed to evidence considerable public support for
regulation by the government in many spheres. When asked, for
example, whether "the federal government is doing more than it

should, less than it should, or about the right amount to regulate major corporations in areas like product safety and other things that have to do with protecting the public," 70 percent of the respondents replied either "about right" or "less than it should." When asked about ten specific types of government regulation, a majority of respondents supported present or even stricter government regulations.

In this example, questions were asked in the survey that were not used in the reported analysis. A more insidious form of falsification is not to ask a question at all because of prior knowledge or anticipation that it may produce negative results.

### Use of Single Questions on Complex Issues

As we have stressed in our discussion of questionnaires, there is a danger in relying on answers to single questions. Especially as the issue becomes more complex, it is more and more difficult to capture a respondent's attitude reliably with a single question. When scales or indices are used instead of single questions, the data almost always become more stable and easier to interpret. The media as well as advocacy researchers dislike scales and indices because they are more abstract than a single question and thus harder to explain and understand. If one is attempting to measure trends over time, however, the trends will have less "noise" and be easier to follow when multiple questions are used. One solution to this dilemma is to show both individual question results and a summary measure based on the combined questions.

As one example, in a study of integrated neighborhoods (Bradburn, Sudman, and Gockel, 1970, p. 399), we asked the following questions about contact with neighbors and then constructed a summary scale:

> Which of these things has anyone in your family done in the past few months with members of families who live in this neighborhood:
>
> Stopped and talked when we met
> Had an informal chat together in their home or our home

Had dinner or a party together at their home or our
home
Got together on other occasions
Went out together for dinner or a movie
Attended the meeting of a neighborhood organization
or group together

To form a meaningful scale, the researcher must first decide
which questions to combine. A number of different procedures can
be used for this purpose, some fairly simple and some highly
sophisticated. In all these procedures, the researcher must consider
the intercorrelations of the potential questions. Items that do not
correlate with the other items would be omitted from the final draft
of the questionnaire, or at least not included in the scale. More
complex multivariate procedures involve factor analysis, Guttman
scaling, and Rasch models. The intent of all these procedures is to
identify unidimensional scales—that is, scales that are measuring
only one thing and not a mixture of attitudes.

In developing a scale, one may weight the individual
questions equally, so that a scale score is a simple sum of answers;
or one may use complex weights. All else equal, we prefer the
simpler scales, in which an individual's score is simply the sum of
answers, rather than more complex procedures, which are sometimes difficult to explain and understand. Normally, the scales are
developed during the pilot phase of a study, not during the final
analysis.

Ultimately, each scale must be evaluated for reliability and
validity. A scale is considered reliable if the various items all
measure the same thing (as indicated by the intercorrelations among
the questions). A scale is considered valid if it measures what it
claims to measure and not something else. Validity is more difficult
to demonstrate than reliability is. The simplest demonstration is
*face validity;* that is, one can point out that the questions appear
to relate to the concept being measured. Thus, in the preceding
example, it seems fairly clear that all the questions relate to
neighboring. The other ways of demonstrating validity are through
convergent and divergent procedures. Convergent validity means
that the scale is related to other variables and scales to which a priori

we expect it to be related. Divergent validity means that the scale is not so highly related to another scale that we are really measuring something else. It is often as difficult to prove validity as it is to write questions that everyone agrees tap the key dimensions.

## Treating the "Don't Knows" and Undecideds

It may seem a minor issue, but survey results can sometimes differ substantially depending on whether the "don't know" and undecided respondents are included or excluded. A simple example (cited by De Boer, 1980) illustrates this point. This question was asked by CBS in 1977:

> Do you think that Jimmy Carter should have pushed for closer ties with communist China even though that meant breaking off relations with the Chinese Nationalists on Taiwan?

The following results were obtained:

| Carter | Percent | Percent excluding "no opinion" |
|---|---|---|
| Should | 28 | 40 |
| Should not | 40 | 60 |
| No opinion | 30 | |
| | 100 | 100 |

The first column gives the reader a sense that attitudes on this issue are mixed; the second column, which excludes the "no opinion" respondents, makes it appear that opinion is pretty firmly on the "should not" side. It seems obvious that the greater the fraction of "no opinion" respondents, the more necessary it is to show them in the results. A large fraction of "no opinion" responses means that the public does not have a clear position yet on an issue, and this is important to know. On the other hand, if only a few respondents (for example, fewer than 10 percent) are undecided, they could be omitted with no real distortion and the table made easier to read. Even here, it would be important for the report to indicate somewhere—in the table or a footnote or in the report itself—the fraction of "no opinion" answers.

### Reports of Sampling Variability

Since surveys are based on samples and not on complete censuses, the reader of survey results has a right to expect estimates of sampling variance. The absence of such estimates makes it impossible to tell, for example, whether there has been a significant change in opinion from one period to the next or whether the change could simply have been caused by chance.

There are two important limitations to estimates of sampling variability. The first, as noted earlier, is that sampling variability is not the only possible cause of error in surveys. Sample biases and response effects resulting from questionnaire wording are often far more serious sources of error, although difficult to measure (see Chapter Nine). Thus, estimates of sampling variance should be considered *minimum* estimates of error instead of total estimates.

The second point to remember is that statistical significance and practical importance are not the same thing. Statistical significance depends on sample size. In large national surveys, differences between groups of a few percent may be highly significant statistically. Whether these differences are of practical importance is a matter for the policy makers and other users of the data to decide. Frequently, especially in social science journals, researchers will stress the statistical significance while ignoring any consideration of importance. Conversely, some samples may be too small to detect statistical significance, but the observed differences over time have important policy implications. In this case, the survey designer can make the statistical tests more powerful by increasing the sample size.

### Comparing Different Groups

For many purposes, one may be interested in comparing subgroup behavior as well as in total estimates. In some cases, the differences between subgroups may be more interesting or important than the totals. Tables 7 and 8 give examples of typical methods used for presenting comparative data. Table 7 is taken from the *Gallup Report* and shows data in full form, as they are typically presented in a *Gallup Report*. Each line in the table represents a subgroup, and the answers all add across to 100 percent. Each percentage on a line is based on the number of interviews given in the final right-hand column. Note that the "no opinions," which are in the range of 0–2 percent, are also included.

The reader interprets this table by looking up and down to compare the groups. Thus, the reader would note that 50 percent of people aged fifty and older have a great deal of confidence in the church or organized religion, as compared to 39 percent of those under fifty; that 51 percent of people in the South have a great deal of confidence as compared to 33 percent in the East; that differences by race are fairly small; and so on.

Table 8, a Census Bureau report from the Current Population Survey, shows comparisons in condensed form. Thus, it shows the percent registered but not also the percent not registered, since these groups must add up to 100 percent if the "don't knows" are omitted, as is done here. Similarly, it shows the percent who voted and omits the percent who did not vote. Again, the reader compares up and down. It can be seen that voting increases with age and education, is lower in the South than elsewhere, and does not differ by sex.

The Census Bureau's format is preferred when there are only two possible answers, while the Gallup method is used when three or more answers are possible. Some researchers might add to the Gallup data a column showing total percentages of 100, so that the reader would know immediately in which direction the data are percentaged.

A reader will sometimes be faced with data that are percentaged incorrectly or not percentaged at all. In this case, it will be very difficult to make comparisons. To understand the data, one must correct or compute the percentages. The thing to remember is to compute the percentages by using as the denominator the variable that is being compared—age, race, gender, or any other independent variable. One should *not* use the total number of answers of a certain type as the denominator. It makes little sense

**Table 7. Confidence in Church/Organized Religion.**

Question: I am going to read you a list of institutions in American society. Would you tell me how much confidence you, yourself, have in each one—a great deal, quite a lot, some, or very little?

The Church or Organized Religion

*May 17-20, 1985*

|  | Great deal | Quite a lot | Some | Very little | None | No opinion | Number of interviews |
|---|---|---|---|---|---|---|---|
| **NATIONAL** | 42% | 24% | 21% | 11% | 1% | 1% | 1,528 |
| *Sex* | | | | | | | |
| Men | 36 | 27 | 22 | 13 | 1 | 1 | 755 |
| Women | 48 | 21 | 20 | 9 | 1 | 1 | 773 |
| *Age* | | | | | | | |
| Total under 30 | 39 | 26 | 24 | 10 | 1 | * | 320 |
| 18-24 years | 38 | 28 | 24 | 9 | 1 | * | 138 |
| 25-29 years | 40 | 23 | 23 | 13 | 1 | * | 182 |
| 30-49 years | 38 | 25 | 23 | 12 | 1 | 1 | 593 |
| Total 50 & older | 50 | 21 | 18 | 10 | * | 1 | 608 |
| 50-64 years | 48 | 23 | 18 | 10 | * | 1 | 302 |
| 65 & older | 52 | 18 | 18 | 10 | 1 | 1 | 306 |
| *Region* | | | | | | | |
| East | 33 | 24 | 28 | 13 | 1 | 1 | 388 |
| Midwest | 44 | 26 | 20 | 9 | * | 1 | 398 |
| South | 51 | 24 | 14 | 9 | 1 | 1 | 444 |
| West | 39 | 20 | 25 | 15 | 1 | * | 298 |
| *Race* | | | | | | | |
| Whites | 42 | 23 | 22 | 11 | 1 | 1 | 1,334 |
| Nonwhites | 45 | 27 | 18 | 8 | 1 | 1 | 184 |
| Blacks | 47 | 26 | 18 | 7 | * | 2 | 151 |
| Hispanics | 42 | 25 | 21 | 10 | 1 | 1 | 104 |

*Less than 1 percent.
Source: *Gallup Report*, no. 238, July 1985, p. 4.

**Table 8. Characteristics of the Voting-Age Population Reported
Having Registered or Voted: November 1982.[a]**

| Characteristic | Number of persons | Percent registered | Percent voted |
|---|---|---|---|
| Total, 18 years and over | 165,483 | 64.1 | 48.5 |
| Race or Spanish origin: | | | |
| White | 143,607 | 65.6 | 49.9 |
| Black | 17,624 | 59.1 | 43.0 |
| Spanish origin | 8,765 | 35.3 | 25.3 |
| Sex: | | | |
| Male | 78,044 | 63.7 | 48.7 |
| Female | 87,437 | 64.4 | 48.4 |
| Age: | | | |
| 18 to 24 years | 28,823 | 42.4 | 24.8 |
| 25 to 44 years | 66,881 | 62.5 | 45.4 |
| 45 to 64 years | 44,180 | 75.6 | 62.2 |
| 65 years and over | 23,398 | 75.2 | 59.9 |
| Region: | | | |
| Northeast | 36,356 | 62.5 | 49.8 |
| North Central | 41,891 | 71.1 | 54.7 |
| South | 55,357 | 61.7 | 41.8 |
| West | 32,879 | 60.6 | 50.7 |
| Residence: | | | |
| Metropolitan | 113,061 | 62.6 | 48.3 |
| In SMSAs of 1 million or more[b] | 64,442 | 62.8 | 48.5 |
| In SMSAs of under 1 million | 48,619 | 62.3 | 48.0 |
| Nonmetropolitan | 52,422 | 67.2 | 49.1 |
| Years of school completed: | | | |
| Elementary:   0 to 8 years | 22,365 | 52.3 | 35.7 |
| High school: 1 to 3 years | 22,324 | 53.3 | 37.7 |
| 4 years | 65,186 | 62.9 | 47.1 |
| College:     1 to 3 years | 28,751 | 70.0 | 53.3 |
| 4 years or more | 26,858 | 79.4 | 66.5 |
| Occupation: | | | |
| White-collar workers | 53,408 | 72.7 | 57.8 |
| Blue-collar workers | 28,220 | 55.8 | 39.1 |
| Service workers | 13,000 | 56.9 | 41.1 |
| Farm workers | 2,597 | 66.7 | 51.3 |

[a]Numbers in thousands, civilian noninstitutional population.
[b]SMSA = Standard Metropolitan Statistical Area.
*Source:* United States Bureau of the Census, 1983b, p. vii.

to report the fraction of all "yes" answers given by those in the thirty-five to forty-four age group, since this fraction depends on two things: the size of this group and the percentage in this group that said "yes." If the percentaging is done correctly, the percentage of interest is found directly, as in our examples. (For a more complete discussion of this point, see Zeisel, 1968.)

As one illustration of unpercentaged data, consider Table 9, from the Current Population Survey. (In the report, the data are percentaged correctly.) One cannot tell very much about the differences between groups simply by looking at the raw numbers. If one percentaged incorrectly (up and down, instead of across), Table 10 would result. This table is not totally meaningless, since it shows that those aged eighteen to twenty-one constitute the largest percentages of those enrolled in college. But the table is still difficult to interpret without making comparisons in several rows or columns simultaneously.

Table 9. College Enrollment by Sex and Age, 1982.[a]

|  | Enrolled | Not enrolled | Total |
|---|---|---|---|
| Males |  |  |  |
| 14–17 years old | 112 | 7,380 | 7,492 |
| 18–19 | 1,376 | 2,585 | 3,961 |
| 20–21 | 1,346 | 2,610 | 3,956 |
| 22–24 | 1,115 | 5,051 | 6,166 |
| 25–29 | 968 | 8,913 | 9,881 |
| 30–34 | 492 | 8,508 | 9,000 |
| 35 years old and over | 490 | 44,492 | 44,982 |
| Total 14 and over | 5,899 | 79,539 | 85,438 |
| Females |  |  |  |
| 14–17 years old | 141 | 7,117 | 7,258 |
| 18–19 | 1,553 | 2,509 | 4,062 |
| 20–21 | 1,343 | 2,871 | 4,214 |
| 22–24 | 945 | 5,542 | 6,487 |
| 25–29 | 891 | 9,464 | 10,355 |
| 30–34 | 637 | 8,811 | 9,448 |
| 35 years old and over | 900 | 51,869 | 52,769 |
| Total 14 and over | 6,410 | 88,183 | 94,593 |
| Total all persons | 12,309 | 167,722 | 180,031 |

[a]Figures in thousands.
*Source:* United States Bureau of the Census, 1983a, p. 2.

Table 10. College Enrollment by Sex and Age, 1982.

|  | Percent (down) | | |
|  | Enrolled | Not enrolled | Total |
|---|---|---|---|
| **Males** | | | |
| 14–17 years old | 0.9 | 4.4 | 4.2 |
| 18–19 | 11.2 | 1.5 | 2.2 |
| 20–21 | 10.9 | 1.6 | 2.2 |
| 22–24 | 9.1 | 3.0 | 3.4 |
| 25–29 | 7.9 | 5.3 | 5.5 |
| 30–34 | 4.0 | 5.1 | 5.0 |
| 35 and over | 4.0 | 26.5 | 25.0 |
| **Females** | | | |
| 14–17 years old | 1.1 | 4.2 | 4.0 |
| 18–19 | 12.6 | 1.5 | 2.3 |
| 20–21 | 10.9 | 1.7 | 2.3 |
| 22–24 | 7.7 | 3.3 | 3.6 |
| 25–29 | 7.2 | 5.7 | 5.8 |
| 30–34 | 5.2 | 5.3 | 5.2 |
| 35 and over | 7.3 | 30.9 | 29.3 |
| Total | 100.0 | 100.0 | 100.0 |

Table 11, which is percentaged correctly, makes it clear that the rates of college attendance are about equal for men between eighteen and nineteen years old (34.7 percent) and between twenty and twenty-one years old (34 percent) whereas, among women, those between eighteen and nineteen have the highest attendance rates. In the older age groups, the rates of attendance drop sharply— which is not surprising but can be seen much more clearly in Table 11 than in Table 10. Note that, in practice, the final two columns of Table 11 could be omitted with no loss of information.

We have stressed this point because a surprising number of published tables are percentaged incorrectly.

### Statistical Significance

Once differences are observed between groups, it is natural to ask whether they occurred by chance or are statistically significant.

### Table 11. College Enrollment by Sex and Age, 1982.

|  | Percent (across) | | |
|---|---|---|---|
|  | Enrolled | Not enrolled | Total |
| **Males** | | | |
| 14–17 years old | 1.5 | 98.5 | 100.0 |
| 18–19 | 34.7 | 65.3 | 100.0 |
| 20–21 | 34.0 | 66.0 | 100.0 |
| 22–24 | 18.1 | 81.9 | 100.0 |
| 25–29 | 9.8 | 90.2 | 100.0 |
| 30–34 | 5.5 | 94.5 | 100.0 |
| 35 years old and over | 1.1 | 98.9 | 100.0 |
| **Females** | | | |
| 14–17 years old | 1.9 | 98.1 | 100.0 |
| 18–19 | 38.2 | 61.8 | 100.0 |
| 20–21 | 31.9 | 68.1 | 100.0 |
| 22–24 | 14.6 | 85.4 | 100.0 |
| 25–29 | 8.6 | 91.4 | 100.0 |
| 30–34 | 6.7 | 93.3 | 100.0 |
| 35 years old and over | 1.7 | 98.3 | 100.0 |

Perhaps the most common error is to scan the results of many comparisons in order to find a difference that appears to be large. When such a difference is located, a statistical test probably will find it significant. It may not be obvious what is wrong with this procedure; therefore, a brief discussion may be helpful.

If one looks at a large number of differences between groups, standard tests are virtually certain to find some of those differences statistically significant. There is a small probability that a single sample difference will appear to be significant when the underlying real difference is zero. When one looks at many comparisons, a sample difference that has a small probability of occurrence is very likely to show up even if no differences are really there.

We do not suggest that users of survey data should refrain from examining large numbers of comparisons. This method is often helpful in generating hypotheses. However, one should not attempt to generate and test hypotheses from the same data set. If a researcher wishes to test hypotheses, he should formulate these hypotheses in advance, using data from previous studies. The data from the new study can then be used to test the hypotheses with tests of statistical significance. If no data exist, an alternative method is to split the data from a survey randomly in half. Then the first half can be used to develop the hypothesis and the second to test the hypothesis.

As discussed above, one should be careful not to confuse statistical and practical significance. If the samples are large enough, differences between groups may be statistically significant without being of practical importance. Thus, for sufficiently large samples, the fact that 53 percent of men compared to 52 percent of women favor a political candidate may be statistically significant. It is doubtful that such a small difference, even if real, would have political significance. On the other hand—especially in small subgroups of the population, such as Hispanics—the sample sizes may be too small to make group comparisons statistically significant, but the underlying differences may be of practical importance.

### The Noncomparison Problem

One often sees descriptions of the characteristics or attitudes of special groups, such as the Moral Majority, unwed mothers, college students or professors, and persons in jail. It is difficult to know what to make of such findings unless these special groups are compared to the rest of the population. Naive researchers will study *only* the special group and say that they are not interested in the rest of the population, but it is only through comparisons that one can really understand the group being studied.

Some examples make this very clear. Suppose we conduct a survey about handguns and find that 75 percent of all persons in jail agree that handguns should be legal. The obvious next question is whether these prisoners are more or less in favor of handguns than other people are. Without some comparison group, one does not know whether their views are similar to those of everyone else or are special.

Some questions, of course, apply only to special groups. College students might be asked about their satisfaction with instruction or extracurricular activities, prisoners about prison food, and so on. No outside group can answer such questions, although the answers can be compared with answers given by people in similar circumstances at different times or places. It is not always necessary for researchers to gather all the comparative survey data themselves. The data from a special group can be compared with data on the general population gathered by another researcher. In this case, however, the question wording and context, as well as the time period covered, must be reasonably similar.

### Explaining Results: Some Examples

Social scientists—indeed, all people who examine social science results—do not want simply to observe behavior and attitudes; they also want to explain them. In this section, we discuss some basic issues that make these explanations difficult. We use a series of examples to illustrate the problem. These examples raise two major questions that must always be considered when one attempts to explain survey results: (1) Are there other relevant variables that have not been measured or considered and that could explain, fully or in part, the observed results if they had been included? (2) If there is a causal relation between two variables, what is the direction of the causality? Does $A$ cause $B$; or is there an equal probability, or at least some possibility, that $B$ causes $A$; or are $A$ and $B$ mutually interacting (that is, $A$ causes $B$, while simultaneously $B$ causes $A$)?

The same problems that occur in surveys do not occur in experiments, where it is possible to manipulate the order of causality and to control or randomize for extraneous factors. Most surveys are conducted on issues where no experimentation would be possible; therefore, regardless of how well the data are analyzed, there will always be some residual uncertainty. This residual uncertainty is a cause of disagreements among social scientists and is especially responsible for the misuse of surveys to support advocacy positions.

The following examples will, we hope, help readers become alert to possible alternative explanations and to mistrust facile analyses that ignore them. Nevertheless, we hope that readers will not swing completely the other way and refuse to believe any survey results. When all or most other plausible variables have been included in the analysis and the direction of the causality has been thoroughly explored, the explanation should be accepted, at least until it is overturned by new results.

*Example 1: The Use of Asafetida Bags to Prevent Colds.* In the nineteenth century, many schoolchildren wore asafetida bags tied around their necks to prevent colds. These bags contained foul-smelling plants and herbs. Children wearing these bags seemed less likely to get colds than children who did not wear them. This observation demonstrated that the bags gave off medicinal vapors that prevented colds—or did it?

Although this is not really an example of survey analysis, it charmingly illustrates the need to consider other factors. From the perspective of twentieth-century medical knowledge, we are aware that the fumes from the asafetida bags have no medicinal properties. They almost certainly, however, discourage other children or persons from getting too close to the unfortunate wearer and, by thus reducing the risk of contact, reduce the risk of infection.

There are still other possible explanations. Parents who made their children wear asafetida bags were probably more careful in other ways about their children's health and took precautions, such as cleaning the house carefully, making their children wash their hands before meals, and serving more nutritious food. Finally, we are not really certain that children wearing asafetida bags had fewer colds. Having a cold is somewhat subjective, and parents, thinking their child protected, may have been less likely to pay attention to cold symptoms.

We started with this example because no one today would disagree with the analysis. For each of the other examples, however, all based on current survey research, similar kinds of mistaken explanations are observed.

*Example 2: The Effect of Exit Polls on Voting.* In some elections, sample surveys have shown that people who did not vote in the election were more likely to have heard the results of exit polls on television. This finding proves that exit polls reduce the probability of voting—or does it?

Jackson (1983) conducted a survey of voters and nonvoters in a particular election. The voters were asked when they had voted. Nonvoters were asked whether they had heard about exit poll results before the polls closed in their state. From the responses, he estimated the effect of the poll results on voting. That is, if a person had not voted before the first exit poll results were announced, how likely was that person to vote? Jackson concluded that up to 12 percent of voters could have been affected by the early news if they had heard about it. Only about one in six had actually heard the exit poll results.

Jackson assumed that his analysis resembled a natural experiment, with some subjects receiving the news at a time when it could alter their behavior (the experimental group). Unfortunately, he failed to consider that the behavior supposedly affected, voting, might actually have been the cause of whether or not news was heard. That is, a voter was possibly less likely to be at home or someplace else where election news could be heard. Although a relationship may exist between hearing news and voting, the causality is not clear. It could go in both directions; that is, some people did not vote because they heard the exit poll results, while others did not hear the exit poll results because they were voting.

*Example 3: The Effect of Overweight on Success.* A recent survey of 15,000 executives found that those who were "overweight" were paid significantly less than others, the penalty to the obese being in some cases as much as $1,000 a pound (Bowles and Gintis, 1976). Is any other explanation possible?

We do not have the data for this study and are unable to determine whether any other factors were considered. The following questions occur: Is it possible that all or some of the respondents became overweight because they were unsuccessful, rather than the other way around? It is known that many unhappy people use food to compensate for their unhappiness. If persons feel frustrated at work, they might begin to overeat and gain weight. For an unambiguous measure of overweight, one would need to have a weight history and an employment history and to trace them over time. Even here, other factors might need to be considered.

Consider first the size of the community. Suppose that people in smaller communities or rural areas have a greater tendency to be overweight. Also suppose that incomes of executives are lower in these smaller communities and rural areas. Then the apparent relationship between economic success and overweight would vanish with controls for size of community.

Another possible explanation might be the gender of the respondent. It is not clear how overweight was measured, but it could have been a self-report of the respondent. Suppose that, regardless of actual weight, women are more likely to report themselves as being overweight. We also know that women, in general, are paid less than men. Thus, the differences observed could have been gender differences in income rather than differences caused by overweight.

Similarly, income differences could be related to racial differences, regional differences, or educational differences—all of which might also be related to likelihood of being overweight. None of these are mentioned in the brief discussion in the book, but all these plausible alternative explanations would need to be eliminated before one could have any strong belief that lack of economic success is directly caused by overweight.

*Example 4: The Effect of IQ on Economic Success.* Bowles and Gintis (1976, pp. 121–122) make the following claim: "The intergenerational transmission of social and economic status operates primarily via noncognitive mechanisms, despite the fact that the school system rewards higher IQ, an attribute significantly associated with higher socioeconomic background. The unimportance of IQ in explaining the relationship between socioeconomic background and economic success, together with the fact that most of the association between IQ and income can be accounted for by the common association of these variables with education and socioeconomic background, supports our major assertion: IQ is not an important criterion for economic success."

Thus far, we have discussed a series of examples where insufficient attention was given to alternative explanations. In this example, so much attention is paid to alternative explanations that the conclusion (namely, that IQ is not an important criterion for economic success) is not only counterintuitive but also, as we shall show, incorrect. We shall use data provided by Bowles and Nelson (1974) to illustrate this example. The data are taken from the Current Population Survey and are reasonably reliable, although not all information is available and information on parents' social class is always subject to some distortion. In the 1974 paper, Bowles and Nelson propose the causal model shown in Figure 2. This causal model is typical of those that have been used to attempt to determine the achievement process, and we have no quarrel with it. Indeed, the use of causal models is a major improvement over other methods for describing complex multivariate relationships.

In words, the model in Figure 2 simply states the following relationships:

> Adult income and occupational status are related to socioeconomic background, years of schooling, and adult IQ.
> Years of schooling is related to socioeconomic background and childhood IQ.
> Adult IQ is related to childhood IQ and years of schooling.
> Childhood IQ is related to genotypic IQ and socioeconomic background.
> Socioeconomic background and genotypic IQ are mutually related.

Of course, this model does not fully explain income or occupational factors. Indeed, models of achievement typically explain less than half of the total variation. Other unmeasured factors also play significant roles. In this respect, the model is similar to most social science models, which—even at their most powerful—give only partial explanations.

Using multiple regression methods, one can measure the magnitude of the relationships at each step. The relationship between genotypic IQ and childhood IQ cannot be made directly, so it is omitted here. The authors point out that some fraction of childhood IQ is caused by socioeconomic background, but this relationship does not really change their argument. There is also no direct measure of adult IQ, so it is also omitted. A simplified model

**Figure 2. Causal Model of IQ, Socioeconomic Background, Schooling, and Economic Success.**

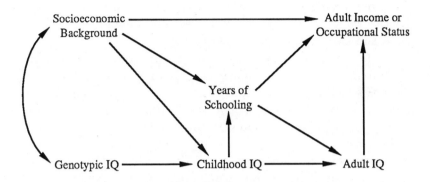

*Notes:* The model applies to people of the same sex, race, and roughly the same age. Additional variables would be required to take account of these important aspects of the income determination process. Arrows indicate the assumed direction of causation. The one double-headed arrow represents statistical association with no implied causation.

*Source:* Bowles and Nelson, 1974, p. 41.

**Figure 3. Simplified Causal Model of IQ, Socioeconomic Background, Schooling, and Occupational Status.[a]**

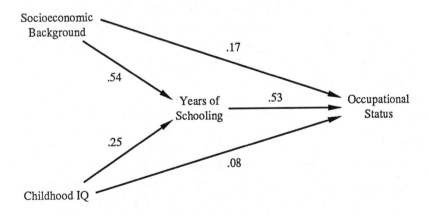

[a]Numbers on lines are normalized regression coefficients.
*Source:* Adapted from Bowles and Nelson, 1974, p. 43.

with estimates for white males aged forty-five to fifty-four is given in Figure 3. The numbers shown on the lines are normalized regression coefficients, and their magnitude is an indication of the relative importance of the different variables. Bowles and Nelson show similar results for other age groups.

In words, what these results say is that both socioeconomic background and childhood IQ are factors in determining how many years of school a person obtains, but socioeconomic background is more important. Years of school is the most important factor in explaining occupational status; the direct effects of socioeconomic status are next in importance, and IQ has the smallest direct effect. Note, however, that both socioeconomic background and IQ have total effects that are the sum of the direct effects and the indirect effects through years of school.

The same result is found for the explanations of adult income, although the exact measures vary, as they do also for different ages. Bowles and Nelson (1974) conclude that socioeconomic background is more important than IQ, but they do not deny that there is an IQ effect.

In their 1976 book, however, Bowles and Gintis choose to present their data in another way—because, they claim, the data are easier to understand in this new presentation. In each case, they show information in twenty bar charts, arranging data in deciles by family socioeconomic background. One of these bar charts is shown in Figure 4. We leave it to the reader to decide whether this figure is easier to read than the earlier figures are. What we want to do is to discuss this figure and try to explain why it seems to show different results, although the data are taken from exactly the same source.

Figure 4 is headed "Educational Attainments Are Strongly Dependent on Social Background Even for People of Similar Childhood IQs." The blank bars (indicating years of school achieved by decile of socioeconomic background) show that years of school rise steadily as one goes from the first to tenth decile on socioeconomic background. The striped bars indicate that this relationship continues to exist even when IQ is controlled for. This figure does *not* demonstrate, however, that IQ is unrelated to schooling. It simply says that socioeconomic background is

**Figure 4. Educational Attainments Are Strongly Dependent on Social
Background Even for People of Similar Childhood IQs.**

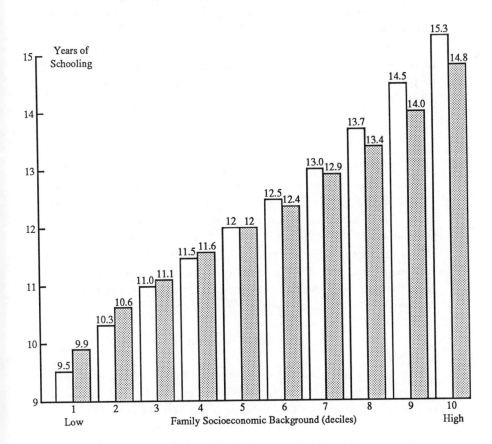

*Notes:* For each socioeconomic group, the left-hand bar indicates
the estimated average number of years of schooling attained by all men
from that group. The right-hand bar indicates the estimated average
number of years of schooling attained by men with IQ scores equal to the
average for the entire sample. The sample refers to "non-Negro" men of
"nonfarm" backgrounds, aged 35–44 years in 1962.
*Source:* Bowles and Gintis, 1976, p. 31.

important. One could equally well construct a figure comparing years of school for persons in different deciles on IQ and note that there was a steady increase in years of school even when socioeconomic background was controlled for.

One can only conclude that Bowles and Gintis presented their results in this format in order to win an argument rather than to provide a complete description of the complex multivariate relationship.

### Summary

The intent of this chapter has been to alert readers to the possible ways in which data analysis may be used to make the results appear favorable to the point of view of those presenting them. For this reason, survey results cannot always be accepted at face value. On the other hand, it would be equally unwise to reject all results just because data are sometimes distorted. Most survey analysis is undistorted and is produced by disinterested researchers. Still, the same warning holds in the marketplace of ideas as in the marketplace for goods and services: *Caveat emptor.*

### Additional Reading

For beginners, we believe that books that give both good and bad examples of uses of statistics are especially helpful. We recommend *Statistics: A Guide to the Unknown* (Tanur and others, 1978); *Statistics: A New Approach* (Wallis and Roberts, 1956); Volume 1 of *Surveying Subjective Phenomena* (Turner and Martin, 1984); and an old classic, *How to Lie with Statistics* (Huff, 1954). Another classic book on straightforward statistical presentation is *Say It with Figures* (Zeisel, 1968).

In addition to these books, some readers may also wish to look at articles in *Public Opinion* and the *Public Opinion Quarterly* for illustrations of how survey data are presented.

# 9

# Understanding Sources of Error

All measurements are subject to error, and surveys, which are a complex form of measurement, are subject to a variety of types of errors. It is rarely, if ever, possible to make an error-free measurement, but authors presenting the results of measurements do not always remind the reader of this fact or spend much time discussing the potential errors in the data. Therefore, the user of survey data needs to understand the sources of error and the limitations that such errors may put on interpretations of the data.

Measurements reported in survey results are best thought of as estimates of some value. For example, if you read in the newspaper that 68 percent of the population support making football the national sport, 24 percent oppose, and 8 percent have no opinion, you should interpret those figures as the researcher's best estimate of the true distribution of opinion on this topic. Sometimes estimates may be given as a range (68 percent plus or minus 3 percent), to acknowledge that there is some known range of error in the estimate; but most often results are given as single figures or point estimates.

The word *error*, as used here in relation to surveys, has two rather distinct meanings. One meaning refers to the precision of the estimate—that is, the width of the range within which the researcher feels confident that the true value lies. Thus, an estimate that 68 percent, plus or minus 2 percent, of the population support making football the national sport is a more precise estimate than one which says that 68 percent, plus or minus 10 percent, of the population support football as the national sport. In both cases, 68 percent is the best estimate, but one is given more precisely than the other. There are a number of factors, to be discussed later in this chapter, that affect the variability of estimates but do not affect the estimates in a systematic fashion.

The second meaning of the word *error* refers to factors that affect estimates in a systematic fashion. Such factors are said to bias the results; that is, they produce results that are systematically different from the true value. The concept of precision is different from the concept of bias or validity. One may have biased results that are quite precise, or unbiased estimates that are not very precise, or any other combination of the two.

Errors in surveys are conventionally divided into sampling and nonsampling errors. Nonsampling errors themselves can be further divided into errors arising from the execution of the sample (for example, by failure to obtain responses from all the respondents selected for the sample, or by failure to obtain the responses to all the items on the questionnaire) and errors caused by other factors (for example, bias in question wording, as discussed in Chapter Seven, or respondents deliberately lying, or interviewers making mistakes in the way questions were asked).

### Sampling Error

As discussed in Chapter Six, sampling is a process by which members of a larger population are selected according to known rules of probability that enable measurements on the sample to be used to estimate the values as if they had been taken on the entire population. Since sampling is a process based on rules of probability, many different samples could be drawn to estimate population values. Thus, if a researcher were selecting a sample of 1,000 adults out of a population of 200 million, there are many possible combinations of a thousand people who could constitute a probability sample of the adult population, even if the researcher did not allow anyone to be in more than one sample.

The concept of sampling error is possible to grasp intuitively. Suppose one took ten samples, each consisting of a thousand different persons selected according to probabilistic rules, and asked them the question about football as the national sport. It is unlikely that the proportion supporting football as the national sport would be exactly the same in each of the ten samples. This difference between repeated samples is what we mean by sampling error. We know from sampling theory that, if the samples are properly drawn, the probability that an observed proportion will be larger than the true proportion is the same as that it will be smaller than the true proportion. We also know that, as the sample sizes and number of replications increase, the mean of the estimates from the different samples will converge on the true proportion for the population. By extension, as the size of a single sample increases, the estimate of a value such as a mean or proportion based on the sample values will usually get closer and closer to the true value in the population. The rate at which this convergence occurs, however, is not a straight-line function of sample size but rather is a function of the square root of the sample size. Thus, after a certain point, increasing the sample size yields less and less in increased precision and is not worth the extra cost in taking the larger sample.

Sampling error always exists, unless one conducts a census, but it is error in the sense of lack of precision rather than bias and can be reduced when the sample size is increased. It is possible to estimate a range of values that will include the true value with a specified probability, calculated on the basis of the sample observations and the size of the sample. This range of values is usually referred to as the "confidence limit" or the "margin of error" in surveys. Confidence limits exist at many different levels of confidence, the most common ones used being the 95 percent and 99 percent confidence levels. Thus, a statement that 68 percent of the population favors football as the national sport, with a 95 percent confidence level (or margin of error) of plus or minus 3 percent based on a sample of 1,000 persons, means that we are 95 percent confident that the true value in the population, if we were to do a complete census, would be between 65 and 71 percent. If we wanted to be more confident of the result, we would have to extend the range—so that, for example, in this case, we could be 99 percent confident that the range 63.5–72.5 percent would include the true value for the population. On the other hand, we would have zero confidence that the value would be *exactly* 68 percent or any other exact percentage.

Although there is a relationship between the size of the sample and the width of the confidence limits, there is no relationship between the proportion the sample is of the population (except in some instances where the sample is larger than 25 percent of the population) and the size of the confidence limits. It is commonly believed that the larger the population, the larger the sample size must be in order to achieve the same level of precision. A sample of the size 1,000 can estimate the value as precisely for a population of 100 million as for a population of 100,000 or 10,000. Except when the sample size is greater than 25 percent of the population size, the only aspect of the population that affects the width of confidence limits is the heterogeneity or variability of the population.

### Sample Bias

As we have seen, the concept of sampling error applies to the precision of estimates rather than to bias or error in the second sense of the term. Bias enters samples when the samples are not picked by means of probabilistic rules or when there is failure to obtain data from some members of the sample. Bias in samples is more difficult to quantify because its measurement depends on knowing the true values in the population, values that are often unknown and must be estimated from the sample. For samples of the United States population, many characteristics of the population are known through census data, so that characteristics of the sample distributions can be matched through known characteristics of the population. When such population characteristics are known, biases in these characteristics in the sample can be corrected by appropriate weighting, so that the distribution of these characteristics in the sample will match those in the population. Such weighting, however, cannot correct for all biases in the sample. The degree to which weighting according to such known characteristics as sex, race, age, education, and geographical region of the country actually corrects potential biases in the data for other characteristics is dependent on the assumption that these characteristics are the important ones affecting the distribution of opinions that are being measured.

In practice, bias in samples comes from two major sources. The first is failure to obtain interviews (or responses to all questions) from all the respondents in the sample—that is, the degree to which the completion rate is less than 100 percent. In practice, no sample survey can obtain data from all respondents. Some will be unavailable during the interview period, some cannot be found or contacted, and some will refuse to cooperate. While surveys sponsored by the federal government, such as those conducted by the Bureau of the Census or sponsored by some of the major federal statistical agencies, obtain completion rates from 85 to 95 percent, most other surveys have considerably lower completion rates. Commercial or low-budget surveys often have completion rates of 30–40 percent and occasionally, particularly with mail surveys, even lower completion rates. While it is arguable whether surveys with completion rates as low as 30 or 40 percent can be corrected through weighting, many surveys do rely heavily on weighting to correct for deficiencies in completion rates. Survey reports rarely mention the actual completion rate and the amount of weighting done to correct the data, but such information is absolutely necessary; without it, we cannot evaluate a survey for potential error or limitations in interpretations.

As pointed out in Chapter Six (in the section headed "Really Terrible Sampling"), a more serious type of bias in surveys occurs when probability sampling methods are abandoned altogether and the researcher depends on convenience samples; that is, when samples are picked because individuals happen to be easy to interview or because they have volunteered to participate in the survey. Such "surveys" are frequently conducted among the readers of newspapers or magazines; constituents of members of Congress; or those tuned in to a particular television program, who may be asked to call a special number to register their opinions about some question that is posed on the program. Because responses to those "surveys" are often very large, in the tens or hundreds of thousands, it is difficult for people to believe that they do not have some validity. How can a sample of a few hundred possibly be more valid than a "sample" of 50,000 or 100,000? Besides the fact that, in such self-selected polls, individuals can send in multiple responses, the principal problem is that respondents are selecting themselves rather than being selected according to probabilistic rules. When respondents select themselves to participate in surveys, rather than being selected by an impersonal method, there is a very real possibility that their interest in participating in the survey is prompted by their views on particular topics; and such a correlation between their views and their decision to participate will seriously distort the distribution of the responses.

In the following "dial-in poll" conducted by a major television network, the effects of self-selection can be seen clearly because at the same time a telephone survey with a randomly selected set of households was conducted by the network's polling organization. The dial-in poll was conducted in the fall of 1983 after a controversy about whether the United States should make financial contributions to the United Nations. The question asked was: "Should the United Nations continue to be based in the United States?" The "dial-in" produced over 185,000 calls; 33 percent said that the United Nations should continue to be in the United States, and 67 percent said it should not. In the telephone survey, where respondents were picked by probability methods, the results were 72 percent in favor of continuation and 28 percent opposed, based on a sample of about 1,000 respondents.

In this example, we can see that the viewers of the program who were phoning in their opinions were a very biased sample and had quite different opinions from the nation as a whole. Although the report of this experiment does not give sufficient information about possible biases in the telephone random sample because of noncompletion of calls or how much weighting there is in the reported data to correct for these biases, this source of bias will be relatively small compared with that of self-selection. When samples consist of those who are self-selected, larger sample sizes may well result in greater rather than less bias and a larger rather than a smaller error. This is the lesson that was learned in 1936, when the *Literary Digest*—on the basis of more than 2 million returns— predicted that Alfred Landon would win the 1936 election against Franklin Roosevelt, whereas Roper, Gallup, and other pioneers in scientific surveys, using what would now be considered rather crude sampling methods, correctly predicted the election on the basis of samples of a few thousand. It is a lesson, however, that apparently has to be learned over and over again.

## Nonsampling Errors

There is no comparable theory of nonsampling error paralleling the concept of sampling error. In this section, we will discuss a number of sources of nonsampling error; but such errors cannot be quantified unless experimental variations are built into the actual studies, and such experiments are rarely done except for explicitly methodological purposes. All we can do in this section is to alert readers to some of the most common problems, so that they may be sensitive to possible sources of error when reading reports of surveys.

We noted earlier that surveys are concerned with two distinct types of data: factual data, for which there are, in principle, true values that may be checked by outside observers; and data about psychological states, such as thoughts, feelings, beliefs, and opinions, which are not directly verifiable by anyone other than the respondent. Error in the sense of precision or variability is a term that can be applied to both types of data. Bias, however, in the sense of a systematic departure from some "true" value, is technically applicable only to factual or behavioral data that have, in principle, true values. For subjective states, there is no "true value"; bias must be defined by the purposes of the study or by the theoretical views of the researcher rather than by some external criterion. While it is more nearly correct to speak of response effects rather than response errors, for purposes of easy exposition, we shall refer to all these types of nonsampling errors as response errors.

The data collection process in surveys has three distinct elements: the questionnaire itself, which provides not only the stimuli but also the categories or form in which the responses are to be made; the interviewer and data processing operations by which the responses are recorded and put into a form that can be tabulated by computers; and the respondent, who provides the answers to questions asked. Each of these elements may be contributing factors to response errors.

*The Questionnaire.* In Chapter Seven, we discussed the importance of questionnaire wording for collecting the data appropriate for the research questions to be addressed in a particular survey. We noted there some of the ways in which question wording can affect the distribution of answers. Question-wording effects can be the greatest single source of bias in surveys. Some of the more blatant forms of bias in wording are obvious to all but the most committed respondents and thus are avoided by most people who make up questionnaires. Some of the subtler forms of bias in question wording are presented in Chapter Seven. The reader should review that chapter in the context of this chapter's discussion of measurement errors. There are, however, a few other aspects of form and order of questions that contribute to response errors.

The order in which questions are asked may create a context for interpreting them; therefore, when the order is changed, the context—and hence the respondents' interpretation—also may change. One type of order effect may appear when there are logical implications between questions. Because people generally want to appear consistent in their attitudes, their responses to a series of questions may be more consistent than they would be if the questions were scattered or asked independently. For example, a question that asks about attitudes toward import quotas for goods from Japan may influence responses to a question about Japanese policy on import quotas for goods from America. Typically, when the question that has the most support ("It's all right for the United States to put restrictions on imports from Japan") comes first, it will increase the support for the less-endorsed question ("It's all right for Japan to put restrictions on imports from the United States"). When the order of the questions is reversed, the responses are not affected. Since neither order is obviously the correct one, a way to handle this problem is to use two forms of the questionnaire and to reverse the order of the questions on each form. If there are no differences in response, the results from the two forms can be combined. If there are differences, they would need to be described and interpreted.

Order also appears to affect the interpretation of questions about topics that have both general and specific aspects. That is, responses may differ depending on whether questions about the specifics come before or after questions about the general phenomenon. For example, a general question about a woman's right to have an abortion is affected by whether it comes before or after questions about a woman's right to have an abortion under specific conditions—for example, when the mother's life is in danger, when the fetus is defective, or when the pregnancy was the result of rape. Here again, the effect seems to be asymmetrical, with only the general question being affected. More respondents will express support for abortion when the general question is asked alone or before the questions about abortions under specific conditions. The questions about the specific conditions do not appear to be affected by the placement of the general question about abortion.

An explanation for this order effect is suggested by the norms of natural conversation. In a natural conversation, questioners ask only for the information they need, and respondents give answers that are not redundant, or the back and forth of the conversation can clarify any apparent redundancies. In a series of survey questions about abortion, respondents may assume that, when the researcher asks further questions, he is seeking information that has not already been obtained. Therefore, when a general question about abortion comes at the end of a list of attitudes about abortion under specific conditions (rather than at the beginning of the list), respondents may interpret the question as excluding these specific conditions. When the conditions are excluded, support for abortion is reduced (Schuman and Presser, 1981).

Some surveys ask about a number of instances of a similar type. For instance, the respondent is shown a list of magazines or of potential presidential candidates and is asked about each item on the list. When such a list becomes long, the order of the items on the list may become important. Items near the beginning of the list may be read or listened to more carefully than items later in the list. Items placed near the beginning of the list tend to get the most favorable responses, and items in the middle of the list get the least favorable responses. When list order may be a problem, careful researchers use two or more forms of the list and randomize the order on the various forms (Becker, 1954).

Order effects can be quite substantial (sometimes as high as 10–20 percentage points) and can substantially alter one's interpretation of the data. For example, when the general question about abortion is asked by itself or before the questions about abortion under specific conditions, one would conclude that a majority of Americans are in favor of abortion. When it is asked after the questions about specific conditions, one would conclude that a majority are against abortion in general. Since questions have to be asked in some order, the existence of order effects presents a dilemma for the pollster. Empirical studies of the existence and magnitude of order effects and the judicious use of split ballots can help pollsters resolve such problems.

*Interviewer Effects.* Interviewers have long been thought of as a possible source of error in interviews. The most obvious possibility is that interviewers may, in fact, falsify the interviews in part or in whole and just make up the answers on their own. Since face-to-face interviewers work by themselves with only indirect supervision, "curbstoning," as it is called in the trade, is an ever present worry for survey organizations. Good survey organizations therefore engage in validation procedures. That is, someone in the organization will recontact some of the respondents to verify that the interview actually took place and to verify the answers to a sample of questions.

With the advent of centralized telephone interviewing, supervision of interviewers has become much easier. Typically, telephone-interviewing installations are constructed so that supervisors can monitor interviews on a random basis without the interviewer's knowledge. Thus, a supervisor can monitor the work of interviewers almost continuously and identify interviewers who are asking questions improperly or appear to be acting in a way that will bias answers.

Good training and supervision of interviewers is essential to reliable data collection. Studies of interviewer effects indicate that interviewer behavior, particularly that of inexperienced or untrained interviewers, usually increases the variability of responses rather than producing a bias; that is, they tend to add some "noise" to the data. Even then, however, controlled studies indicate that interviewers make a rather small contribution to the variability of the data.

There is one dramatic exception to the generalization that well-trained and well-supervised interviewers do not make significant contributions to response bias. This exception occurs in instances where characteristics of the interviewers and of the respondents are related to the content of the questions. For example, when questions about race relations are being asked, the race of the interviewer may contribute to response bias if the respondent is a member of a different race. To a lesser extent, a similar interaction is found between the gender of the interviewer and of the respondent for questions related to sexual behavior and attitudes. Matching the race of the interviewer and the respondent appears to be important only when the topic is about racial relations. Similarly, matching the gender of the respondent and the interviewer seems to be important only when the topic is about sex.

Readers may be surprised to learn that interviewers are a relatively small source of response errors, particularly in light of the many horror stories about falsification of interviews. It is obvious that interviewers can contribute enormously to response error if they act improperly. The conclusion about the relatively small impact of interviewers is valid only if the interviewers are well trained and supervised by the survey organization. When quality control through supervision breaks down, interviewers may contribute so much error that the survey is totally worthless. A survey organization's reputation depends on quality control.

*Respondent Effects.* "How do you know the respondent isn't lying?" is a question that is frequently asked of pollsters. The specter of respondents deliberately misleading researchers is one that haunts survey organizations. For a number of reasons, however, respondents in general do not tend to lie about their opinions or behavior. First, participation in interviews is voluntary, and respondents are free to (and do) refuse to participate in surveys. Second, respondents are approached in a way that suggests that they have something worth hearing and that the interview provides an opportunity for them to make their views known to the larger world. Finally, if questionnaires are well constructed and the interviewers are well trained, respondents are put at their ease and can go through the interview with a minimum of irritation and frustration. Thus, respondents seem to enjoy a well-conducted interview in which they can talk about things of interest to them.

Apart from badly designed questionnaires and poorly trained interviewers, the major problem facing the pollster regards questions that may have socially desirable or undesirable answers. If respondents are approached in a serious manner by a courteous interviewer, they can be motivated to participate responsibly in a survey. However, their desire to be good respondents and answer questions as fully and as truthfully as possible may conflict with their desire to present themselves in a good light to the interviewer. Such a conflict may arise when respondents are asked sensitive questions—for instance, about illegal or embarrassing behavior. In these instances, well-trained interviewers adopt a number of techniques to reduce respondents' fears of appearing to be odd or deficient in some way. They are trained to ask these questions as if they are standard questions, to give no indication of nervousness, and to record all responses as if they are perfectly legitimate and well within the interviewer's range of experience. Questionnaire designers also have a number of techniques at their disposal to try to reduce the apparent social desirability of different answers to questions. We discuss these techniques in *Asking Questions* (Sudman and Bradburn, 1982, chap. 3).

There remain, however, considerable individual differences in the degree to which people are sensitive to the opinions of others, even strangers such as interviewers, and their desire to appear in a socially desirable stance. On surveys dealing with sensitive topics, questions are sometimes put in to try to measure the degree to which individuals are prone to give socially acceptable answers regardless of their true opinions or behavior. These techniques are still controversial, and there is, no doubt, still a considerable amount of misreporting on surveys involving extremely sensitive topics. (For a discussion of some of these techniques, see Bradburn, Sudman, and Associates, 1979, chap. 6.)

In recent years, some newspaper columnists, who believe that polls are too powerful, have suggested that respondents should lie about their voting intentions when called by pollsters. The evidence to date is that none of these campaigns to undermine the accuracy of polls by encouraging deliberate lying has had a measurable effect on election polls.

Of course, respondents may contribute to response error in ways other than by deliberately lying. Sometimes they may have no real opinion about an issue but will still select a response from those offered when there is no explicit "no opinion" or "don't know" category. For this reason, we have strongly suggested in Chapter Seven that attitude questions provide for an explicit "don't know" category. In addition, in response to questions about behaviors in the past, respondents may simply have forgotten what they or other family members did or bought. Finally, they may misinterpret the question, either because they did not understand some of the language or because they were not paying sufficient attention. If the question is an open-ended one, the respondent may not be able to express his opinion clearly enough so that it is intelligible to the interviewer or researcher. All these factors may contribute to response errors even though the respondent is not deliberately lying. Again, many of these sources of error can be minimized by careful questionnaire construction and thorough training of interviewers, who should be alert to the possibility that respondents do not understand the questions. Interviewers then probe the response to make sure that respondents have really understood the question as it was intended.

## Summary

In this chapter, we have surveyed a number of sources of response errors that may threaten the reliability or validity of surveys. A large literature in survey methodology has addressed many of these sources of error, and researchers have made considerable progress toward improving measurements.

Potential sources of bias, such as question wording and question order, which might appear to produce so much error in polls as to undermine their credibility, fortunately do not affect all respondents to the same degree. When respondents have well-developed attitudes—that is, when issues have been discussed for a long time and people have made up their minds—responses are relatively insensitive to wording effects. On the other hand, on issues that are new to the public agenda or are not salient to the public, many respondents may not have well-developed attitudes of their own. They are thus more likely to look to the question wording for cues to help them make judgments. In these cases, question-wording effects may be substantial.

The purpose of this chapter has been to make readers aware of some of the principal limitations to interpreting survey data and, we hope, to make them more critical consumers of poll data. Even though we have discussed a number of sources of error, the reader should not conclude that surveys are so hopelessly error prone that we can learn nothing from them. Many sources of error work in opposite directions and tend to cancel out one another. Many of the error types contribute to decreased precision of estimates but do not contribute importantly to overall bias. However, a user of polls taken at different times should be cautious about concluding that differences between them indicate a real trend. Only when method-ological differences do not exist or can be ignored is it possible to make statements about changes in the real world that are not simply artifacts. And, finally, it cannot be emphasized too much that many surveys are well done and many are poorly done. Only when users learn how to tell the difference and to demand that surveys be done well will the average level of surveys improve.

## Additional Reading

A short introduction to measurement error that is a little more technical than the material in this chapter is Bradburn's "Response Effects" in the *Handbook of Survey Research* (Rossi, Wright, and Anderson, 1983). A much more extensive discussion is presented in our earlier books *Response Effects in Surveys* (Sudman and Bradburn, 1974) and *Improving Interview Method and Questionnaire Design* (Bradburn, Sudman, and Associates, 1979).

*Questions and Answers in Attitude Surveys* (Schuman and Presser, 1981) contains an excellent summary of experimental work on attitude questions. An extensive discussion of measurement problems appears in *Surveying Subjective Phenomena* (Turner and Martin, 1984).

# 10

# Should Polls Be Banned?

The wide and growing use of polls and opinion surveys and the general public's willingness to participate in polls have not quieted the critics of the polls. Some people still argue that polls should be banned or greatly restricted. Obviously, we do not share this view, nor do most people. In response to poll questions, overwhelming majorities of respondents indicate that they enjoyed the experience and thought that the time spent was worthwhile (Sharp and Frankel, 1981). The possibility of restrictions, however, is not purely a theoretical issue. Opinion polls are already severely restricted during the final weeks of elections in several European countries, and there have been attempts to do the same in several states—including California, Maryland, and Washington. Some communities have banned or attempted to ban face-to-face interviewing, and there is some discussion about restricting telephone interviewing as well. The American Association for Public Opinion Research was sufficiently concerned about this legislative activity that it set up a Committee on the Regulation of Survey Research in 1985.

Critics who favor restricting polls and surveys give four major reasons for their position: (1) Voting polls unduly and unfairly influence the electoral process, either causing voters to change their minds or to refrain from voting entirely. (2) Polls invade the privacy of persons who do not wish to be bothered, and the data revealed to interviewers are sometimes used to harm the respondent. (3) The polls do a disservice to the democratic process by oversimplying the issues and placing too much pressure on elected officials. (4) The polls are so unreliable that the results they publish are meaningless. We discuss each of these charges in detail.

Although we oppose the regulation of legitimate polls, we are well aware that polls have been used for illegal or unethical purposes. We end this chapter with a description of some of the most common of these phony polls and indicate what is being done and what might be done to eliminate them.

### Do Polls Unduly Influence Elections?

In discussing whether polls unduly influence elections, one must distinguish between preelection polls and the network exit polls that are conducted on election day so that predictions can be made early on the night of an election. Both preelection polls and exit polls have been attacked, primarily by candidates or political parties in local areas who have lost close elections. If the poll results had not been reported, critics claim, the election results would have changed. Sometimes, but not usually, there are additional concerns if the poll results do not predict the election with sufficient accuracy.

Is there any truth to the claim that polls influence elections? If the question is asked in this form, the answer must be "Yes, polls and many other things influence elections." What must be determined is the magnitude of the effect. Let us consider the preelection and exit polls separately over a range of elections.

*Preelection Polls: Effects on Turnout.* It has been observed, to no one's surprise, that close elections increase turnout, all else being equal. Information on the closeness of an election is provided mainly by the preelection polls, although the exit polls also provide information to some potential late voters. Thus, the effect of the preelection polls depends on the situation. If the polls predict a close election, they encourage voter participation and increase turnout. If they predict a runaway race, potential voters either may not vote at all or may ignore parts of the ballot while voting other parts. Voting or not also depends on the importance of the office. Thus, among registered voters, the closeness of the race will produce only minor changes in turnout in the vote for president of the United States, but closeness has greater influence as the office becomes less critical to the voter.

Many factors besides closeness influence the decision to vote: weather, campaign activity, the attractiveness of the candidates, to name a few. Perhaps most important is the decision to register, which could, at most, be only slightly influenced by preelection polls. Thus, banning preelection polls would be very unlikely to increase voter turnout and might well have the opposite effect.

The absence of polls would not, in itself, lead to the absence of news about the closeness of an election unless there is also a complete news blackout, since reporters and political experts would make forecasts as they did before polls were introduced. At least in the United States, it is very difficult to see how laws banning the publication of preelection poll results could be held constitutional, since these laws appear to violate First Amendment rights of free speech.

*Bandwagon Effects.* Almost everyone loves to be on the winning side, and it is claimed that polls persuade voters to change their votes, especially when their candidate is far behind. The data gathered to support this claim have been very weak, although again we would agree that some voters may at some times have chosen to vote for the favorite on the basis of poll results. Again, there will be little reason to expect a bandwagon effect if the polls predict a close election. Even if one candidate is slightly ahead, voters would be unlikely to switch on the basis of the poll results, since there is now sufficient recognition that polls do not always predict perfectly.

The main bandwagon effect should be observed when one candidate is reported substantially ahead of the other(s). Even here, many voters will vote counter-bandwagon to reduce the leading candidate's margin of victory, so that the candidate does not regard his or her victory as a "mandate" and thereby become less responsive to constituent views. On the other hand, undecided voters and voters who only weakly favor another candidate may vote for the leader so that they can be on the winning side. Because of the differing situations and the countervailing forces, no strong bandwagon effects have been found, although some researchers have shown weak effects (Aldrich, 1980, chap. 5).

The greatest concern arises when a poll showing a candidate far ahead is in error, either deliberately or inadvertently. Then the actual outcome of the election may be affected by the incorrect poll data. Indeed, this is a stratagem adopted by candidates and parties who publish their own poll results in an effort to influence an election. The media polls cannot deliberately slant their results for long and remain credible, especially if there are multiple polls covering the same election.

One effect that the polls do have is on the amount of money contributed to a candidate's campaign. Especially in primary elections, candidates who receive low poll ratings find it difficult to raise funds and frequently drop out of the running. Even in national presidential elections, it has been alleged that poll results influence contributions. In a close election, some contributors may make donations to both parties, whereas they contribute only to the winner in a runaway race. As an example, it was claimed that Hubert Humphrey's poor showing in the early polls in 1968 made it very difficult for him to raise money for television advertising. This lack of funds might well have contributed to his loss in what was ultimately a close race.

In the absence of polls, voters would be left to the mercies of the candidates, parties, and political pundits to give them a sense of how the race was proceeding. Although polls may have their problems, they are clearly more accurate and unbiased than these alternative sources.

*Exit Polls.* There has been much greater criticism leveled against exit polls than against the preelection polls. In the past, on the assumption that later voters would behave like early voters, some stations made projections of elections even before the polls closed for a state or locality. Currently, all the networks have agreed not to make projections for a given area until the polls in that area close. There is still, of course, the possibility that reports from areas where the polls close early (the eastern areas of the United States) can affect later poll results from the West Coast—but only if the exit poll results differ from the preelection polls. If they do not differ, then prospective voters would have no reason to change their intended behavior. They would either vote or not, and if they voted, they would vote for the candidate whom they intended to vote for.

If the exit polls differed from the preelection polls, persons who had not voted when they heard the results could still change their minds. If the exit polls predicted a close election, persons who had not planned to vote would be encouraged to vote. If a runaway election were predicted from the exit polls, some people might not vote who had intended to vote. Their failure to vote would clearly not affect the runaway election but could have a small effect on other races on the same ballot. For example, the 1980 presidential election had been predicted close by most polls, but the exit polls predicted a strong victory for Ronald Reagan. Some analyses done by one of us (Sudman, 1986) suggest that about 1–5 percent of voters on the West Coast might have been affected. Even if only a few voters actually changed their behavior, many voters on the West Coast felt that the value of their vote had been diminished because results from other areas were known with a high degree of certainty before West Coast polling places closed.

Most of the critics of exit polls suggest that the release of exit poll results be delayed until all polls close everywhere. However, a delay of this sort would essentially eliminate their usefulness to the networks for election-night news coverage; therefore, these polls probably would not be funded, although the results are reported the next day in major newspapers and are used extensively by political scientists and students of elections because they provide information on why people voted as they did and the social characteristics of voters for the different candidates. The networks have vigorously resisted additional restrictions on broadcasting of exit poll results, again claiming First Amendment rights.

A few communities have challenged exit polls because they destroy the sanctity of the ballot box. To date, the courts have rejected these challenges. It must be remembered, moreover, that participation in the exit polls is purely voluntary on the part of the voter and that most voters are eager to participate.

Although we oppose restrictions on exit polls, we recognize that the case in their favor is weaker than the case for the preelection polls. In addition to their news value, many political scientists think that the preelection polls increase the overall public awareness of and interest in elections and thus encourage rather than inhibit political participation. The same argument cannot be made for the exit polls, except in a retrospective sense. We believe, however, that those who are concerned about political alienation might better spend their time revising the election methods so that all polls are open at the same time. It is the wide range of poll-closing hours that is primarily responsible for feelings by some voters that because they voted late their vote didn't count.

### Do Polls Invade People's Privacy?

Concerns about government invasions of privacy peaked in the United States during the Watergate hearings, but invasion of privacy has continued to be an issue ever since. These concerns are even stronger in Europe. The major concern is that high-speed computers and administrative data bases enable government officials to obtain detailed information about individuals that can be used against them. For a time, little distinction was made between these administrative data bases and sample surveys, but it is now generally recognized that most surveys do not place respondents at any undue risk of loss of privacy.

There are three major distinctions between administrative records and most surveys:

1. The topics of most surveys deal with innocuous attitudes and behavior.
2. Respondents can refuse to answer any questions and can distort answers in socially desirable directions, as we noted in Chapter Nine.
3. The ethical codes of survey organizations require that data be summarized and not revealed at an identifiable level. Names and addresses of respondents usually are separated from data as

soon as processing is completed, and these identifiers are destroyed as soon as there is no need for them. If the identifiers must be retained for future interviewing, survey organizations keep them in secure places and limit access to those who are fielding the study.

A very small fraction of all surveys do present serious privacy issues. Some examples from the past illustrate the problem. A social researcher conducted a survey among members of a teenage gang in Chicago. Later the results of that survey were subpoenaed by a prosecutor, who used some of the data to attempt to prove that members of the gang had fraudulently obtained government funds. Similarly, a prosecutor in New Jersey attempted to subpoena survey results (in this case, from the Income Maintenance Experiment conducted by Mathematica Policy Research) in order to determine whether any of the participants in that experiment were defrauding the government. The judge refused to subpoena the questionnaires because the prosecutor had not established sufficient grounds for the search and granting the subpoena would almost certainly destroy a very large and important experiment.

In general, the types of surveys that raise serious confidentiality issues have the following characteristics: (1) The topic deals with behavior that is potentially illegal or, at the least, could cause harmful consequences to the respondent, such as loss of work or expulsion from school. (2) The population is limited and well defined (for example, a group of employees at a firm or a group of students at a specific school), so that personal identification is possible. (3) The study requires that personal identifiers be retained for a considerable time, either for future reinterviews or so that data may be validated. Even in these special cases, it is possible to conduct surveys and retain respondent confidentiality, but special steps are necessary. For federally funded projects on sensitive issues, federal regulations now enable researchers to obtain an explicit exemption from any possible subpoena by demonstrating the value of the study for policy purposes. Researchers without this exemption have made arrangements to send identifying information outside the United States to Canada or Europe to prevent the possibility of subpoenas. It is our impression that, as a result of these actions, there have been no recent efforts to subpoena any survey data.

Some guardians of public privacy, however, would go far beyond the issues that we have been discussing and would attempt to prevent interviewers from knocking on doors or calling on the telephone without prior consent in writing of the respondent. They attempt to link surveys with door-to-door or telephone selling efforts and argue that a community has a right to ban these activities if it chooses to do so. Pollsters, of course, have been vigorously opposed to such efforts and have almost always been successful in making clear the distinction between legitimate polls and selling efforts. Polling organizations are especially concerned about sales efforts disguised as polls, since they blur the distinction between seeking information and attitudes and selling. We believe that any efforts to bar survey interviews would almost certainly violate First Amendment rights to freedom of speech.

All survey organizations recognize, however, that the respondent has a right to refuse to be interviewed and that substantial numbers exercise that right on every survey. Interviewers seek only the opportunity to explain the survey, so that the respondent can decide whether or not to participate. In this connection, survey organizations are faced with two ethical and practical issues: how much to tell the respondent about the interview in advance and how hard to press for cooperation. At one time, many in the survey community strongly believed that respondents should be told all about the study before starting the interview. They soon found that most respondents became impatient with the long explanations and wanted to get on with the interview. The current thinking is to make the introduction reasonably short and to provide additional information in the body of the interview as necessary. In most cases, the purpose of the questionnaire is immediately evident, and long explanations are not needed or wanted.

Some pollsters still are uncertain whether to tell the respondent how long the interview will last. If the interview is standard and does not have much branching, so that the length of the interview is known, we believe that the respondent should be told. If it is a long interview, respondents need to know whether they have the time available to respond at the time of the contact. If not, the interviewer can arrange for the interview at a more convenient time. If there is substantial branching, however, the interviewer will not know in advance how long the interview will last. In this case, the respondent can only be told that "it will depend on what your answers are."

High-quality survey organizations attempt to improve the quality of their sample cooperation by persuading initial refusers to cooperate. Generally, about one-third of initial refusers will cooperate at a different time with a different (usually more skilled) interviewer. These reinterview attempts are made very selectively to people who give "soft" refusals, such as "I'm too busy now." "Hard" refusals, such as "I don't want to be bothered" or "I never give interviews," are not contacted again. There is a fine line between making additional efforts and harassing a potential respondent. Sensible researchers make every effort to avoid harassment, since it can only backfire in the future.

*Effects of Painful Questions on Respondents' Emotional Health.* Critics allege that some questions asked in surveys can actually cause respondents acute distress or illness. Thus, asking people to report on a painful event, such as the illness or death of a loved one, can again open psychic wounds that have healed. We are not aware that this has ever happened, although we would not deny the possibility. Because the survey is under control of the respondent, it is highly unlikely that such a situation would continue beyond an initial painful question or that the interview would be significantly different from questions or comments the respondent would be exposed to in the course of normal daily activities. On the other side of the coin, survey researchers are frequently told by respondents that the interview has been therapeutic. Many people find it helpful to talk about a painful event with a sympathetic listener.

*Confidentiality: Protection for Groups.* Some social scientists believe that they always owe confidentiality protection to groups as well as individuals. Thus, they would never reveal the names of the organizations, the neighborhoods, or even the cities where the study was conducted. The issue is more complex than that. There are times when confidentiality should be maintained, but there are other times when it is useful or even vital to reveal the group names. Several factors need to be considered: Was confidentiality promised? Was information obtained from individuals about themselves or from informants reporting about the group? Could revealing the name of the group make it possible to identify either individuals within the group or the informant?

At one end of the spectrum, a researcher conducting surveys in which a small number of profit-making organizations are asked about their current and planned activities would certainly need to promise and maintain confidentiality, in order to prevent their competitors from gaining useful information. At the other end of the spectrum, a researcher conducting household interviews on purchasing behavior in one or a few cities is not required to conceal the names of the cities. If the users of such a study are intended to generalize from it to a broader population, they will need to know the places where the study was conducted so that they can make judgments about the quality of the sample. That is, one must balance the need for information to determine data quality with the potential harm to individuals and groups.

Let us spell out some suggestions on cases that fall between these extremes. If group confidentiality was promised, in order to obtain cooperation or for any other reason, the researcher should, of course, keep the promise. If the information was obtained from informants and is so detailed that some readers of the study would be able to guess who provided the information, then the group name should be suppressed. Similarly, if the group is sufficiently small so that information about the group might lead to disclosure about individuals, group information should be suppressed.

There is also an implicit promise of confidentiality to organizations that are selected as parts of large national probability samples. Thus, a university that makes its list of students available for a national study of college seniors' career choices expects that analyses will be by university type rather than by specific institutions. For example, an analysis might compare students in private research universities with those in public institutions, but not the students at the University of Chicago with those at the University of Illinois. There is no objection, however, to listing the schools that participated in a discussion of the sample design.

Generally, when information is obtained from individuals in households about their own attitudes and behavior, and the responses are then combined to provide group information, we see no need to promise or provide group confidentiality in addition to individual confidentiality, if the sample sizes are sufficient to maintain individual confidentiality. We do not believe that data should be suppressed simply because the results are unfavorable to any public figure, institution, or group. The fact that citizens of a city think the mayor has done a bad job should not be grounds for suppressing the name of that city. The fact that most of the residents of a neighborhood see problems in their neighborhood should not be grounds for suppressing the name of the neighborhood. The fact that an ethnic group is described unfavorably in some way should not be grounds for suppressing data about that group.

We believe the researcher should vigorously resist any effort of community or group leaders to censor results that they fear may have a harmful effect on their communities or groups. The ultimate use to which a survey will be put is always uncertain. What is certain is that censorship of negative results destroys the researcher's independence and credibility. Individual respondents deserve confidentiality; the community or group does not.

## Do Polls Oversimplify Issues?

Since the earliest days of the polls, critics have accused them of oversimplifying the issues and presenting simplistic perspectives. As an example of this concern, here is a quote from TRB in the *New Republic* (Sept. 30, 1985, p. 4):

### VOX POP CROCK

The usual complaint about polls is that they lead to democratic excess. They put representative government on too short a leash. Perpetually informed of what the voters think on every issue, politicians follow instead of leading. My complaint is different. Polls undermine democracy, even here where we have real elections. That's because polls don't measure public opinion. They create it, often with building blocks of ignorance, prejudice, and simple muddle. Worse, they reinforce the impression among voters and politicians alike that untethered opinion is what democracy is about.

Some polls solemnly report people's opinions about the unknowable. A *Washington Post*/ABC News poll in July revealed that 54 percent of Americans don't expect President Reagan's cancer to recur before he leaves office. Thirty-three percent think it will recur, and only 12 percent have no opinion. According to a poll taken by *Newsweek* in August, 52 percent of the public now believes that an AIDS epidemic among the general population is either "very likely" or "somewhat likely." The more you know about cancer or AIDS, the more you know that the correct answer to these questions is "don't know." Yet only a few courageous citizens dare to have no opinion. It seems almost unpatriotic.

Equally silly and more nefarious are questions like: "Do you think most poor people are lazy or do you think most poor people are hard-working?" Thus a *Los Angeles Times* poll last April. Perhaps it's reassuring that 51 percent said hard-working and 26 percent said lazy. But only 23 percent got the right answer, which is "not sure." How can you be sure about such a preposterous generality? Yet the very act of taking the poll and publicizing the results gives legitimacy and weight to empty prejudices.

At the other extreme are polls asking people's opinions about indisputable questions of fact. According to a Gallup poll this month, 11 percent of taxpayers are of the opinion that their taxes will go up under Reagan's tax-reform plan. Forty-six percent believe their taxes will go down. In fact, the vast majority of people's taxes will go down. Perhaps more seriously, a recent Cambridge Reports poll concluded that almost one person in five believes, incorrectly, that few if any cancers are treatable. . . .

No poll allows you to express reasoned views. You're not allowed to ask, "What do you mean by 'lazy'?" or "Does 'somewhat' mean more or less than 20 percent?" There is no answer category for "this question makes no sense" or "I reject your premises." That is because polls don't seek reasoned opinions. Vague attitudes are what they want, and what they impose on the political system as reflections of "public opinion."

Even the granddaddy poll question about presidential popularity is essentially unanswerable. The classic formulation is, "Do you approve or disapprove of the way President Reagan is handling his job?" I think Reagan has done brilliantly at "handling his job." I just disagree with him about nearly everything. What am I supposed to say?

At their sleaziest, polls take a subject on which the vast majority of people are completely ignorant, implant a prejudice, call it an opinion, and serve it up as a basis for policy. The insurance industry hired the distinguished pollsters Yankelovich, Skelly and White to study public opinion about the proposal in Reagan's tax-reform plan to tax the so-called "inside buildup" in whole life insurance policies. The poll showed that 49 percent had never even heard of Reagan's tax reform, let alone this "inside buildup" business. But the pollster read a long description of the "inside buildup" provision, explaining that "taxes would be paid whether or not the person actually obtained any money" and that "a typical 35-year-old man" would owe $5,800 in increased taxes. People were asked their reaction to "this new tax" (actually, of course, part of a general tax cut for individuals). Surprise, surprise, 72 percent opposed it.

Near the beginning of the survey, 62 percent

said they were familiar with the concept of whole life insurance. By the end, 71 percent were "aware that you can borrow the cash surrender value of a whole life insurance policy," and even more were dead set against the government's monkeying around with whole life's current tax advantages. Eighty-three percent said that ending the tax advantage would make whole life insurance "less desirable." The insurance people hail this recognition of a mathematical trusim as proof that Americans are against closing their loophole.

It's ridiculous to suppose that anyone can form a valid opinion about an issue like the taxation of "inside buildup" in whole life insurance policies based exclusively on information supplied by a pollster. There is no loophole in the tax code that Yankelovich et al. couldn't manufacture a majority in defense of, for their usual fee. It's time to stop listening to these people. Better yet, it's time to stop talking to them.

The major problem with TRB's critique is that it is not limited to some polls but indicts *all* polls. Certainly, some polls attempt to create opinion out of ignorance. Most notably, the polls used for advocacy purposes, as discussed in Chapter Three, can certainly be challenged. In TRB's account, the poll dealing with public attitudes toward tax reform does seem to "implant a prejudice, call it an opinion, and serve it up as a basis for policy." Even in this example, however, we think there is useful information for policy makers. For example, the pollsters found that half of the sample had not heard of Reagan's tax reform proposals. That finding should suggest to policy makers that the president needed to explain the proposals to the public. By now, the reader will know what is problematic about the survey cited by TRB. It is a good illustration of an advocacy survey that needs to be treated critically before any conclusions can be drawn from it. We are as opposed to the uncritical acceptance of all survey findings as we are to their uncritical rejection.

In general, we think that public opinion polls probably are not useful for eliciting opinions on complex issues and details. The public will never be expert enough to comment on and judge all the details of an issue such as tax reform. Polls can, however, provide general information on public perceptions of the current fairness of taxes and of the perceived need for reform, as well as opinions about major proposals for specific reforms as these become widely discussed.

Some of the objections to poll questions are simply objections to the fact that all language is basically ambiguous. There is probably no question that is completely free of measurement error, as we discussed earlier. TRB objects to the question "Do you approve or disapprove of the way President Reagan is handling his job?" because "I think Reagan has done brilliantly at 'handling his job.' I just disagree with him about nearly everything." If TRB told that to an interviewer, the interviewer would probe for an answer to the question, write down comments, and let a coder or supervisor ultimately decide how it should be coded. We would code this response as "disapprove" and so would most coders, since approval would mean approval of both the president's programs and the methods for implementing those programs. This question, which TRB thinks is unanswerable, has been answered by overwhelming majorities of respondents, although—as with any question—there will always be a few people who cannot answer. The answers to this question have had significant impacts on presidential actions, although, as we argued earlier, it is basically presidential policies and their success that determine presidential popularity, and not frantic efforts at public relations.

Those who know most about an issue tend to find some survey questions oversimple, but the questions are typically designed for a general public with lower levels of detailed knowledge. For surveys of elite groups, more sophisticated questionnaires are both possible and necessary.

TRB argues that a question such as "Do you think most poor people are lazy or do you think most poor people are hardworking?" gives legitimacy and weight to empty prejudices. He claims that the only possible right answer is "not sure." We disagree vigorously. That is, TRB is treating this question as an information question when in fact it is an opinion question. Survey researchers often ask opinion questions in this form to make the respondent more comfortable in answering the question. The correct answer to the knowledge question is "not sure," but the reality is that people do have prejudices and that they act on them. Any student of the polls since their inception knows that there has been a continuing ambivalence on the part of the American public on how the poor should be treated. A substantial fraction of the public has always believed that poverty is the fault of the victim. Measuring the size of this segment of the population is important, since it tells policy makers something about the public's acceptance of new social welfare programs. The answers to the poll question may not be "right," but they are stable and do reflect a reality that must be accounted for. In rejecting this question, TRB failed to distinguish between findings that are untrustworthy and findings that are distasteful because they disagree with his point of view.

To sum up, thousands of polls are conducted annually. Some oversimplify issues, whereas others present issues in too much detailed complexity. As with all other sources of information, polls must be carefully evaluated and not simply accepted or rejected out of hand, especially when one suspects that the polls are being used for advocacy purposes.

As we have argued earlier, it is often as useful to know that public attitudes are unformed as to know what the formed attitudes are. It would be nice if respondents were willing to admit ignorance on an issue rather than formulating an instant attitude. We know, however, that many respondents do not wish to appear ill informed and will respond on the basis of minimal cues from the question. It is the responsibility of the pollster to measure knowledge accurately and not to report "non-findings." In Chapter Seven and in *Asking Questions* (Sudman and Bradburn, 1982), we advocate the use of explicit "don't know" answers, so that respondents are not pushed into giving opinions when they do not have them.

### Are Poll Results Meaningless?

We believe that most polls can provide useful information if used with proper caution. Measurement errors are not unique to surveys but are found in every science, including such hard and apparently "exact" sciences as astronomy, physics, and chemistry. In many research applications in the physical sciences, such as measuring the thermal conductivity of copper or the effects of the rotation of the earth and moon on the intensity of cosmic rays hitting the earth, the relative measurement errors are as great as or greater than in survey research. The key question that must always be asked is "What is the precision of the data relative to the uses to which they will be placed?" From this perspective, much of the work done by pollsters is sufficiently accurate for the needs that surveys address. Polls are most often criticized not because of measurement error but because the findings disagree with the critic's personal view on a proposed policy. The controversy over "Star Wars" illustrates that "hard" science findings are also likely to be disputed by people who are on different sides of a policy issue.

### Are the Polls in Trouble?

We have discussed the major reasons that some critics think polls should be banned or restricted. Looking into our crystal balls, we do not see any significant efforts to ban the polls in the near future. The critics are currently a small minority, and the uses of polls continue to grow, especially by political parties and candidates for office. The exit polls will continue to face the closest scrutiny, and there is some possibility of additional restrictions on exit polls.

There is still substantial evidence that the public enjoys reading about polls; trusts poll results, perhaps a bit too much; and is willing to provide information. William Granger in the *Chicago Tribune Magazine* (June 8, 1986, p. 8) describes Louie from Milwaukee:

> Today the alleged surveys are supposed to be scientific, with a plus-or-minus error percentage built in. They are solemnly quoted by pundits and politicians alike as accurate measures of what the great unwashed are thinking at any given moment.
> Louie does not believe it.

He is a middle-aged man bursting with opinions, and no one asks him what he thinks. Not even the ladies in the shopping centers, not even the egregious talk-show hosts who rattle on and on about the price of laxatives without knowing their value.

Louie from Milwaukee, opinionated and with half a lifetime of experience to back up those opinions, is virgin territory. How many more Louies are there in the world, ready for plowing?

I read the newspaper opinion column and see the same old names of contributors; I listen to the call-in shows and hear the same cranks whine about the menace of socialized medicine. What I am longing for, as a snowbird longs for Orlando in January, is to hear from the Louies of the world.

Louie longs, too, and it is more personal with him.

To date, the public is not resisting interviews, but special groups are. For example, many physicians who are bombarded with mail and personal interviews are now refusing to be interviewed or are demanding large monetary payments for cooperation. There have been discussions of methods for reducing the burden on oversampled groups such as physicians by centralizing the sampling lists and omitting from those lists those who had recently cooperated on another study. To date, however, nothing has been done to implement such a policy.

The major reason for concern is that cooperation rates have been slowly declining for the past several decades. This decline could reflect disenchantment with the polls, but two other reasons seem to us to be much more likely. First, the increased concern with crime has made it harder to contact many respondents. Less often noted, but of greater importance, is the increased number of women working full time. Consequently, survey organizations are having trouble finding interviewers who wish to work part time—just when the demand for interviewers has increased. Given the shrunken supply and the increased demand, the quality of interviewing has declined somewhat in the past several decades. Since working women are also more difficult to find at home and to persuade to cooperate than unemployed persons, all these factors lead to lower overall cooperation. Thus, the greatest dangers to the polls are in social and technical developments that are independent of public attitudes toward the polls.

## Use of Polls for Illegal and Unethical Activities

We have argued against the regulation of legitimate polls, but we favor regulation of phony polls that mislead the public and bring legitimate polls into disrepute. In most cases, no new legislation is required, simply the enforcement of existing laws against fraud. The phony polls are used mainly to gain access into a home so that something can be sold. For years, encyclopedia salesmen used this method. They would start with some questions about the importance of education and then swing into a pitch for the encyclopedia they were selling. After vigorous activity by the polling industry to have this declared an unfair business practice, the use of phony questionnaires to sell encyclopedias has pretty much ceased, although there may still be a few isolated cases.

Phony questionnaires have mainly been used for door-to-door selling, but also on the telephone and through the mails. The use of mails for this purpose has been discouraged by vigorous post office activities against fraud. The American Association for Public Opinion Research and other professional polling organizations continue to monitor phony polls and, when necessary, will use persuasion and legal methods to have such polls eliminated.

A more subtle variation of the phony poll is the use of a survey to screen for potential customers. A major automobile company once called thousands of people and asked them questions about their satisfaction with their current cars. Respondents thought that this was a legitimate survey but were surprised and angered to learn that the information they provided was turned over to a salesman for a local dealership, who tried to sell them a new car. After vigorous protests, this process was ended and has not been tried by others to our knowledge.

One hears from time to time of the use of phony polls for clearly illegal purposes. Several sexually disturbed persons have combined questions about sexual activity with their obscene phone calls. Some people refuse to give information about their households because they fear that the information will be used by burglars, but we have never heard of a case where this actually happened. For such activities, no new legislation is needed. The acts are already covered by the law and are relatively rare, although they have a disproportionate effect on public confidence in polls because they receive wide news coverage and public attention.

In recent years, phony polls have been used most extensively for fund-raising purposes by voluntary organizations, such as the Republican National Committee, the League of Women Voters, and the American Civil Liberties Union. Fund raisers for these organizations have learned that including a poll along with a solicitation for funds increases the amount of money that is returned. It is clear that the poll results are not used. Indeed, the questions are frequently worded in ways that strongly bias the answers toward the position of the organization, so that any tabulation of the results would be essentially meaningless.

Pollsters believe that such polls for fund-raising purposes are clearly unethical, although not illegal. While protest letters have been sent to organizations using these methods and a few have agreed not to use them in the future, we can see no end to this misuse until it becomes ineffective. When those who are being solicited for their views recognize that the organization really is not interested in what they have to say, but is cynically using a poll to increase contributions, the method will finally be discarded.

It is important to distinguish between phony polls used for fund raising and legitimate surveys of members of an organization. Most organizations periodically poll their members (and sometimes nonmembers) to determine their attitudes on current and future policies. When these polls are conducted, there is not a simultaneous plea for funds, and every effort is made to keep the questions unbiased and to obtain a high cooperation rate.

To summarize: Both the polling of membership and fund raising are legitimate enterprises of voluntary organizations. Combining these activities makes both illegitimate. It would be quixotic to expect legal restrictions, given the political power of the organizations that use this method. Ultimately, the organizations will regulate themselves if sufficient numbers of their members protest.

## Summary

In this chapter, we have discussed four major charges made against polls: that they influence elections, that they invade privacy, that they oversimplify the issues, and—most sweeping—that they are meaningless. The most valid of the charges is that polls, along with many other factors, influence the election process. We believe that the polls along with the media deserve the protection of the Bill of Rights. Banning the polls would simply return us to the time when the same predictions were made, but with much less accuracy. Those who are concerned that exit polls inhibit late voters might better spend their time revising election methods.

Concerns that polls invade respondent privacy have lessened as it has been recognized that most people enjoy the process; that most polls deal with perfectly harmless topics; and that respondents always have complete liberty to refuse to be interviewed, to refuse to answer any question, or to distort answers if they wish. Nevertheless, pollsters recognize and defend respondents' rights to confidentiality.

There is some truth to the claim that the polls as well as the media oversimplify complex issues. The public cannot be expected to be expert enough to comment on details that may puzzle even the specialists. The public can, however, provide the broad guidelines that can direct the actions of policy makers through responses to well-designed surveys.

Finally, we believe that poll results are meaningful and important, even though they contain measurement errors. When polls are criticized, it is usually because of concern with the outcomes rather than the measurement errors.

There continues to be high public regard for the polls and little likelihood that they will be banned or restricted in the near future. The polls have been and will always be dependent on this public support, since without it the polls could not obtain sufficient cooperation to make the results useful.

# 11

# Effects of Polls on Elections, Governments, Business & Media

---

In Chapter Ten, we attempted to respond to some of the major criticisms that have been leveled against polls. In this final summary chapter, we step back and evaluate what the effects of polls have been on our society. On the whole, we will argue, these effects have been beneficial, although the polls clearly have not achieved all the noble goals that were envisioned for them a half century ago.

We start with a discussion of the impact of polls on the electoral process and on elected and nonelected government officials. We then discuss the effects the polls have had on the political participation of individual voters. We turn next to the effects of polls on commerce and the media. We close this chapter with predictions of the future of polling in the United States and elsewhere.

### Effects of Polls on the Electoral Process

Polls have had a major effect on the way that candidates are selected by the political parties. In the era before the polls, most candidates were selected by a relatively few power brokers in the proverbial "smoke-filled rooms." Since the polls began, they have played an ever-increasing role in candidate selection. No candidate will be slated if poll results indicate that he or she lacks sufficient name recognition or if the attitudes of those who know the candidate are negative. Even if such a candidate chose to run, it is highly unlikely that that candidate would receive sufficent campaign contributions to make an effective campaign possible. Most contributors, even if their motives are disinterested, are loath to throw their money away on a losing campaign.

Because of several changes in the electoral process during the past twenty years, polling has become increasingly important to candidates. Political parties do not exert as much influence in elections, particularly in the selection of candidates for president. Reforms in both major parties after 1968 increased the importance of primaries and party caucuses in selecting delegates to the nominating convention. Thus, primaries and party caucuses have taken on a preelectoral role for candidate selection. As a result, potential candidates for president are required to run in many elections before the nominating convention in order to secure the necessary convention votes. Polls have become one of the major techniques used by candidates to help them plan effective campaigns in the different states and give credibility to their claims to be serious candidates. Since money is necessary to pay for publicity, campaign activities, and polling, campaign contributions take on increased importance in political campaigns.

Paradoxically, because of the increased openness and democratization of the nomination process, individuals with little experience or party backing can organize a credible campaign for office; at the same time, candidates are now more dependent on those who will finance their campaigns—including individuals or groups with strong special interests. Thus, what might be seen as a process that should make candidates responsible to the majority may actually make them dependent on a small minority.

One result of this process is to reduce the number of candidates with low or moderate incomes. Candidates with large incomes can still choose to run in a primary, figuring that—even if they lose, as the polls predict—they will receive name recognition for future campaigns. And, of course, current campaign methods, which feature expensive television advertising, also favor rich over poor candidates.

Some people argue that the new methods of selecting

candidates are inferior to the older methods, where political experts at least occasionally selected candidates because they had outstanding political skills. This argument is incapable of being proved or disproved. What is obvious, however, is that candidates selected by the current methods use opinion polls extensively and are much less beholden to a small group of party leaders and insiders. On the other hand, they may be more dependent on a small group of campaign contributors who represent a few special interests.

As we pointed out earlier, given the great importance of the preelection polls to the candidates, there is every temptation to modify the procedures or the actual data so that the individual looks like a viable candidate. To the extent that these polls are only used internally by the party or candidate to make campaign decisions, the results are self-correcting. That is, the election itself will demonstrate whether a poll was badly done or falsified, and the organization conducting such a poll will lose its reputation for reliability. Along the way, some superior or more ethical candidates may be eliminated. That is the penalty suffered by the party leaders and contributors who accept falsified or poor-quality results.

The general polling and survey field also suffers a loss of credibility because many people do not distinguish among polls. Therefore, if one poll is discredited, these people will distrust all polls. At the least, we hope that our readers will recognize that polls must be evaluated on their individual merits. Almost every poll sponsored by a candidate rather than by an independent source is probably better considered guilty until proven innocent.

### Effects of Polls on Elected Officials

Polls have made it possible for elected officials to find out what their constituents think about major issues and about the officials themselves. As we stressed earlier, political leaders must listen to constituents in order to educate and persuade them to support policies that are in the public interest. Slavish adherence to the public will is not the goal, but no major domestic or foreign program can be implemented successfully if it does not have substantial public support.

Presidents and congressmen pay a great deal of attention to the president's popularity as measured by public polls. Some have argued that periodic polls that measure the public's opinion about how well the president is doing his job are an analogue to votes of confidence in a parliamentary system. When the president enjoys great approval, he is effective in getting his program through Congress. When he slips in the polls, his ability to govern, particularly his ability to take unpopular positions, is weakened. Those who believe that political leaders are too dependent on popularity lament this power of the polls to limit presidential effectiveness. Those who feel that the presidential system places too much power in the hands of the president welcome the ability of the public to prevent the usurpation of power. If power corrupts, polls can be a forceful antidote.

Regardless of one's own opinion about whether the polls play a positive or negative role in our political life, it is clear that they are a force that must be reckoned with. They are one major means by which public opinion makes itself felt, and they act as a counterweight to other means, such as the mass media or politicians at all levels of government. The increasing reliance on polls by politicians everywhere suggests that they may have become the single most important source of knowledge about public opinion and have limited the role of other sources that might appear to be more partisan or reflect vested interests.

*Lobbies.* The continued influence of special-interest lobbies has distressed some political observers, who hoped that opinion polls would reduce that influence. Ironically, campaign reform laws, designed to limit the amount of money that any one contributor can make to a political campaign, have increased the influence of political action committees (PACs), which now are the major source of funding for individuals running for office. Although no candidate is simply a tool of any lobby, all elected officials will certainly continue to listen to major contributors. Also, lobbyists represent special areas of expertise that must be consulted in a complex society. It is not the presence of lobbies that should be distressing; it is the absence of other sources of information.

Before opinion polls were available, only one side of an issue might be heard. In the absence of data, the lobbyists could claim that theirs was the popular view. Today, the lobbyist who makes this claim requires poll data to back it up. Although polls are sometimes misused for persuasive purposes, the widespread availability of poll data on major public issues provides an effective check to unjustified claims.

The political process in the United States operates under a system of checks and balances. The executive, legislative, and judiciary branches serve as checks and balances on each other; the various special-interest groups also check and balance one another. In turn, the polls enable public opinion to provide checks and balances on special interests.

*Organized Campaigns.* New technology makes it very easy for a small group to organize a petition, letter, telegram, or telephone campaign in which a political leader will receive thousands of messages urging a specific position. Almost all politicians have been suspicious of such mass persuasion efforts but, in the absence of additional information, have sometimes been swayed by them. Public opinion polls can actually improve the effectiveness of such campaigns if they show that general public attitudes support them. If public opinion is on the other side of an issue, however, the polls prevent small minorities from suggesting that their views are the majority's views.

Well-reasoned letters from constituents can still have an impact on their representatives, since they represent strength of position. As we have pointed out, one of the failings of many polls is that they do not measure how strongly people feel about an issue. It continues to be the case, and we think it should be, that those who are best informed and feel most strongly about an issue are given greater weight than the less well informed and interested. Here also, the polls help the political leader to know whether the letters represent broader attitudes on an issue or are limited to a minority group.

*Personal Influences.* Polls have significantly reduced the impact that persons close to political leaders have on their decision making. The effects of personal influence have been both deliberate and unconscious. We all tend to associate with people who are like us and who share our views. In the absence of other information, we may soon begin to believe that everyone thinks as we and our friends do. Political leaders associate mainly with other leaders and with successful and influential persons. It is difficult for them to know what the grass-roots views are. Even when they return to their constituencies for meetings, they are likely to talk with those who share their views. While the media are a significant balance to the effects of cronyism, political figures have often been critical and suspicious of the media. Only the polls provide a believable alternative to relying heavily on close friends to provide the voice of the people.

### Effects of Polls on Nonelected Officials

It might be argued that the effects of polls have been even greater on nonelected officials than on elected officials. The election process itself is a mechanism for removing from office politicians who misread or ignore the public will, but no such mechanism exists for civil servants. Prior to the use of surveys and polls, civil servants developed their programs with limited knowledge of the effects these programs would have; and after a program was begun, there was limited knowledge of its effectiveness.

Surveys have now become the major source of information for both program development and evaluation. To give specific examples, surveys conducted by various agencies in the Department of Health and Human Services played a major role in the development of specific procedures used for Medicare reimbursement. Since the introduction of Medicare, a series of large surveys have been conducted periodically to measure the impacts of Medicare (and other health programs) on the costs and delivery of health care services and the general health of the population in the United States. The monthly Current Population Survey is the major source of information on the unemployment rate and is used both as a measure of the effectiveness of current economic programs and as a trigger for changes if unemployment rises beyond an acceptable level. It seems fair to say that every major federal program is monitored by surveys of the target groups. This does not mean, however, that all civil servants use polls with equal intensity and skill. Some administrators are strong believers in data and use them as part of their daily decision-making process, while others rely much more heavily on their own experiences and judgment. Even here, the availability of outside data acts as a check against programs that are substantially off target.

The effect of polls and surveys on state and local government programs has been far less than at the federal level, partly because of cost considerations. The cost of such surveys, while large, is a trivial part of the federal budget but is much more significant at the state and local levels. The costs of state and local surveys are only slightly less than the cost of a national survey, but the resources available are much smaller. Also, the general level of sophistication in the use of polls and surveys for program development and evaluation has been higher at the federal than at the state and local levels.

The use of surveys at the state and local levels is likely to increase sharply in the next several decades. There is now a growing sophistication by local program staff on the use of research methods, especially surveys. With smaller budgets, state and local governmental units can obtain information that can be useful for policy purposes even if not at the same level of accuracy as achieved by the U.S. Bureau of the Census.

Conservatives often argue that many government programs should be abolished; but even here survey data are needed to help policy makers determine whether a program is or is not effective. Given our complex society, it is unlikely that the level of governmental activity will be substantially reduced in the future. Therefore, government programs still will need to be monitored, and surveys will be a major component of the evaluation process.

There are, of course, other sources of information for evaluating government programs. Records are one major source, but they tell only part of the story. That is, medical records and bills give a partial picture of the effect of an illness on an elderly person. To find the current health and financial status of that person, as well as the impact of the illness on other household members, survey data are required.

Finally, it can be argued that the availability of an outside evaluation mechanism, surveys and polls, sensitizes nonelected officials to their responsibility to the public and makes them behave differently than if they were completely isolated. Even in totalitarian regimes such as the Soviet Union and China, surveys and polls are conducted to evaluate services such as housing. While public opinion in these countries plays virtually no role in establishing domestic or foreign policies, it does play a role in determining how these policies have been implemented by the government bureaucracies.

### Effects of Polls on Individual Citizens

The average person has been intrigued by the polls since their inception and has given them a warm welcome. Most people report that they enjoy being surveyed, although the actual percentages depend on the topic and method of data collection. The unethical uses of phony polls to sell something or to raise money provide indirect evidence of favorability toward polls. While these uses are distressing to pollsters, they demonstrate the generally positive attitudes of the public toward the polls.

Most people recognize that poll data make a substantial contribution to the political system and that government officials do pay attention to them. The extensive coverage of the polls in the news media has been especially important in shaping this view. It is also true that most people enjoy being asked for their views by a sympathetic interviewer who listens carefully and records what they say. Thus, we would conclude that the polls bring the average citizen closer to those who govern.

Our view, however, is not a unanimous view. As we pointed out in the last chapter, some voters may feel disenfranchised when the polls reveal either on election day or during the campaign that their candidate is lagging behind, and a small percentage of these people may not vote as a result. Among the many reasons for not voting, however, polls are fairly unimportant, although they receive substantial publicity.

Many researchers have attempted to demonstrate the presence of a bandwagon effect—that is, a movement by the public during an election campaign toward the candidate shown to be ahead by the polls. The election results, however, have shown very mixed results. Sometimes the candidate with a substantial lead in the polls increases that lead during the actual election, sometimes that lead is narrowed, and sometimes the results are just as predicted. Overall, these changes provide no support for a bandwagon theory. There have been some efforts to demonstrate that the polls have differential effects on voter turnouts, but again the actual election results do not show this effect. Note that all these objections are toward the use of polls in predicting the winner of an election. Few object to their use in determining public attitudes or behavior.

A much more difficult question to address is whether polls have had an effect on other more active forms of political participation, such as contributing money to political campaigns, working for political candidates, becoming aware of the major issues, and attempting to persuade the public and political leaders about the correctness of a position. Our general feeling is that they have not. While the polls have caused more citizens to be aware of and to pay some attention to issues, there is little to suggest that polls by themselves have increased the number of strongly committed political activists. The question is difficult because those who are politically active tend to be extensive users of poll data; but, as best as can be determined, the strong political interest precedes rather than follows the use of poll results.

Some critics have accused the polls of superficiality because the questions about complex issues are general and oversimplified. It is certainly true that most polls reported in the media are simple and fail to probe the nuances of issues. But we do not know whether this superficiality is attributable to the limitations of public understanding, as is sometimes alleged, or to the media's lack of interest in reporting more complex analyses. Private polls conducted for political purposes often probe more deeply in an effort to find out how to shape a campaign message or effectively sell a particular viewpoint.

There is certainly a place for additional polls or additional questions for those who are well informed and hold strong views. Standard polls of the general population may pay too little attention to these groups, although they are tapped in special surveys of "elites."

Are there any other ways in which the polls affect the individual citizen? One major effect is to dispel collective ignorance. A large majority of all citizens may share the same view on a public issue, but a well-financed minority may attempt to spread the idea that the contrary position is favored by the majority. In the absence of poll data, the majority may remain silent and inactive and permit the minority to prevail. The presence of poll results can hearten the majority, so that they can organize to promote their majority position and inform decision makers about what the majority wants.

Polls and surveys may have similar effects on behavior. When poll data reveal that previously taboo activities for teenagers, such as sexual activity or drug or alcohol use, are common practices, the reported usage goes up still more. This behavioral bandwagon effect may be caused, in part, simply by a greater willingness to report accurately, but additionally those who had earlier refrained because of fear of being different now have this fear removed or reduced. Of course, teenagers also get information from peers, movies, and the media about what other teenagers are doing.

If one believes, as many parents do, that teenage sexual activity or drug and alcohol use are bad things, then the polls, as well as the mass media, must share the blame for increases in such behavior. If, on the other hand, one believes that reducing cholesterol intake, dieting, and quitting smoking are good things, then the polls can take some of the credit. No one can guarantee that the behaviors reported in the polls and the subsequent consequences of the publication of these results are always desirable. Similar to the mass media reports of news, the polls sometimes ennoble and sometimes diminish the human spirit. We believe that the alternative of censorship or ignorance of the true state of public opinion and behavior is worse than any of the consequences of reporting accurately what the poll results are.

## Effects of Polls on Businesses and Consumers

There is no question that polls and surveys are a vital part of the information-seeking mechanisms used by all but the smallest businesses. Businesses clearly recognize the value of information about consumers in improving their competitive positions and profits. The issue we discuss in this section is whether polls help businesses serve consumers better or whether poll data are used to manipulate consumers into buying things that they do not need or would otherwise not buy.

The answers to this question depend very little on the polls themselves and much more on attitudes toward business and marketing. If one believes, as we do, that legitimate businesses can continue to exist and to be profitable only if they satisfy consumer needs, then the role of the polls is obvious. A firm cannot satisfy consumer needs if it does not know what those needs are. Thus, surveys are used to provide information that enables a business to serve the consumer better.

If one believes, however, that businesses manipulate consumers into purchasing unneeded or harmful items, then the polls must also be held responsible as one of the tools of the devil. We do not believe that marketing and advertising based on survey data can force people into continuing to buy products that they do not wish to buy. Marketing based on polls can be used to get people to try a new product, but only satisfaction with product performance can make people continue to use it. Most firms depend on customer satisfaction for their own continuing prosperity, and many place heavy emphasis on surveys of their own customers to uncover and thus be able to correct quickly any causes of dissatisfaction.

There are, of course, "quick-buck" firms that attempt to make their sales and profits from single purchases before consumer dissatisfaction surfaces and the product or service is withdrawn from the market. While such firms could use surveys to improve their appeal to consumers, they usually do not do so. They are generally too small to afford and too unsophisticated to use marketing research.

Some critics have raised questions about the use of surveys in the marketing of products such as cigarettes, alcohol, and even high-cholesterol dairy products, given the known health dangers of using these products. We do not wish to argue here whether these products should be made illegal, except to point out that the attempts to ban all consumption of alcoholic beverages during the prohibition era resulted in "speakeasies" and "bathtub gin" and a general disrespect for law. In any event, since these products still are legal, and since consumers are left to make up their own minds about whether to use them, the use of market research as a tool for obtaining information about consumers should certainly be considered a legitimate activity. Of course, we do not mean that these surveys should include false or misleading statements, which are already prohibited by law. Individuals who feel that the sale of a product is immoral should disassociate themselves from that product. The great temptation to judge (unfavorably) the morals and ethics of the legal behavior of others may make one feel self-righteous but is otherwise unproductive.

### Effects of Polls on the Media

We have noted that the media, both broadcast and print, are heavy users of poll data as news. It is reasonable to ask whether the use of polls has improved the quality or quantity of significant information that the public receives. One thing that polls have clearly done is to reduce the media reliance on commentators who claimed to be able to interpret public attitudes. Before the polls, these experts would base their analyses primarily on intuition and judgment, along with very limited information. For example, postelection analyses were based on selected precinct voting records, along with some limited information about the demographic composition of the precincts. The availability of the exit polls has made possible a much richer as well as more accurate evaluation of the reasons why people voted as they did.

For measuring the public pulse before polls, commentators would talk with small and very biased samples of persons, many of whom were acquaintances. Obviously, the polls provide far more valid and reliable information.

If there is any objection to the media use of polls, it is that they tend to present the information in limited and incomplete fashion. This is slightly more true for television and radio than for print media, but the differences are minimal. The media argue that time and space limitations prevent them from giving a more complete description of the results. Specifically, the broadcast media hardly ever mention how the study was conducted, beyond sometimes giving the sample size and sampling error. There is no discussion of the cooperation rate, or of potential problems with sample bias, or of questionnaire effects. Newspapers tend to be a bit better, but even here it is often difficult to determine the quality of the survey or poll. Much too often, news editors assume that all polls are equally reliable regardless of source or methods used.

While this concern is a serious one to professional pollsters, there is an even more significant limitation. Most of the time, the media present the poll results in only the simplest way. Again, time and space limitations are given as the reason; and again, television is worse than the print media. The results are usually given only on a question-by-question basis, with hardly any attempt to combine items into scales that would give more reliable results. Attempts at reporting results by important subgroups or to relate attitudes on different topics are limited, and only the simplest descriptive statistics are used. The media claim that the public just could not understand anything more complicated.

We argue that many listeners and readers (although not all) would be interested in and could understand more detailed poll information. If this information were made available, it might increase the level of knowledge of the public beyond the superficial level that is the result of the current limited information. On the other hand, the media may be right and the public may be getting all the poll details it wants. There is no way that information can be forced on an unwilling listener or reader. We would point out, however, that there are millions of people who have had some training in statistics, either in college or high school, and would welcome additional details so they could better understand poll results.

## Effects of Polls on Debates of Public Issues

We regard the use of polls in public debates as a mixed blessing. On the one hand, it is far better to know public attitudes on controversial issues, such as abortion and nuclear disarmament, rather than simply to have both sides making unsupported statements that they represent the majority. For example, it is likely that—in the absence of poll results showing that a majority of Americans favor legalized abortion, at least within limits—the vocal minority in the right-to-life movement would have been much more successful than they have been in promoting antiabortion legislation.

On the other hand, the problem with the use of the polls in public debates is that each side may commission its own poll to prove the position it already holds or, at the least, to discredit the poll results of the other side. When polls are conducted with the aim of proving a point, the questions will be worded and the methods selected so that the results will come out as desired. If the results are still not satisfactory, they will then be quietly buried so that they cannot be used by the opposing side. Any neutral person using poll data commissioned by either side of a controversial issue must be aware of the possibility that the data are suspect. If both sides present results that differ substantially, the consequence is that neither of the two polls is believed and that all polling methods become suspect.

The sophisticated or cynical user of poll results may be unwilling to use any poll results unless they come from a neutral source, such as one of the media or university polls. At the least, as with candidate polls, polls conducted by an association that supports a specific view are best treated as guilty until proven innocent.

## The Future of Polls and Surveys

With some trepidation, we speculate about the future of polls and surveys in the next half century. We certainly expect that there will be substantial changes in methods of data collection. In the first half century of the polls, probability sampling methods were developed and questionnaire design and interviewing methods improved. The dominant form of data collection was face-to-face interviewing. Currently, telephone interviews, usually conducted with the aid of a computer terminal, have mostly supplanted the face-to-face interview. As more and more households and business firms have their own computers linked to other computers by phone wires, it will become possible to use electronic mail procedures to conduct interviews via computer. A simpler version of this procedure would be to mail floppy disks to persons with computers and to have them insert the disks in their computers and answer the questions as directed. This method would allow consumers to react to drawings of new product packages or new advertisements. The rapid development of portable battery-operated computers will replace the paper-and-pencil version of questionnaires even if the interviewing is done face to face.

Aside from technology, the greatest advances in methodology are likely to occur in questionnaire construction. Recent studies linking survey methodology to work in cognitive psychology should produce important additional insights into reasons why people answer as they do and how to improve data quality.

More important, we do not expect that most of the uses or the effects of polls we have discussed earlier will change very much. At the federal level, polls are already so widely used that there is little room for extensive additional use. Of course, the topics of the polls and surveys will change continuously as the major issues that face government change. At the state and local levels, there is still substantial unused capacity for the use of polls; and it is natural to expect that polls will be used more extensively, both because of the greater sophistication of local political leaders and government employees and because costs may decrease as new methods are developed.

We do not envision substantial changes in the reporting of the polls by the mass media. There will, however, be more extensive availability of poll data in the rapidly growing electronic data sources. That is, poll data will be archived and readily available to anyone who wishes to have them, but the user will need to request the data and pay a small fee to obtain the results. Thus, those most interested in a topic will be able to obtain almost instant access via their computers and telephone hookups to detailed information. The ready availability of archived poll data allows for greater reporting of trend data, which may be more meaningful than the simple reporting of current poll data. When the same questions are asked over time, one can see how opinion has changed (or not). Even simple questions about support for particular issues become richer in interpretation when responses can be viewed in conjunction with changes in events over time. There is some movement on the part of the media in reporting trends in opinion. More such reporting should be encouraged.

There is, of course, always the possibility that at some future point the public desire for privacy will become so strong that all uninvited contacts will be outlawed or made very difficult by new technology. If this occurs, polls and surveys will also become difficult or impossible because the laws or technologies do not distinguish between sales calls, solicitations for money, and opinion polls. The ease of polling by telephone may expand its use to the point that it becomes self-defeating and the public becomes so annoyed by the deluge of survey callers that everyone will refuse to cooperate. One hopes that people will become more discriminating and be willing to select the worthwhile polls from the others rather than reject polls altogether.

We do not believe that polls themselves will be singled out for legal banning, although the results are sometimes displeasing to individual lawmakers. The extensive use of the polls by politicians and the generally positive feelings toward the polls by the general public offer reasonable assurance of their continuing vitality, at least in democratic societies.

### Have the Polls Fulfilled Their Promise?

The ambitions of the founders of polling were noble. They wanted to make public opinion a major force in the governance of our society. These ambitions have been largely fulfilled. As a result, special interests have a less significant role than they did fifty years ago, although they still have great power.

The polls, like democracy, are imperfect. There continue to be trivial uses of polls. There are incompetent and deliberately dishonest uses of polls. There are still methodological issues that limit the usefulness of polls. With all these limits, however, the polls have been and will continue to be the best way of measuring the voice of the people.

# Glossary

**Analysis of variance.** A widely used statistical procedure that compares variability across groups to that within groups, to determine how likely it is that group differences are caused by chance.

**Area probability sample.** A method for obtaining a general population or household sample when no list is available. The sample is selected in stages. At the first stage, counties or groups of counties usually are selected. At subsequent stages, locations within counties, blocks within locations, and households within blocks are chosen. The method uses available census data on size of places and ultimately requires listing of individual households.

**Bayesian statistics.** Statistical methods that incorporate the prior subjective probability distribution of the decision maker or researcher with the new evidence collected. In standard statistical methods, prior probabilities are ignored.

**Bias.** The difference between the value reported and the true value. Response bias for behavioral reports is the difference between the respondent's reports and the respondent's actual behavior. (See also **Validity.**) Sample bias results from the omission or unequal selection of members of the population without appropriate weighting. Sample bias is usually the result of respondents' unavailability or refusal to cooperate, but it is sometimes caused by a faulty sample design.

**Closed and open questions.** Closed questions give the alternative answers to the respondent, either explicitly or implicitly. Closed questions may have two alternatives (dichotomous questions), such as "yes" or "no" or "male" or "female"; or they may have multiple choices, such as "Democrat," "Republican," or "Independent" or "strongly agree," "agree," "disagree," and "strongly disagree." In contrast, an open question does not provide answer categories to the respondent. An example would be "What do you think is the most serious problem facing the nation today?"

**Clustering.** A sampling method in which small geographical areas—such as cities, blocks, schools, or hospitals—are selected at a first stage, and individuals from these units are then selected as the ultimate respondents. The purpose of clustering is to reduce the costs of locating and contacting the respondents.

**Computer-assisted personal interviewing (CAPI).** An interviewing method in which the interviewer carries a lightweight portable computer into a household. The advantage is that the computer carries out complex branching and editing commands and reduces interviewer clerical errors. See also **CATI.**

**Computer-assisted telephone interviewing (CATI).** A telephone-interviewing method in which questions appear on a computer screen and answers are entered directly into the computer keyboard. The method reduces interviewers' clerical errors and speeds up data processing.

**Confidence limits.** The upper and lower values of statistical estimates. The 95 percent and 99 percent confidence limits are those most widely used. For example, 62–68 percent might be given as the 95 percent confidence limit for an estimate of those who favor a policy. This means that the sampling procedure used had a 95 percent chance of producing a set of limits that encloses the actual proportion of the population who favor a policy. Sometimes referred to in the media as the margin of error.

**Data archives.** Organizations that store results from previous polls and surveys and make them available for secondary analysis of data and design of new questionnaires.

**Demographic characteristics.** The basic classification variables—

gender, age, marital status, race, ethnic origin, education, occupation, income, religion, and residence—that characterize an individual or a household.

**Guttman scales.** A series of questions intended to measure attitudes or behavior along a given dimension. In a perfect Guttman scale, all respondents agreeing to a less common response would be expected to agree to a more common response. Thus, the total number of agreements is a measure of intensity. For example, in a Guttman scale of neighboring, respondents who report intimate contact with neighbors would also be expected to report more casual contacts. The total number of types of contacts is taken as the measure of neighboring.

**Linear models.** A family of statistical procedures for explaining an attitude or a behavior as the sum of a group of variables multiplied by appropriate constants. Many important statistical procedures, such as linear regression and analysis of variance, are based on linear models.

**Margin of error.** See **Confidence limits.**

**Multivariate methods.** Statistical procedures for explaining an attitude or a behavior as the function of a group of other variables. Linear models are a subtype of multivariate methods.

**Open questions.** See **Closed and open questions.**

**Order effect.** A change in the distribution of responses to a question caused either by the position of the question after earlier questions on the same topic or by the order in which the alternative answers are given to the respondent.

**Panel study.** A data collection procedure in which information is obtained from the sample units two or more times, either by repeated interviews or by diaries. Since panels can track individual changes, they provide more reliable as well as more detailed information over time than independent samples do, but they are more difficult to recruit and maintain.

**Primary sampling units (PSUs).** The geographical areas chosen at the first stage of a cluster sample. These are typically counties or standard metropolitan statistical areas (SMSAs); but other geographical units, such as telephone exchanges or schools, also can be used.

**Probability samples.** Samples selected in such a way that each unit in the population has a known, nonzero, chance of being included.

**Random digit dialing (RDD).** The selection of telephone numbers for a telephone sample by computer generation from the list of working telephone exchanges. RDD procedures have the advantage of including unlisted numbers, which would be missed if numbers were drawn from a telephone book.

**Rasch models.** A psychometric procedure for measuring both the difficulty of individual items in a scale and differences between individuals on some latent trait. The method has been used most often on tests of knowledge and ability, but it is also appropriate for measuring attitudes and behavior.

**Reliability.** The degree to which multiple measures of the same behavior or attitude agree. These multiple measures may be over time or at the same point in time.

**Response errors (bias).** The difference between what the respondent reports and the respondent's actual behavior. Response error for attitude questions is an ambiguous concept.

**Sampling error/variance.** The difference between estimates obtained from repeated samples of the same population using identical procedures. The use of the term *error* does not mean that a mistake has been made. Sampling variance is merely the square of sampling error.

**Standard metropolitan statistical areas (SMSAs).** Geographical areas defined by the Bureau of the Census, containing a central city with more than 50,000 people. SMSAs are usually a single county, but larger ones may include several counties. In New England, the definitions are based on townships. In 1983, the terminology changed to metropolitan statistical area (MSA) and consolidated metropolitan statistical area (CMSA).

**Statistical significance.** Statistical measures are used to test hypotheses that two (or more) estimates are really different from one another or that some estimate is really different from zero—that is, that the differences obtained in the survey are not the result of chance variation. When the outcome of a statistical test has statistical significance, the investigator is willing to say that the estimated differences between two groups (for example, in the percent supporting some policy observed in the survey) are real and not chance differences. Statistical significance is usually stated as being at some level—for example, at the 95 or 99 percent level. Statistical significance is not the same as practical significance. If samples are sufficiently large, differences between estimates may be statistically significant but of no practical significance. Conversely, if samples are small, differences in estimates may be of practical importance but may not be statistically significant; that is, it is likely that the observed differences are due to chance.

**Stratification.** A sampling method that divides the total population into subgroups (strata), which may be sampled and from which estimates may be obtained in different ways. Stratification is used to reduce the sampling error.

**Validity.** A valid instrument or scale is one that measures what it claims to, and not something else. The concept is clearest with respect to behavioral questions, where an outside validation source is possible. Examples include the use of financial or medical records to check on reporting of assets or illness costs. Validity measures have also been suggested for attitudinal questions.

**Waksberg method.** A sampling procedure used to improve the efficiency of random digit dialing telephone samples. The method is used to eliminate consecutive groups of telephone numbers that are not in use.

**Weighting/self-weighting.** The adjustment of sample results to account for sampling procedures and possible sample biases caused by noncooperation and incomplete data. Weighting assumes that universe estimates are available from the Census Bureau or elsewhere. If each unit has an equal probability of selection, and no adjustments are made for other factors, the sample is self-weighting.

# References

Aldrich, J. H. *Before the Convention: Strategies and Choices in Presidential Nomination Campaigns.* Chicago: University of Chicago Press, 1980.

Becker, S. L. "Why an Order Effect?" *Public Opinion Quarterly,* 1954, *18,* 271–278.

Blumenthal, S. "Marketing the President." *New York Times Magazine,* Sept. 13, 1981, pp. 42–43ff.

Booth, C. *The Life and Labour of the People of London.* (17 vols.) London: Macmillan, 1889–1903.

Bowles, S., and Gintis, H. *Schooling in Capitalist America: Educational Reform and the Contradictions of Economic Life.* New York: Basic Books, 1976.

Bowles, S., and Nelson, V. "The Inheritance of IQ and the Intergenerational Transmission of Economic Inequality." *Review of Economics and Statistics,* 1974, *56,* 39–51.

Bowley, A. L., and Burnett-Hurst, A. R. *Livelihood and Poverty.* London: G. Bell, 1915.

Bradburn, N. M., Rips, L. J., and Shevell, S. K. "Answering Autobiographical Questions: The Impact of Memory and Inference on Surveys." *Science,* April 10, 1987, *236,* 157–161.

Bradburn, N. M., Sudman, S., and Associates. *Improving Interview Method and Questionnaire Design: Response Effects to Threat-*

*ening Questions in Survey Research.* San Francisco: Jossey-Bass, 1979.

Bradburn, N. M., Sudman, S., and Gockel, G. L. *Racial Integration in American Neighborhoods: A Comparative Survey.* NORC Report No. 111-B. Chicago: National Opinion Research Center, 1970.

Cantril, H. *The Human Dimension: Experiences in Policy Research.* New Brunswick, N.J.: Rutgers University Press, 1967.

Cochran, W. G. *Sampling Techniques.* (2nd ed.) New York: Wiley, 1963.

Converse, J. M. *Survey Research in the United States: Roots and Emergence, 1890–1960.* Berkeley: University of California Press, 1987.

Converse, J. M., and Presser, S. *Survey Questions: Handcrafting the Standardized Questionnaire.* Newbury Park, Calif.: Sage, 1986.

Curtin, R. T. "Indicators of Consumer Behavior: The University of Michigan Surveys of Consumers." *Public Opinion Quarterly,* 1982, *46,* 340–352.

De Boer, C. "The Polls." *Public Opinion Quarterly,* 1980, *44,* 272.

Deming, W. E. *Sample Design in Business Research.* New York: Wiley, 1960.

Dillman, D. A. *Mail and Telephone Surveys.* New York: Wiley, 1978.

Drew, E. "A Reporter at Large (Washington, D.C.)." *New Yorker,* Aug. 27, 1979, pp. 45–73.

Erdos, P., and Morgan, A. J. *Professional Mail Surveys.* New York: McGraw-Hill, 1970.

Evans, R., and Novak, R. *Nixon in the White House.* New York: Random House, 1971.

Ferber, R. (ed.). *The Handbook of Marketing Research.* New York: McGraw-Hill, 1974.

Fowler, F. J. *Survey Research Methods.* Newbury Park, Calif.: Sage, 1984.

Gallup, G. *The Gallup Poll: Public Opinion, 1935–1971.* (3 vols.) Wilmington, Del.: Scholarly Resources, 1972a.

Gallup, G. *The Sophisticated Poll Watcher's Guide.* Princeton, N.J.: Princeton Opinion Press, 1972b.

Gallup, G. *The Gallup Poll: Public Opinion, 1972-1977.* (2 vols.) Wilmington, Del.: Scholarly Resources, 1978.

Gallup, G. *The Gallup Poll.* Wilmington, Del.: Scholarly Resources, 1979-present (annual volumes).

Gallup, G., and Rae, S. F. *The Pulse of Democracy.* New York: Simon & Schuster, 1940.

*Gallup Report.* "Confidence in Church/Organized Religion," July 1985, no. 238, p. 4.

Graber, D. A. "Reading Between the Lines of Consumer Confidence Measures." *Public Opinion Quarterly,* 1982, *46,* 336-339.

Granger, W. "Louie from Milwaukee." *Chicago Tribune Magazine,* June 8, 1986, p. 8.

Groves, R., and Kahn, R. *Surveys by Telephone: A National Comparison with Personal Interviews.* Orlando, Fla.: Academic Press, 1979.

Hansen, M. H., Hurwitz, W. N., and Madow, W. G. *Sample Survey Methods and Theory.* (2 vols.) New York: Wiley, 1953.

Honomichl, J. "How Much Spent on Research? Follow Me." *Advertising Age,* June 21, 1982, pp. 48, 52.

Huff, D. *How to Lie with Statistics.* New York: Norton, 1954.

Jackson, J. E. "Election Night Reporting and Voter Turnout." *American Journal of Political Science,* 1983, *27,* 613-635.

Jahoda, M., Lazarsfeld, P., and Zeisel, H. *Die Arbeitlosen von Marienthal.* Frankfurt am Main: Suhrkamp, 1975. (Originally published 1933.)

Jewell, M. E., and Patterson, S. C. *The Legislative Process in the United States.* (3rd ed.) New York: Random House, 1977.

Johnson, L. B. *The Vantage Point: Perspectives of the Presidency.* New York: Holt, Rinehart & Winston, 1971.

Kinsley, M. "The Art of Polling: How You and Union Carbide Came to Agree." *New Republic,* June 20, 1981, pp. 16-19.

Kish, L. *Survey Sampling.* New York: Wiley, 1965.

Ladd, E. C. "Polling and the Press: The Clash of Institutional Imperatives." *Public Opinion Quarterly,* 1980, *44,* 574-584.

Lavrakas, P. J. *Telephone Survey Methods: Sampling, Selection and Supervision.* Newbury Park, Calif.: Sage, 1987.

Lazarsfeld, P. "The American Soldier: An Expository Review." *Public Opinion Quarterly,* 1949, *13,* 377-404.

Linden, F. "The Consumer as Forecaster." *Public Opinion Quarterly*, 1982, *46*, 353–360.

Lippmann, W. *Public Opinion.* San Diego, Calif.: Harcourt Brace Jovanovich, 1922.

Lippmann, W. *The Phantom Public.* New York: Macmillan, 1925.

Lockhart, D. (ed.). *Making Effective Use of Mailed Questionnaires.* New Directions for Program Evaluation, no. 21. San Francisco: Jossey-Bass, 1984.

Lockley, L. C. "Notes on the History of Marketing Research." *Journal of Marketing*, 1950, *14*, 733–736.

Martin, E., McDuffee, D., and Presser, S. *Sourcebook of Harris National Surveys: Repeated Questions, 1963–1976.* Chapel Hill: Institute for Research in Social Science, University of North Carolina, 1981.

Mayhew, H. *London Labour and the London Poor.* New York: A. M. Kelly, 1967. (Originally published 1861.)

Moser, C. A., and Kalton, G. *Survey Methods in Social Investigation.* New York: Basic Books, 1972.

Murray, J. R., and others. *The Impact of the 1973–74 Oil Embargo on the American Household.* NORC Report No. 126. Chicago: National Opinion Research Center, 1974.

Neyman, J. "On the Two Different Aspects of the Representative Method: The Method of Stratified Sampling and the Method of Purposive Selection." *Journal of the Royal Statistical Society*, 1934, *97*, 558–606.

Noelle-Neumann, E. "Wanted: Rules for Wording Structured Questionnaires." *Public Opinion Quarterly*, 1970, *34*, 191–201.

Parten, M. *Surveys, Polls and Samples.* New York: Harper & Row, 1950.

Payne, S. *The Art of Asking Questions.* Princeton, N.J.: Princeton University Press, 1951.

Rich, W. "The Human Yardstick." *Saturday Evening Post*, Jan. 21, 1939, pp. 8–9ff.

Robinson, C. *Straw Votes: A Study of Political Prediction.* New York: Columbia University Press, 1932.

Roper, B. W. "The Predictive Value of Consumer Confidence Measures." *Public Opinion Quarterly*, 1982, *46*, 361–367.

Rossi, P. H., Wright, J. D., and Anderson, A. B. (eds.). *The Hand-book of Survey Research.* Orlando, Fla.: Academic Press, 1983.

Rowntree, B. S. *Poverty: A Study of Town Life.* London: Macmillan, 1902.

Schlaifer, R. *Probability and Statistics for Business Decisions.* New York: McGraw-Hill, 1959.

Schuman, H. "Ordinary Questions, Survey Questions, and Policy Questions." *Public Opinion Quarterly,* 1986, *50,* 432–442.

Schuman, H., and Presser, S. *Questions and Answers in Attitude Surveys.* Orlando, Fla.: Academic Press, 1981.

Sharp, L. M., and Frankel, J. "Correlates of Self-Perceived Respondent Burden: Findings from an Experimental Study." Paper presented at annual meeting of the American Statistical Association, Detroit, Aug. 10–11, 1981.

Sheatsley, P. "NORC: The First Forty Years." In *Report, 1981–82.* Chicago: National Opinion Research Center, 1982.

Skott, H. E. "Attitude Research in the Department of Agriculture." *Public Opinion Quarterly,* 1943, *7,* 280–292.

Social Science Research Council. *Report of Committee on Analysis of Pre-Election Polls and Forecasts.* New York: Social Science Research Council, 1949.

Sorenson, T. C. *Kennedy.* New York: Harper & Row, 1965.

Stephan, F. F., and McCarthy, P. *Sampling Opinions.* New York: Wiley, 1958.

Stolarek, J. S., Rood, R. M., and Taylor, M. W. "Measuring Constituency Opinion in the U.S. House: Mail Versus Random Surveys." *Legislative Studies Quarterly,* 1981, *6,* 589–596.

Stouffer, S. A., and others. *The American Soldier.* Vol. 1 of *Studies in Social Psychology in World War II.* (4 vols.) Princeton, N.J.: Princeton University Press, 1949.

Sudman, S. *Reducing the Costs of Surveys.* Hawthorne, N.Y.: Aldine, 1968.

Sudman, S. *Applied Sampling.* Orlando, Fla.: Academic Press, 1976a.

Sudman, S. "Sample Surveys." *Annual Review of Sociology,* 1976b, *2,* 107–120.

Sudman, S. "Do Exit Polls Influence Voting Behavior?" *Public Opinion Quarterly,* 1986, *50,* 331–339.

Sudman, S., and Bradburn, N. M. *Response Effects in Surveys: A Review and Synthesis*. Hawthorne, N.Y.: Aldine, 1974.

Sudman, S., and Bradburn, N. M. *Asking Questions: A Practical Guide to Questionnaire Design*. San Francisco: Jossey-Bass, 1982.

Survey Research Laboratory, University of Illinois. "Academic Research Organizations in the United States and Canada." *Survey Research*, 1987, *18* (3–4), 13–16.

Tanur, J., and others. *Statistics: A Guide to the Unknown*. (2nd ed.) Oakland, Calif.: Holden-Day, 1978.

TRB. "Vox Pop Crock." *New Republic*, Sept. 30, 1985, p. 4.

Turner, C. T., and Martin, E. (eds.). *Surveying Subjective Phenomena*. (2 vols.) New York: Russell Sage Foundation, 1984.

United States Bureau of the Census. *School Enrollment: Social and Economic Characteristics of Students: October 1982*. Current Population Reports, Series P-20, No. 408. Washington, D.C.: U.S. Government Printing Office, 1983a.

United States Bureau of the Census. *Voting and Registration in the Election of November 1982*. Current Population Reports, Series P-20, No. 383. Washington, D.C.: U.S. Government Printing Office, 1983b.

United States Bureau of the Census. *Statistical Abstract of the United States, 1987*. Washington, D.C.: U.S. Government Printing Office, 1987.

Waksberg, J. "Sampling Methods for Random Digit Dialing." *Journal of the American Statistical Association*, 1978, *73*, 40–46.

Wallis, W. A., and Roberts, H. V. *Statistics: A New Approach*. New York: Free Press, 1956.

White, T. H. *The Making of the President, 1964*. New York: Atheneum, 1965.

Williams, D., Howard, L., and Maier, L. "Tax Credits for Tuition." *Newsweek*, April 26, 1982, p. 86.

Zeisel, H. *Say It with Figures*. (5th ed.) New York: Harper & Row, 1968.

# Index